California
SPORTS
ASTOUNDING!

La Jolla
Shores
PRESS

Contact information for La Jolla Shores Press

E-mail: lajollashorespress@gmail.com

ISBN: 978-1-7379981-0-5 (print)
ISBN: 978-1-7379981-1-2 (ebook)

Ordering Information:
Special discounts are available on quantity purchases by sports teams, corporations, associations, and others. For details, contact:

E-mail: lajollashorespress@gmail.com

SPORTS
ASTOUNDING!

Fun, Unknown, and Surprising Facts
From Statehood to Sunday

Dan Cisco
THE CALIFORNIA SPORTS GUY

Dedication

For my parents, who gave me a happy life in sunny San Diego. They shared their love of sports, especially distance running. Hey! In this next life, when I see you again, can you give me some fast twitch muscles?

Table of CONTENTS

OPENING STATEMENT

Sports Fans,

Welcome to your favorite sports book about California! When you finish this book, you will be able to impress your friends, amaze your family, and maybe even conquer your enemies—on a quiz show—with your sublime knowledge of sports in the Golden State.

Books, newspapers, websites, and other interesting sources have been scoured to bring you the fun and unknown facts about California's huge sports genealogy.

Over 65 sports are included!

Do you like the Olympics, professional, college, and high school sports? You will find men's and women's sports covered at all those levels.

This is the first statewide sports history book and the first to chronicle selected highlights from statehood in 1850 to Sunday. You can now enjoy the largest compilation of California sports history in a single volume.

The fun facts and Q&As don't stop coming, and you'll be entertained with facts like:

- The interesting name that was originally chosen for the Oakland Raiders.
- The surprise person who introduced karate to California.
- The interest level for tennis and the X-Games when they first appeared in California.
- The California NFL team with the greatest comeback in regular season history.
- Finding out if your athletic ancestor from the 1800s makes an appearance.
- What sport was called "Basket Ball" before basketball.

- Some of the most interesting surfing facts from historic California newspapers.
- The quirkiest and most memorable mascots ever created.
- The number of California hall of famers from every sport imaginable.
- The first appearance of each sport, notable events, athlete birthdays, and more.

The information presented is accurate to the best of my knowledge, but your input will help me expand coverage for the next edition. Please tell me about your favorite sports, athletes, and coaches. What content would you like added? Please send your comments and suggestions through the website below. Thanks!

Dan Cisco
a.k.a. the California Sports Guy
www.californiasportsastounding.com

JANUARY
ASTONISHING

They All Came a Runnin'
January 1, 1912

A notice for the Cross City Race, now known as Bay to Breakers, first appeared December 14, 1911 in the *Stockton Independent* as follows:

> H. L. Baggerly, sporting editor of the *San Francisco Bulletin*, announces a "cross-city race," for New Year's Day, which promises to be an event of state-wide interest. The running race will start from the ferry and finish at the famous Cliff House, a distance of about seven miles. All amateur runners, 18 years or over, living in California, are eligible to enter. A dozen or more suitable prizes will be distributed. As the race will be conducted by the *Bulletin*, absolute fairness is assured in the recognition of merit. Lovers of outdoor sport about the bay are confident that the race will prove a very interesting event and among the younger athletes there is a clamor for entry admissions.

The annual race, which is typically held on the third Sunday in May, starts at the northeast end of downtown San Francisco, near The Embarcadero, and ends at Ocean Beach, on the Pacific coast. One hundred and seventy-five entries were received from towns as far away as Los Angeles, Monterey, and Sacramento. The *San Francisco Call* described it as "the first cross city race ever attempted on this coast." One hundred and twenty-one runners finished. Robert Jackson "Bobby" Vlught, a St. Mary's College student, won in 44 minutes, 10 seconds.

Seventy-four years later, the 7.46-mile race in the modern era emphasizes fun, exercise, costumes, and still has room for elite runners. On May 18, 1986, 110,000 participants helped set a Guinness World Record for largest footrace in the world. Past examples that add to the fun each year include centipede racing teams of 13 runners strung together, tortilla tossing at the starting line, and runners dressed as salmon.

Q: In the 1966 Bay to Breakers, Frances "Fran" Krauskopf Conley was the first female champion with a time of 60:07. Why was her 239th place finish listed in the newspapers as an "unregistered runner?"

For more running, visit www.californiasportsastounding.com

A: Women were not allowed to compete officially. Conley finished ahead of 38 men.

CALIFORNIA SPORTS BIRTHDAYS
More Fun for January 1

Q: Clifford "Cliff" Bourland, born in 1921, sprinter, won a gold medal in the 1948 Olympics in what event: javelin, decathlon, or the 4 x 400 relay?

....

Did You Know?

Six-year-old Mary Etta Boitano ran 1:01:12 to win the women's division of the 1969 Bay to Breakers race. Eleven-year-old Boitano added three more victories starting in 1974. Boitano, who trained with her family and the South End Rowing Club, would go on to set world age group records in the marathon.

A: Bourland, a native of Los Angeles, won gold in the 4 x 400 meters relay.

NOTABLE EVENT
January 1, 1918

With most college football players fighting overseas in World War I, the Rose Bowl in Pasadena was played with military teams and the approval of President Woodrow Wilson. The Mare Island Marines from Vallejo played Camp Lewis, WA Army. This was more than a game—it was a display of patriotism. Game time temperature was 83 degrees. The *Riverside Daily Press* noted, "While the east shivered in zero-degree weather on New Year's Day, three persons were overcome by the heat during the game. Most of the women were attired in filmy summer gowns, while many men wore white duck. The Marines prevailed 19-7 at Tournament Park becoming the first California team to with the Rose Bowl. Less than a month after the game, the majority of the players from both teams were scheduled to go overseas."

Perfect Game
January 2, 1851

San Francisco's Marty Judnich, a member of the South End Rowing Club, researched the early history of handball in the city. His work, along with the research of authors Bob Barde and Pat Cunneen provided the Northern California Handball Association website with the origins of the sport:

Handball has a long and glorious history in Northern California, dating back to the Great California Gold Rush. Among the many who came to Northern California in search of gold were the Irish, who brought the "Perfect Game" with them.

By 1851, an Irish saloon was operating in San Francisco and listed in the San Francisco City Directory under the heading: "Ball Courts and Alleys." These classifications were commonly used to describe handball courts in Ireland and England. Handball courts, more commonly known as handball "alleys" in Ireland, were often built adjacent to the pub and would utilize one of the pub walls as the front wall of the court. The pub was Thomas Cullen's Saloon and Shamrock Ball and Racket Court located at 543 Market Street; this may well be the oldest listed handball court in the United States, predating Phil Casey's court on DeGraw Street in Brooklyn, New York by some 37 years. The Shamrock court is certainly the oldest known handball court in California, built at least 150 years ago.

Seven-time national champion Mike Linnik promotes the sport through the Northern California Handball Association. He has also served as the San Jose State University handball coach. Notable places to play in San Francisco include Golden Gate Park, the Olympic Club, and the South End Rowing Club.

The Los Cab Sports Village in Fountain Valley and the Los Angeles Athletic Club are among the well-known venues in Southern California. Handball is played statewide mainly at recreation centers, private clubs, and YMCA's.

Q: Who is also credited with building the first handball court in San Francisco: Juan Miguel Aguirre or Billy Ryan?

For more handball, visit www.californiasportsastounding.com

A: The *San Francisco Call* published an obituary on September 2, 1897 for Juan Miguel Aguirre, which recognized him as having "built the first handball court here, locating it at what is now Post Street, between Kearny Street and Grant Avenue.

It is related that a great game was played at this court in the fifties between a Basque and an Irishman for a purse of $1000, in which the Basque won."

CALIFORNIA SPORTS BIRTHDAYS
More Fun for January 2

Q: Daniel "Ed" Carmichael, born in 1907, won a bronze medal in what gymnastic event at the 1932 Olympics: triple Salchow, horse vault, or parallel bars?

....

Did You Know?

Maynard Laswell of the Los Angeles Athletic Club won the National Four-Wall Handball Singles Championship in 1924, 1925, and 1926. In 1955 he became the first Californian to be inducted into the United States Handball Association Hall of Fame.

A: The Los Angeles native won a bronze medal in the horse vault. Teammate Al Jochim won the silver medal.

NOTABLE EVENT
January 2, 1933

The defending Rose Bowl champions, the USC Trojans, won again with a 35-0 shutout of the Pittsburgh Panthers. USC quarterback Cotton Warburton scored twice as the Trojans finished the season unbeaten at 9-0. The Trojans, coached by Howard Jones, beat the Tulane Green Wave 21-12 the previous year.

California in the Mountain West
January 4, 1999

When the Western Athletic Conference suddenly disbanded, the Mountain West Conference started operations the first week of January. Colorado State University President Dr. Albert Yates, with the help of presidents of eight universities, founded the conference in 1998. The San Diego State Aztecs were the only charter member from California. The remaining charter members consisted of the United States Air Force Academy Falcons, the Brigham Young University Cougars, the Colorado State University Rams, the University of New Mexico Lobos, the University of Nevada, Las Vegas Rebels, the University of Utah Utes, and the University of Wyoming Cowboys.

The San Jose State Spartans and Fresno State Bulldogs joined in 2012. The following year Fresno State defeated Utah State 24-17 in the inaugural Mountain West Football Championship Game, held at Bulldog Stadium in Fresno.

San Diego State baseball pitcher Stephen Strasburg earned the number one pick in the 2009 MLB draft, as the Mountain West became one of three conferences to have the number one selection in each of the NFL, NBA, and MLB drafts since the MW was founded.

Q: Which of the three California schools has the most NCAA Division I championships: San Diego State, Fresno State, or San Jose State?

For the Mountain West and other college conferences, visit www.californiasportsastounding.com

A: San Jose State has 10 championships: men's golf (1948), boxing (1958 to 1960), cross country (1962 and 1963), men's outdoor track and field (1969), and women's golf (1987, 1989, and 1992).

CALIFORNIA SPORTS BIRTHDAYS

More Fun for January 4

Q: Dave Scott, born in 1954, won how many Ironman Triathlon World Championships: one, four straight times, or six times total?

....

Did You Know?

Fresno State and San Diego State have a football rivalry dating back to November 29, 1923. San Diego State won the first game 12-2 on their home field at Balboa Stadium.

A: Scott, who was born in Davis and whose nickname is "The Man," won the Hawaii event six times: in 1980 on Oahu, with the rest in Kona on the Big Island from 1982 to 1984, and 1986 to 1987. He was an Ironman Hall of Fame charter inductee in 1993.

NOTABLE BIRTHDAYS

January 4

1964: Dot-Marie Jones, born in Turlock, All-American in the shot put at Modesto Junior College and Fresno State. 15-time women's world arm wrestling champion, including 11 in a row from 1983-1994.

1985: Eric Weddle, native of Fontana, NFL free safety, NFL 2010's All-Decade Team, Super Bowl LVI champion with the Los Angeles Rams.

Van Ness Tennis
January 5, 1885

California's oldest tennis club is located in San Francisco. The Van Ness Avenue Lawn Tennis Club, which was founded in September 1884, was renamed the California Tennis Club. On January 5, 1885, the *Daily Alta California* announced that "A name has finally been given the new lawn tennis club which makes its headquarters at the lot on the corner of Van Ness Avenue and Sutter Street. Henceforth, the organization will be known as the California Tennis Club. The recent severe rains have seriously interfered with the proceedings of the Club, no meeting having taken place since the first week in December. Last Saturday afternoon, however, a partially clear sky caused the members to venture forth, and a very successful meeting was held. The grounds were in splendid condition, and a number of spirited contests were indulged in. No more applications for membership to the club will be entertained, as the maximum number of 80 is now complete."

Mary Therese Austin founded the club and encouraged a "fun and healthy outlet of an exuberant exchange across the net." The California Tennis Club is the oldest private tennis club west of the Mississippi River.

Q: How many Cal Club members have been inducted into the International Tennis Hall of Fame: none, two, or six?

For more tennis, visit www.californiasportsastounding.com

A: Six. Margaret Osborne Du Pont, Clarence Griffin, William Johnston, Alice Marble, Maurice McLoughlin, and Helen Wills.

CALIFORNIA SPORTS BIRTHDAYS
More Fun for January 5

Q: Carolyn Schuler, born in 1943, swimmer, winner of two Olympic gold medals in 1960, represented which California swim club: Mission Viejo Nadadores or Berkeley YMCA?

. . . .

Did You Know?

The Association of Centenary Tennis Clubs, consisting of 100-plus year old clubs from around the world, has three members from California. The California Tennis Club (1884), Berkeley Tennis Club (1906), and the Sutter Lawn Tennis Club (1919).

A: Schuler, a native of San Francisco, swam for the Berkeley YMCA.

NOTABLE BIRTHDAYS

January 5

1967: Brian Blutreich, born in Mission Viejo, track and field athlete, won six All-American honors at UCLA in the discus and shot put from 1986-1990.

1921: Harold "California Comet" Davis, Salinas native, sprinter, attended UC Berkeley, undefeated from 1940-1943 in the 220 yard event, ran 100 yards in 10.2 seconds at the 1941 Compton Relays which tied the world record set by Jesse Owens, National Track and Field Hall of Fame inductee 1974.

Tiny Aerial Life Preserver
January 9, 1914

Twenty-one-year-old Miss Tiny Broadwick, four foot eight, 98 pounds, made the first parachute jump by a woman. Broadwick jumped from a plane piloted by Los Angeles stunt flyer Glenn L. Martin at a height of 850 feet. The observer aboard was *Los Angeles Times* reporter Bonnie Glessner. Broadwick wore Martin's patented invention, the "aerial life preserver," which contained a 14-pound pack and a parachute with 110 yards of silk. Broadwick's demonstration jump landed safely at the Griffith Park aviation field.

Q: How fast can a solo skydiver fall?

For more parachuting, visit www.californiasportsastounding.com

A: The terminal velocity of a falling human being with arms and legs outstretched is about 120 miles per hour in the standard face to earth position.

CALIFORNIA SPORTS BIRTHDAYS
More Fun for January 9

Q: Thomas Curtis, born in 1873, was the first Californian to win an Olympic medal. What was his sport: weightlifting, track and field, or swimming?

Did You Know?

Skydive Perris, between Los Angeles and San Diego, is one of the largest skydiving centers in the world. The center has hosted many world records including the largest formation of women (181), the largest formation of Wingsuiters, the largest sequence of formations by women, and more. Skydive Perris is one of only two skydiving centers in the world to have an indoor skydiving simulator.

A: Track and field. The San Francisco native won the 110-meter hurdles at the 1896 Olympics with a winning time of 17.6 seconds.

NOTABLE BIRTHDAYS

January 9

1943: Rod Curl, born in Redding, professional golfer, first Native American to win a PGA Tour event, won the 1974 Colonial National Invitation by one stroke over Jack Nicklaus.

1975: Justin Huish, born in Fountain Valley, archer, 1996 Olympic gold medalist in the individual and team events

Stone Cold
January 9, 1959

Curling slid into California in 1907 when the San Francisco Scottish Curling Club was founded. Their first games were held on a wooden floor at the Pavilion skating rink in San Francisco.

California's first curling rink opened in Mountain View on January 9, 1959. Canadian Dick Sherwin built the Peninsula Curling Rink at a cost of $250,000. The first bonspiel, or tournament, drew 96 entrants from Alameda, San Francisco, San Mateo, and Santa Clara counties. Players filled the rink as all four sheets of ice were in use during the tournament.

Q: What is California's oldest curling club?

For more curling, visit www.californiasportsastounding.com

A: The San Francisco Bay Area Curling Club is the oldest arena curling club in America. The club was founded in 1958.

CALIFORNIA SPORTS BIRTHDAYS
More Fun for January 9

Q: Marcus Peters, born in 1993, NFL cornerback, led the league in interceptions in what year: 2015, 2017, or 2019?

Did You Know?

The Southern California Curling Center near downtown Los Angeles opened in 2021 as America's largest curling venue west of Fargo, North Dakota. The home of the Hollywood Curling Club has six sheets of ice, allowing up to six games to be played simultaneously. California's other large curling centers are located in Oakland, San Jose, Sacramento, Valencia, and Carlsbad.

A: The Oakland native led the NFL with eight interceptions in 2015. He was named Defensive Rookie of the Year.

NOTABLE BIRTHDAY

January 9, 1975

Mariano Friedick, born in Tarzana, professional cyclist, 1994 World Championships silver medalist in team pursuit. California teammates Adam Laurent and Dirk Copeland also won medals.

NOTABLE EVENT

January 9, 1977

The first Super Bowl held at the Rose Bowl. Super Bowl XI was attended by 103,438 fans who saw the Oakland Raiders demolish the Minnesota Vikings 32-14.

With longer seasons and playoffs, most Super Bowls are now played in late January or early February. This game from 1977 is the earliest Super Bowl scheduled during a calendar year.

Higher and Higher
January 10-20, 1910

Los Angeles athletic promoter Dick Ferris wanted to introduce a new sports event. First, he needed to garner business support. Ferris got that support from the Los Angeles Chamber of Commerce and the Merchants and Manufacturers Association. The next challenge was the venue. Fields near Santa Anita Park were considered, but tall trees would obstruct the event. Ferris needed an area close to the rail lines to bring spectators in via streetcars from the Pacific Electric Station in Los Angeles. He found a low mesa with good sight lines and no obstructions. An area at Dominguez Hill was selected. This area had been developed by Manuel Dominguez on land once part of Rancho San Pedro, an early Spanish land grant. The Dominguez family owned the site and let him use it for free. Then Ferris invited contestants. These were pilots of monoplanes, biplanes, balloons, and airships.

What transpired was the first major air show in America and was only six years after the Wright brother's first flight at Kitty Hawk, NC. The Los Angeles International Air Meet was held over ten days. $80,000 in prizes drew entrants from France, New York, and California. French pilot Louis Paulhan headed the entries. Eleven airplanes and three airships participated.

A $1,500 prize was offered to the best California-made machine and landed several entries from throughout the state. Monoplanes were entered by San Francisco's Pacific Aero Club and the San Diego Aero Manufacturing Company. San Francisco's Lincoln Beachey flew an airship and San Diego's Waldo Waterman piloted a biplane. Los Angeles residents James Slough Zerbe and A.E. Mueller entered with unusual designs. Zerbe's multiplane, with five separate planes of wings, didn't get off the ground. Mueller's entry, called "Mueller's Monster" by the *Los Angeles Times*, was the world's largest airplane. It measured 75 feet long by 50 feet wide, had a 50-horsepower engine, and weighed a ton.

Halfway through the event, the Los Angeles Times declared it "one of the greatest public events in the history of the West. An impetus has been given to aerial sport in America such as no other form of exhibition ever enjoyed." Promoters estimated that over 250,000 tickets were sold. American aviator

Glenn Curtiss set a new air speed record of approximately 55 miles per hour and the prize for the best quick start. He won $6,500.

A parade was held on the final day and showed the evolution of travel. Heading the group was a prairie schooner hauled by oxen. After that came cowboys, automobiles, burros, carriages, balloons, dirigibles, and finally the various builds of airships.

Q: What Pasadena-born record-breaking woman pilot operated the Rancho Oro Verde Fly-Inn Dude Ranch, a hangout for test pilots at Edwards Air Force Base?

For more air racing, visit www.californiasportsastounding.com

A: Florence "Pancho" Barnes. In 1930 she broke Amelia Earhart's world women's speed record with a speed of 196.19 miles per hour.

CALIFORNIA SPORTS BIRTHDAYS
More Fun for January 10

Q: Vladimir "Spider" Sabich Jr., born in 1945, had 18 top ten finishes in Olympic and World Cup competition in what winter sport: curling, speed skating, or alpine skiing?

Did You Know?

On January 24, 1960, the California Office of Historic Preservation dedicated the site Dominguez Hill at historic Rancho San Pedro as a California Registered Historical Landmark #718 in cooperation with the City of Compton. This is California's first sports related historical landmark.

A: Sabich, a native of El Dorado County, was an alpine ski racer. He was a member of the Red Hornet Ski Club and raced at the Edelweiss ski area, which is now known as Camp Sacramento.

Barry Ball
January 10, 1967

The Cow Palace in Daly City hosted the National Basketball Association All-Star game for the first and only time. Los Angeles Lakers coach Fred Schaus directed the Western Conference All-Stars to a 135-120 win over the Eastern Conference All-Stars. San Francisco Warriors forward Rick Barry scored 38 points and was named game MVP. Eastern Conference coach Red Auerbach made history by becoming the first coach to be ejected in the All-Star Game. Referee Willie Smith gave Auerbach his second technical foul in the third quarter for "vulgar language."

Q: What hall-of-fame sportswriter wrote that San Francisco sports fans love Rick Barry second only to the five o'clock martini?

For more basketball, visit www.californiasportsastounding.com

A: Jim Murray of the *Los Angeles Times*.

CALIFORNIA SPORTS BIRTHDAYS
More Fun for January 10

Q: Adam Kennedy, born in 1976, was an infielder for the 2002 World Series champion Anaheim Angels. Who did the Angels beat in seven games: Los Angeles Dodgers or the San Francisco Giants?

....

Did You Know?

The Cow Palace hosted the American Basketball League's San Francisco Saints from 1961-1962. The team moved to Oakland in 1962 and was renamed the Oaks. Their home games were played at the Oakland Auditorium. Southern California was represented by the Long Beach Chiefs and the Los Angeles Jets. The ABL folded in December of 1962.

A: The Riverside native helped the Angels rally from a two-game deficit and beat the San Francisco Giants 4-3.

NOTABLE EVENT

January 10, 1982

With only 58 seconds left and third down at the six-yard line in the NFC championship game at Candlestick Park, 25-year-old San Francisco 49ers quarterback Joe Montana was chased to the sideline by three Dallas Cowboys. He somehow evaded them and heaved a touchdown pass to a leaping wide receiver Dwight Clark who barely caught the ball with his fingertips in the corner of the end zone and was forever labeled, "the Catch." San Francisco won the game 28-27 over the then-dynasty Cowboys. Two weeks later the 49ers beat the Cincinnati Bengals 26-21 for their first Super Bowl title.

NOTABLE BIRTHDAY

January 10, 1994

Madison "Maddie" Bowman, from South Lake Tahoe, 2014 Winter Olympics gold medalist in the Women's Halfpipe.

NFL-AFL in CA
January 15, 1967

Lamar Hunt, owner of the American Football League's Kansas City Chiefs, used a new term for the NFL-AFL championship game in 1966. The first reference in a California newspaper appeared in the Sacramento Bee on July 18, which quoted Hunt as saying "The NFL-AFL championship football game probably will be played on a neutral site, with the Rose Bowl having the best chance. I think one of the first things we will consider is the site of the Super Bowl—that's my term for the championship game between the two leagues."

Sportswriter Braven "Bud" Dyer of the *Desert Sun* promoted the Rose Bowl as a potential site. "Another game AFTER the Rose Bowl couldn't hurt it. Why, they could sell out the college game two or three times over as it is, and the same thing would apply even if the pros did come in. It will be a shame if the game gets black-balled here. I can see the people of Oakland and San Francisco already bidding for it in the new Oakland Stadium."

Pasadena's City Manager made a bid on November 4, but by that time their Chamber of Commerce, the Pacific-8 Conference and Big Ten Conference had voiced opposition to having the Rose and Super Bowls scheduled so close together. The Chamber of Commerce was concerned that a second bowl game would dilute and not increase income to the City of Pasadena and could jeopardize the Rose Bowl game.

The NFL still had several proposals to consider. Los Angeles officials submitted their bid with the Memorial Coliseum as host stadium. The NFL considered several venues across the country, including the Orange Bowl in Miami, the Sugar Bowl in New Orleans, the Cotton Bowl in Dallas, and Houston's Astrodome. The City of Anaheim applied on November 9 and proposed using the almost new, seven-month-old Anaheim Stadium. Los Angeles was eventually awarded the game on December 1.

On January 15, 1967, the game was held at the Coliseum before 61,946 fans. Tickets were a pricey $12, which prevented a sellout. The Green Bay Packers led by Vince Lombardi beat the Kansas City Chiefs 35-10.

Q: What California majorette group performed during the pregame festivities and after each quarter?

For more football, visit www.californiasportsastounding.com

A: The Los Angeles Ramettes, majorettes who performed at all Rams home games.

CALIFORNIA SPORTS BIRTHDAYS
More Fun for January 15

Q: Michele Granger, born in 1970, softball pitcher and 1996 Olympic gold medalist, was a four-time All-American for which Pac-12 school: UC Berkeley, Stanford, or UCLA?

....

Did You Know?

Braven "Bud" Dyer was a sportswriter and editor for the *Los Angeles Times* from 1925 to 1965. He created a nationally recognized awards program for Southern California amateur athletes. Bud teamed with Bill Schroeder and the Helms Athletic Foundation to record and honor the achievements of Southern California athletes. From 1950 to 1970, Dyer and Schroeder worked closely with the sports organizations in Southern California to create an awards program and build a collection of sports books and memorabilia. The Helms Athletic Foundation later became the International Association of Sports Museums and Halls of Fame, of which Dyer was president. The books and memorabilia collection and awards program are now important parts of the Amateur Athletic Foundation of Los Angeles. Dyer worked with prep sportswriters to honor the top athletes from the California Interscholastic Federation's Southern Section and Los Angeles City Sections.

A: The Placentia native played collegiate softball for the UC Berkeley Golden Bears from 1989-1993. She was inducted into the USA Softball Hall of Fame in 2006.

Onion Valley Snow
January 30, 1861

Ski historians Scott J. Lawson and Rob Russell documented the sport's origins in their 2009 article "The History of Longboard Skiing and Its Revival Races in Plumas County." This article cites several published works that prove Plumas County is the birthplace of downhill competitive ski racing in America and the western hemisphere.

The article was presented to the National Ski Congress and International Ski Association at Mammoth Lakes.

The first reference related to the actual sport of racing for a prize appeared in the *Daily National Democrat* on January 30, 1861 and was titled "Snowshoeing for a Belt" (snowshoes being another name for pioneer era skis). "Over at Onion Valley, Plumas County, says the *Mountain Messenger*, the boys are having gay sport in sliding down the long and steep hill sides on snowshoes. George Swain, the expressman, informs us that the Onion Valley folks have attained a perfection in snow shoeing that is astonishing. A club has been formed, and every Sunday the members assemble and have a lively contest of speed for a champion belt, valued at $25."

Q: Who won the first Alturas Snowshoe Club championship in 1867?

For more skiing, visit www.californiasportsastounding.com

A: Robert "Cornish Bob" Oliver won the race held February 11, concluded after storms on February 16. He registered a speed of 60 mph on the 1,230-foot course.

CALIFORNIA SPORTS BIRTHDAYS
More Fun for January 30

Q: Deltha O'Neal, III, born in 1977, NFL cornerback, and All-American at UC Berkeley. What NCAA season record did he set: 100-meter dash, most pick-sixes, or most tackles?

....

Did You Know?

The book *Lost Sierra: Gold, Ghosts & Skis* by William B. Berry and Chapman Wentworth covers California skiing history and the Alturas Snowshoe Club.

A: The most pick-sixes! The native of Palo Alto has the most interceptions returned for a touchdown in a season, with four in 1999.

NOTABLE EVENTS
January 30

1990: Wayne Gretzky of the Los Angeles Kings set an NHL record by reaching 100 points for the 11th consecutive season. Gretzky earned an assist in the Kings 5-2 win over the New Jersey Devils at the Forum in Inglewood.

1996: Earvin "Magic" Johnson returned to play pro basketball after a four and a half year retirement and led the Los Angeles Lakers to a 128-118 win over the Golden State Warriors at the Great Western Forum.

Big Bear Games
January 30, 1997

California hosted the inaugural Winter X Games. ESPN came to the mountain and committed a lot of resources to the event. The network had a truck and electronic equipment stolen in San Bernardino three days before the event, putting the broadcast in jeopardy. The games were held at Snow Summit Ski Resort at Big Bear Lake from January 30 to February 2. Eleven events were contested from five categories: shovel racing, snow mountain bike racing, ice climbing, snowboarding, and crossover competition. Snow Summit and its 240 skiable acres already had experience with big events, having hosted the Vans Triple Crown of Snowboarding. $200,000 in prize money was enough to attract 150 entries.

ESPN was able to rush new equipment and their televised broadcasts reached 198 countries in 21 languages. They also passed out 3,000 cowbells to spectators to help them cheer for the contestants.

California's Shaun "Palm Daddy" Palmer won the Snowboarder X title. Barret Christy collected wins in the Slopestyle and Big Air Women's event.

Q: What is the elevation at Snow Summit Ski Resort?

For more X Games, visit www.californiasportsastounding.com

A: 8,200 feet. The resort has 18 skiable miles and 27 trails.

CALIFORNIA SPORTS BIRTHDAYS
More Fun for January 30

Q: Bert Bonanno, born in 1940, track and field coach, established a world-class track and field program at what college: San Jose City College, UCLA, or USC?

....

Did You Know?

California was the first state to host the Winter and Summer X Games in the same year. The Winter X Games in January 1997 were followed by the Summer X Games just five months later in San Diego.

A: The Pittsburg, CA native coached at San Jose City College. He developed Millard Hampton, Andre Phillips, Bruce Jenner, and several other Olympians and world record holders.

NOTABLE BIRTHDAY

January 30, 1988:

Keshia Baker, born in Fairfield, sprinter, won a gold medal in the 4 x 400-meter relay at the 2012 Olympics. California teammates DeeDee Trotter, Francena McCorory, and Allyson Felix also won medals. Felix would end her career as the most decorated American track and field athlete in Olympic history, with 11 medals from five consecutive Olympic Games from 2004-2020.

NOTABLE EVENT

January 30, 2022

The Los Angeles Rams overcame a 10 point fourth quarter deficit to beat the San Francisco 49ers 20-17 and win the National Football Conference championship at SoFi Stadium.

FEBRUARY
FUN

Informal Base Ball
February 4, 1851

The San Francisco based *Daily Alta California* reported on the first informal game of baseball played in the state. "A game of base ball [spelled as two words] was played upon the Plaza [San Francisco's central square], yesterday afternoon, by a number of the sporting gentlemen about town."

Two days later, the *Alta* printed this update:

"BASE-BALL—This is becoming quite popular among our sporting gentry, who have an exercise upon the Plaza nearly every day. This is certainly better amusement than "bucking" (passing markers during poker) and if no windows or heads are broken will prove much more profitable."

Q: What was the Plaza also known as?

For more baseball, visit www.californiasportsastounding.com

A: Portsmouth Square.

CALIFORNIA SPORTS BIRTHDAYS
More Fun for February 4

Q: Jason Kapono, born in 1981, was the first NBA player to lead the league in what shooting percentage for consecutive seasons: dunks, free throws, or three pointers?

Did You Know?

Oscar De La Hoya, "The Golden Boy," won 11 world titles in six weight classes, plus an Olympic gold medal.

A: Kapono, a Long Beach native, led the league in three-point shooting from 2006 to 2008.

NOTABLE BIRTHDAY

February 4, 1930

Jim Loscutoff, born in San Francisco, pro basketball player, attended Palo Alto High School and Grant Technical College, played on seven Boston Celtics NBA championship teams 1957 and 1959-1964.

NOTABLE EVENTS

February 4

1969: John Madden was named coach of the NFL's Oakland Raiders. Almost eight years later Madden led Oakland to their first Super Bowl win, a 32-14 trouncing of the Minnesota Vikings at the Rose Bowl in Pasadena.

1987: The Sacramento Kings scored only four points in the first quarter against the Los Angeles Lakers before 14,729 fans at the Forum. The four points were the fewest in a quarter since the NBA introduced the 24-second shot clock on April 22, 1954. The Lakers set an NBA record when they scored the first 29 points of the game and led 40-4 after the first quarter. Sacramento's first points came from Derek Smith who made two free throws with 2:54 left in the first quarter. The Lakers won 128-92.

Leaping Leslie
February 7, 1990

Lisa Leslie, a six-foot-five center of the Morningside High School girls basketball team scored 101 points in only 16 minutes against South Torrance High School. Leslie made 37 of 56 field goal attempts and 27 of 35 free throws. She scored 49 points in the first quarter and 52 in the second, an average of more than six points a minute. The final score was 102-24 when the game was called at halftime. South Torrance had two players foul out and another one injured, so only four healthy players remained. Coach Gilbert Ramirez did not bring his team out for the second half.

Q: Who scored the only other point for Morningside?

For more basketball, visit www.californiasportsastounding.com

A: Sherrell Young.

CALIFORNIA SPORTS BIRTHDAYS
More Fun for February 7

Q: Clarence Crabbe II, born in 1908, known professionally as Buster Crabbe, set how many world and national swimming records: 16 world and 35 national, or 20 world and 38 national records?

Did You Know?

Cynthia "Sippy" Woodhead started her swimming career at the Riverside Aquatics Association. She won gold medals in the 200-meter freestyle, 4 × 100-meter freestyle, and medley relay, and two silver medals at the 1978 World Championships when she was only 14 years old. Sippy was a silver medalist in the 200-meter freestyle at the 1984 Olympics. Woodhead was inducted into the International Swimming Hall of Fame in 1994.

A: Buster, a native of Oakland, set 16 world and 35 national records. He then established a career as an actor in over 100 movies, including *Flash Gordon* and *Buck Rogers*.

NOTABLE BIRTHDAYS

February 7

1953: Dan "Quiz" Quisenberry, born in Santa Monica, MLB pitcher, pitched submarine style and led the American League in saves five times: 1980, 1982, 1983, 1984, and 1985. He was a World Series champion with the Kansas City Royals in 1985.

1957: Carney Lansford, born in San Jose, MLB third baseman 1978-1992, All-Star with the Oakland Athletics in 1988, World Series champion with the Athletics in 1989.

NOTABLE EVENT

February 7, 1987

Dennis Conner and his crew of the Stars & Stripes 87 arrived in San Diego after sailing to victory in the America's Cup races held in Australia. Dennis had lost the Cup in 1983, but regained the trophy with a 4-0 sweep. He sailed for the San Diego Yacht Club, became the first from California to win the prestigious event.

Entertain Rather Than Inform
February 12, 1961

Jim Murray's first sports column for the *Los Angeles Times* was published. Murray had already been a general assignment and rewrite man for the *Los Angeles Examiner* from 1944 to 1948. He helped establish *Sports Illustrated* and was a writer and West Coast editor for the magazine from 1953 to 1961. Jim typed his columns on his treasured 1946 Remington typewriter. Murray's first column for the *Times* was "Let's Dot Some 'I's."

Murray clearly showed readers from day one that he wrote to entertain more than inform.

Murray's satire targeted many cities. San Francisco was "Only a place that calls an earthquake a fire could call what was played in Candlestick Park baseball." Oakland was "A town where the count had been 3 and 2 for twenty-five years. It was like a fighter who needed a knockout to win." Los Angeles was described as "A place that has a dry river, but one hundred thousand swimming pools."

Jim won several awards during his career. He won the National Sportscasters and Sportswriters Association Sportswriter of the Year Award an astonishing 14 times, including 12 consecutively from 1966 to 1977. Jim was inducted into the NSSA Hall of Fame in 1978. The Associated Press Sports Editors gave him the Red Smith Award in 1982 for outstanding contributions to sports journalism. Five years later the Baseball Hall of Fame awarded him the J.G. Taylor Spink Award, the highest accolade given by the Baseball Writers' Association of America. In 1990 Murray won a Pulitzer Prize for Commentary for his 1989 columns. After winning the Pulitzer, he modestly said that he thought the prize winner should have had "to bring down a government or expose major graft or give advice to prime ministers. Correctly quoting Los Angeles Dodgers manager Tommy Lasorda shouldn't merit a Pulitzer Prize."

He lost sight in his left eye but continued to produce quality writing to the end. Jim wrote his last column, "You Can Teach an Old Horse New Tricks," from the Del Mar Thoroughbred Club on Saturday August 15, 1998. He died the next day. The next year, Los Angeles Memorial Coliseum commissioners honored Jim for his contributions to sports in Los Angeles with a Court of Honor plaque. A Golden Palm Star on the Palm Springs Walk of Stars was dedicated posthumously to Murray in 2008.

Q: The National Sports Media Association started the California Sportswriter of the Year Award in 1959. Who was the first winner?

For more sports, visit www.californiasportsastounding.com

A: Melvin Durslag, who wrote for the *Los Angeles Herald Examiner* until 1989. He was inducted into the National Sports Media Association Hall of Fame in 1995.

CALIFORNIA SPORTS BIRTHDAYS
More Fun for February 12

Q: Charles "Chick" Hafey, born in 1903 in Berkeley, had the first hit in the first Major League Baseball All-Star game in 1933. Who was the pitcher: Righty McDonald or Lefty Gomez?

Did You Know?

Jim Murray's widow Linda McCoy-Murray created the Jim Murray Memorial Foundation, which raises money to provide scholarships for second- and third-year undergraduate journalism students. The Jim Murray Memorial Foundation (JMMF) became an official California 501(c)(3) nonprofit corporation on May 17, 1999, to perpetuate Jim Murray's legacy and his love for and dedication to his extraordinary career in journalism. The JMMF coordinates a nationwide essay competition, with winners decided by a panel of nationally known journalists. Over 30 colleges and universities have participated. California has been represented by students from California State University Northridge, San Diego State University, UCLA, and USC.

A: Hall of Fame lefthander Lefty Gomez, a native of Rodeo, CA. Gomez was a five-time World Series champion with the New York Yankees in 1932 and from 1936 to 1939.

Best Big Waves
February 17, 1999

California's best big wave spot is not all fun. This place has huge rocks, occasional shark attacks, water temperature as low as 48 degrees and air temperature that can drop to the 30s. The reward is riding waves that can range from 25 to 60 feet high.

Santa Cruz surfer Darryl "Flea" Virostko won the first big wave competition held at Mavericks Beach, located about 25 miles south of San Francisco. Mavericks is about two miles offshore from the Pillar Point Harbor, and just north of the town of Half Moon Bay. The contest was limited to the world's 24 best big wave surfers. Virostko won again in 2000 and 2004, becoming the first three-time Titans of Mavericks Champion. California's winter months with their optimal winds and swells were the prime time for the contest. Invited surfers flocked to the beach knowing they have to seize the opportunity within a limited time span.

There are some famous moments outside of the contest. On December 19, 1994, 16-year-old Jay Moriarity rode a 10-foot board at Mavericks into heavy winds.

He had a spectacular 35-to-40-foot wipeout called the "Iron Cross"—so named because of his outstretched arms. Santa Cruz photographer Bob Barbour captured the moment. His photo made the cover of the May 1995 issue of *Surfer* magazine. The first woman to surf Mavericks was Santa Cruz resident Sarah Gerhardt who accomplished the feat as a 24-year-old in 1999.

The World Surf League took over the contest in 2018, but cancelled it indefinitely due to various logistical challenges and the inability to run the event.

Q: Who was the next Californian to win at Mavericks: Greg Long, Anthony Tashnick, or Peter Mel?

For more surfing, visit www.californiasportsastounding.com

A: Twenty-year-old Anthony Tashnick of Santa Cruz won the event in 2005, the youngest winner ever.

CALIFORNIA SPORTS BIRTHDAYS
More Fun for February 17

Q: Joseph Hunt, born in 1919, was the first to win which four national tennis tournaments?

....

Did You Know?

The largest surfing contest in the world, the Vans U.S. Open, is a nine-day event held each summer at the Huntington Beach Pier. The event also honors notable people in the world of surfing by adding their names to the Surfing Walk of Fame and to the Surfers' Hall of Fame across from the pier. Over 500,000 surf lovers attend the event.

Lemoore, CA is home to the longest, rideable open-barrel man-made waves in the world. Surfing in the Central Valley? Yes. In 2018, 11-time world surfing champion Kelly Slater teamed with USC professor Adam Fincham, a specialist in geophysical fluid dynamics, to create the wave pool. Kelly Slater Surf Park's pool is 2,000 feet long and 500 feet wide. Waves reach a maximum of 6.5 feet, but can be adjusted to fit beginner, intermediate, and advanced surfers. The Surf Ranch Pro contest in 2018 was the world's first championship tour wave pool event in surfing history. World Surfing League officials renamed it the Freshwater Pro in 2019.

A: The San Francisco native won the U.S. Boys (15 and under), junior (18 and under), NCAA (1941), and U.S. Open singles championship (1943).

NOTABLE BIRTHDAYS
February 17

1987: Soccer player Amy Rodriguez "A-Rod" Shilling of Lake Forest won gold medals at the 2008 and 2012 Olympics, plus a World Cup gold in 2015.

1988: Brian Burrows born in Torrance, sport shooter, 2020 Olympic bronze medalist in mixed trap.

Winter 1960
February 18-29

California welcomed its first Olympics with the winter edition. The VIII Olympic Winter Games were held in Squaw Valley. Local landowner Alexander Cushing, who had already built a lodge and ski life in Squaw Valley, was the driving force in gathering support for the Olympics. After the Golden State was awarded the games, the California Olympic Commission was formed. The commission built the venues and expanded the existing infrastructure. Entrepreneur and Stanford graduate Prentis Cobb Hale directed the Organizing Committee.

The Winter Olympics established several firsts. This was the first to be televised live. CBS introduced the first instant replay. Organizers had the first Olympic Village purpose-built for the occasion. Another first was contributed by famous animator and cartoonist Walt Disney. He led the Pageantry Committee, which organized the opening and closing ceremonies. He also created the Tower of Nations, a huge metal structure topped by the Olympic rings. The tower was the site of all medal ceremonies, the first time they were held in the same location.

America's first "Miracle on Ice" happened as the underdog hockey team shocked everyone as they swept the top four teams in the world—Canada, Soviet Union, Czechoslovakia, and Sweden—to win their first gold medal in the sport. Russia would go on to win every Olympic hockey tournament until 1980 when they lost to Team USA again.

San Mateo's Barbara Roles was the lone Californian to medal. She won a bronze medal in the ladies' singles event of figure skating.

Squaw Valley was renamed Palisades Tahoe on September 13, 2021. The ski resort investigated the term "squaw" and acknowledged its name as a racist and sexist slur that was used by settlers referencing Native American women. Palisades Tahoe, located in Olympic Valley, is the ancestral homeland of the Washoe Tribe.

Q: Barbara Roles won another bronze medal in 1960 at what competition?

For more Olympics, visit www.californiasportsastounding.com

A: Roles placed third in the ladies' singles at the World Figure Skating Championships one week after the Olympics.

CALIFORNIA SPORTS BIRTHDAYS
More Fun for February 18

Q: Joe "Flash" Gordon, born in 1915, MLB second baseman, was the American League MVP in 1942 for what team: St. Louis Browns or New York Yankees?

....

Did You Know?

Blyth Arena was the site of the 1960 Winter Olympics opening and closing ceremonies, ice hockey, and figure skating. The arena was named after Charles Blyth, who chaired the California Olympic Commission. Capacity was 8,500 seats, though 10,000 hysterical hockey fans crammed into the arena to watch the USA score their first win over Russia, 3-2.

A: Gordon, a Los Angeles native, was the 1942 MVP for the New York Yankees.

NOTABLE BIRTHDAYS
February 18

1931: Robert St. Clair, NFL tackle, San Francisco native, All-Pro with the San Francisco 49ers 1955, 1956, 1958, 1960, 1961, and Pro Football Hall of Fame inductee 1990.

1947: Gary Sheerer, water polo player, born in Berkeley, 1972 Olympic bronze medalist and team captain, and USA Water Polo Hall of Fame inductee 1982.

Velocipede Victories
February 20, 1869

Velocipedes, a human powered land vehicle with one or more wheels, most commonly known as a bicycle, were first advertised in the *Sacramento Bee* in 1857. They were sold at Dale & Company on J Street in Sacramento.

The first race was covered in February of 1869 by the Grass Valley newspaper the *Morning Union*: "The Velocipede Race—Mill Street yesterday afternoon was crowded with spectators of the velocipede race. Morris H. Joseph rode his own vehicle, which was made in San Francisco, and Tom Mills rode the one constructed in Grass Valley. Joe had been practicing on his for several days, but Tom, when he commenced the race, bestrode his steed for the first time. The riders mounted in the Empire Stables for the first heat, and went from that place to Main Street, thence down Main to the front of Stokes' Occidental Saloon. Tom Milts won the first heat. The second trial was from above the Exchange Hotel to Stokes.' In this heat Tom's velocipede bucked, and he had to dismount. He picked up the machine, however, and throwing it across his shoulder, made excellent time, barely losing the second heat by a second. The referee, who was not present, declared the race to be a tie, and that all bets are off.

The Grass Valley velocipede consists of a carpenter's sawhorse, under the legs of which, at each end, is placed a wheel. The rider propelled it by having both feet on the ground, and running his level best. The crowd greeted Tom Mills and velocipede with shouts of laughter."

The following month the *Daily Evening Herald* described formal races at the Mechanics' Pavilion in San Francisco "The velocipede race was witnessed by 2,500 people, who appeared greatly interested in the result. The race was won by E. Harris, he made the mile in four minutes and five seconds."

Q: Who was the first Californian to win the prestigious Tour de France bicycle race?

For more cycling, visit www.californiasportsastounding.com

A: Lakewood native Greg LeMond won the race in 1986, 1989, and 1990. He was inducted into the United States Bicycling Hall of Fame in 1996. Greg was the first cyclist to appear on the cover of *Sports Illustrated*.

CALIFORNIA SPORTS BIRTHDAYS
More Fun February 20

Q: Gill Byrd, born in 1961, was an NFL first team All-Pro cornerback in 1989 for which California team: Oakland Raiders, Los Angeles Rams, or San Diego Chargers?

. . . .

Did You Know?

The Amgen Tour of California is an annual professional cycling stage race on the UCI World Tour and USA Cycling Professional Tour. The eight-day race covers between 650 to 700 miles.

A: The San Francisco native played cornerback for the San Diego Chargers from 1983 to 1992.

NOTABLE BIRTHDAY
February 20, 1969

Thomas "Touchdown Tommy" Vardell, born in El Cajon, NFL fullback, played for Stanford University from 1988 to 1991. He scored 39 touchdowns during his collegiate career and never fumbled.

Stars 2 Padres
February 20, 1936

Stars became Padres before the start of the 1936 Pacific Coast League season. San Diego baseball fans had a new minor league team. The *San Pedro News-Pilot* noted "The new San Diego Coast league baseball team, formerly the Hollywood Stars, will be known as the "Padres," owner William Lane announced at a team banquet last night. The choice was made by W. C. Tuttle, league president, Lane and newspapermen present at the affair. Previously the nickname of "Dons," had been favored but was voted down because it is used by San Francisco University."

The Stars, who were tenants of the Los Angeles Angels and played at Wrigley Field, were forced to move after their $6,000 annual rent was raised.

San Diego welcomed the team by renovating a field near the waterfront and West Broadway, installing 8,000 bleacher seats, and renaming it Lane Field. That was their home until 1957, then they relocated to Westgate Park from 1958 to 1967, and San Diego Stadium in 1968.

Major League Baseball awarded San Diego an expansion franchise in 1969. The team joined the National League and retained their nickname. Their first game was held at home on April 8. Dick Selma pitched a five hitter, and the Padres edged the Houston Astros 2-1. The Padres finished their stay in the stadium by winning pennants in 1984 and 1998 but lost in the World Series both times. A new home opened for the Padres in 2004 and they moved downtown to Petco Park.

Three San Diego players are enshrined in the National Baseball Hall of Fame and Museum with their plaques showing the Padres cap. Tony "Mr. Padre" Gwynn won eight National League batting titles. Trevor Hoffman was the first pitcher in MLB history to record 600 saves. Right fielder Dave Winfield was a multiple All-Star and Gold Glove winner.

Q: The Padres set a Major League record in 2020 by hitting a grand slam in how many consecutive games?

For more baseball, visit www.californiasportsastounding.com

A: Four. The Padres hit grand slams in four games August 17 through 20 against the Texas Rangers. Fernando Tatis Jr., Wil Myers, Manny Machado, and Eric Hosmer crushed home runs as the Padres finished the four-game sweep with two wins at home.

CALIFORNIA SPORTS BIRTHDAYS
More Fun for February 20

Q: James Wilson, born in 1922, was the only Major League pitcher to accomplish this feat in 1954: a no-hitter, 25 wins, or 300 strikeouts?

. . . .

Did You Know?

Baseball hall of famer Tony Gwynn started college as a point guard on the San Diego State basketball team from 1978 to 1981. He set the school record of 590 assists in a career, more than 100 ahead of the second-best mark. Tony was also an All-American outfielder for the Aztecs. On June 9, 1981, Gwynn was drafted by the Padres and the NBA's San Diego Clippers. He chose the Padres.

A: San Diego's Jim Wilson, with catcher Del Crandall pitched the only MLB no-hitter in 1954 as the Milwaukee Braves beat the Philadelphia Phillies 2-0 in a home game.

=========

NOTABLE EVENT
February 20, 2011

The 60th NBA All-Star game was held as the Western Conference beat the Eastern Conference 148-143 at Staples Center. Los Angeles Lakers guard Kobe Bryant scored 37 points and won his fourth All-Star game MVP award.

Eleven Laps to a Record
February 21, 1976

The San Diego Indoor Games at the San Diego Sports Arena took place just before the outdoor high school season. This runner was in excellent shape thanks to his two coaches. Jim, his father, and Elmer Runge of Patrick Henry High School. His personal record for the mile run was 4:07. Victory wasn't the goal, but a new personal mark would be great against such a strong field. Waiting for him were world class milers Rod Dixon of New Zealand and Filbert Bayi of Tanzania. The track was a challenge too, with 11 laps to the mile and 50-yard straightaways followed by high banked turns. The good news was that he was running at home, in front of friends and family.

The starting pistol sounded, and he followed the aggressive field. 62.5 seconds for his first quarter mile. He didn't want to crash and fade if the pace was too fast. This pace was slower than expected. 61.2 seconds for the next quarter, and the field rapidly sped up. Then 60.1 seconds, then a final lap of 58.9 seconds. He ran negative splits, the second half of the race faster than the first. The crowd cheered him to the finish line in sixth place with a time of 4:02.7. Thom Hunt had set a new national high school record that lasted almost 25 years.

Hunt progressed on a career lasting several years. He was versatile and competed at every event from the mile, the steeplechase, all the way up to the marathon. In November of 1976 he competed for the Jamul Toads, a team of San Diego runners that won the AAU National Cross Country Championship. Hunt attended the University of Arizona where he was a seven time All-American in cross country and track. In 1981 he set an American record of 28 minutes and 12 seconds for a 10k road race. Hunt also competed in four Olympic Trials.

Hunt became a USA Track and Field certified coach after retiring from competition. He coached nine individual state champions in cross country and track at San Diego Mesa College. Hunt later coached the women's cross country team at Cuyamaca College in El Cajon.

Q: Thom Hunt won World Championship medals at which event in 1976 and 1977?

For more track and field, visit www.californiasportsastounding.com

A: Hunt was a silver medalist at the World Cross Country Championships junior men's race to fellow Californian Eric Hulst in 1976. The next year he won the gold medal as the USA repeated as team champions with a four-point victory over Spain.

CALIFORNIA SPORTS BIRTHDAYS
More Fun for February 21

Q: Jason "J. D." Gibbs, born in 1969, followed his father, an NFL football coach, to what other sport: arena football, soccer, or stock car racing?

. . . .

Did You Know?

Promoter Al Franken presented the Los Angeles Invitational indoor track meet on January 22, 1960. The first ever indoor meet in Los Angeles was held at the new Sports Arena which had opened just six months earlier. Santa Monica's Parry O'Brien set a world indoor shot put record of 63 feet, 1 inch. Sunkist Growers became the sponsor, and the event was renamed the Sunkist Invitational from 1970 to 1995. The Sunkist was the oldest indoor competition west of the Mississippi. Organizers claimed over 100 Olympic gold medalists among their participants. The meet was cancelled in 2003 due to lack of sponsorship.

A: Gibbs, a Los Angeles native, went from football to stock car racing. "J.D." was a driver and co-owner of Joe Gibbs Racing.

======================================

NOTABLE EVENT
February 21, 1992

Kristi Yamaguchi, a native of Hayward, won America's first Olympic gold medal in women's figure skating since 1976. The following month she won the World Figure Skating Championships at the Oakland-Alameda County Coliseum Arena.

A Beach of a Marathon
February 21, 1982

The inaugural Long Beach World Runners Marathon was held. 1,600 runners enjoyed a flat, scenic course starting and ending at the luxury liner R.M.S. Queen Mary in Long Beach Harbor. Long Beach resident Joan Lind, a 1976 Olympic rowing medalist, and the Lakewood High School cross country and swim coach participated.

Martti Kiilholma of Finland ran 2:17:10 to win the men's division, while Tish Husak, a fitness teacher at Long Beach City College, timed 2:58:06 as the fastest woman. Race director Gordon Proctor reported that 1,575 runners finished the course.

Lind finished her first marathon in 3:12.44, placing her as the fourth fastest woman.

Q: What former Los Angeles Lakers head coach finished the race?

For more running, visit www.californiasportsastounding.com

A: Paul Westhead, who coached the Lakers to the National Basketball Association title in 1980 with a 4-2 win over the Philadelphia 76ers.

CALIFORNIA SPORTS BIRTHDAYS
More Fun for February 21

Q: Alan Trammell, born in 1958, MLB shortstop, manager, and coach, was inducted into what California sports hall of fame in 1998: Bay Area Sports Hall of Fame, California Sports Hall of Fame, or the San Diego Hall of Champions?

Did You Know?

The Long Beach Marathon has related events that include a half marathon, 5K road race, a 20-mile bike tour, a kids' fun run, and a health and fitness expo. Over 25,000 people attend over the weekend, making it one of Southern California's largest sporting events.

A: The Garden Grove native was inducted into the San Diego Hall of Champions in 1998.

NOTABLE EVENT

February 21, 1851

The San Francisco-based *Daily Alta California*, five months after statehood, published an advertisement: "SUNDAY EXCURSION TO THE FISHING BANKS. — Whalers Ahoy— The Steamer Goliath, Captain Thomas, will leave Cunningham's Wharf, on Sunday 23rd., at 10 am., for the Farallon Islands. Should the weather be fine, and as she will have experienced whalers on board, together with boats and necessary tackle, it is expected that several whales will be captured, affording all a fine opportunity of enjoying the exciting sport."

Formal Base Ball
February 22, 1860

California's first formal game of baseball, according to New York rules, was played between the San Francisco Base Ball (spelled as two words) Club and the Red Rovers at Center's Bridge. The teams tied at 33 after nine innings, but the Red Rovers refused to continue the game and protested that the pitching of San Francisco player J.C. Willock was illegal. The umpire disagreed and declared the game a forfeit and awarded the victory to San Francisco.

The *San Joaquin Republican* also gave this description on February 26:

"The San Francisco and Red Rover Base Ball clubs went to play a match game this week. They got into a dispute about a "pitch" and the R. R.'s withdrew."

Q: What two other Northern California cities had baseball teams in 1860?

For more baseball, visit www.californiasportsastounding.com

A: Sacramento and Stockton had Base Ball Clubs.

CALIFORNIA SPORTS BIRTHDAYS
More Fun for February 22

Q: Abraham Attell, born in 1883, who was light on his feet, was a world champion boxer in what weight division: heavyweight, welterweight, or featherweight?

Did You Know?

Andrew "Andy" Piercy, born November 1, 1854, was the first California born baseball player in Major League history. The San Jose native played second base in two games for the Chicago White Stockings during the 1881 season.

Point Loma High School in San Diego produced two baseball players who pitched perfect games for the New York Yankees at Yankee Stadium. Don Larsen pitched a perfect game for the Yankees as they defeated the Brooklyn Dodgers 2-0 in game five of the 1956 World Series. It is the only no-hitter and perfect game in World Series history. In 1998 David Wells pitched a perfect game as New York beat the Minnesota Twins 4-0. His victory was the 15th perfect game in Major League history

A: Attell, a native of San Francisco, was World Featherweight Champion from 1906 to 1912 and made a division record 21 title defenses.

NOTABLE BIRTHDAYS

February 22,

1908: Bill Dally, native of Elmira, rower, attended UC Berkeley, 1928 Olympic gold medalist in men's eights.

1971: Lisa Fernandez, born in Long Beach, softball pitcher, All-American at UCLA from 1990 to 1993, ASA National Softball Hall of Fame inductee 2013, three-time Olympic gold medalist 1996, 2000, and 2004.

Trojan Track Trio
February 26, 1900

USC started their track and field program in 1900 with no coach and no captain. Their season ended 0-1 as they lost to Pomona College 52.5 to 42.5 at the Sagehens new track. The *Los Angeles Times* described the oval as "soft, and the bank and sharp curves interfered greatly with the runners in their attempts to lower records."

Dean Cromwell was hired as head coach in 1909 and developed the Trojans into a national powerhouse. He coached from 1909 to 1913, took a break, and returned from 1916 to 1948. His teams won 12 NCAA titles, including an astonishing nine in a row from 1935 to 1943. Cromwell coached several Olympic medalists and world record holders. Notable California born athletes include discus thrower Ken Carpenter, 110-meter hurdler Fred Kelly, pole vaulter Bill Sefton, and sprinters Cliff Bourland and Mel Patton.

Multi-sport athlete Jess Hill was named head track coach in 1949. He had been a fullback on the 1928 USC national championship football team, played as an outfielder in Major League Baseball from 1935 to 1937 and was a national champion in the long jump in 1929. Hill coached the Trojans to the NCAA title at the Los Memorial Coliseum in 1949, plus another title in 1950.

Jess Mortensen took over in 1951—he had been captain of the 1930 NCAA championship track team under Cromwell. Over the next ten years he directed the Trojans to seven NCAA titles, the last in 1961. Mortensen's teams never lost a dual meet, finishing with a record of 64-0. The USC men's program now claims 26 NCAA titles, more than twice as many as runner-up Arkansas.

Q: What did Cromwell, Hill, and Mortensen have in common?

For more track and field, visit www.californiasportsastounding.com

A: They never lost to UCLA in a dual meet. Cromwell was 15-0, Hill recorded three wins, and Mortensen finished his career 11-0 versus the Bruins.

CALIFORNIA SPORTS BIRTHDAYS
More Fun for February 26

Q: Sheila Cornell, born in 1962, Olympic gold medalist in 1996 and 2000 for the USA softball team. What position did she play: catcher, pitcher, or first base?

....

Did You Know?

Director of Track and Field Caryl Smith Gilbert joined the Trojans in 2014. She has coached USC athletes to over 180 first team All-American honors and over 50 school records in just six years. The USC women's team won NCAA championships in 2018 and 2021. Her women's teams are undefeated against UCLA.

A: The Encino native played first base. Cornell was inducted into the National Softball Hall of Fame and Museum in 2006.

NOTABLE BIRTHDAY
February 26, 1968

Jack Thomas "J.T." Snow, born in Long Beach, MLB first baseman for the California Angels and San Francisco Giants, Gold Glove winner 1995 to 2000.

MARCH
MANIA

Desert Tennis
March 1, 2000

International Tennis Hall of Fame inductee and former UCLA player Charlie Pasarell had big plans for the California desert, to build the world's second largest tennis stadium. Pasarell, along with retired South African player Raymond Moore and Indian Wells former mayor Richard Oliphant, raised money for his idea. Riverside County, the city of Indian Wells, International Management Group, and several other organizations helped take the project from groundbreaking to completion in only 17 months. The result was the $75 million Indian Wells Tennis Garden. This impressive facility has 16,071 seats. Only the U.S. Open facility in New York is larger.

The stadium is home to the BNP Paribas Open, also known as the Indian Wells Masters. Both the men's ATP World Tour and the women's WTA Tour participate, making it a "fifth major" or the fifth largest tournament in the world. Over 475,000 visitors attend the event, making it the most attended tennis tournament besides the four majors.

Oracle cofounder and CTO Larry Ellison bought the tournament and stadium in 2009. He upgraded the facility in several areas and expanded it to 29 world class courts. His tournament is the first in the world to install the Hawk Eye replay challenge technology on every court.

Q: What was the name of the 1976 tournament, the first year in California?

For more tennis, visit www.californiasportsastounding.com

A: American Airlines Tennis Games.

CALIFORNIA SPORTS BIRTHDAYS
More Fun for March 1

Q: Pete Rozelle, born in 1926, worked in the athletic department for which Northern California university before becoming the NFL commissioner: Berkeley, Stanford, or the University of San Francisco?

....

Did You Know?

The first NBA games played outdoors in California were held at the Indian Wells Tennis Center from 2008 to 2010. The preseason exhibition games were the idea of Rancho Mirage philanthropist and Phoenix Suns part owner Richard Heckmann. A crowd of 16,236 fans watched the first game on October 11, 2008. Despite winds of 15 mph and 64 degree temperature, the Denver Nuggets outlasted the Phoenix Suns 77-72.

A: Rozelle, a native of Southgate, was a student publicist for the University of San Francisco athletic department. After graduating in 1950, he became the Dons' full-time athletic news director. In 1960 Rozelle was the first Californian to be named NFL commissioner.

NOTABLE BIRTHDAYS
March 1

1922: Fred Scolari, born in San Francisco, basketball point guard, 1952 and 1953 NBA All-Star with the Baltimore Bullets, Bay Area Sports Hall of Fame inductee 1998.

1952: Swaps, a California bred thoroughbred racehorse, 1955 Kentucky Derby champion, 1956 American Horse of the Year, nicknamed the "California Comet" when healthy and the "California Cripple" when injured.

Dedeaux Dynasty
March 5, 1942

A slim young man was the greatest baseball star ever produced at Hollywood High, and one of the greatest at USC. He also ranks among the greatest college baseball coaches, and it all started after USC hired him for the 1942 season. The *Los Angeles Evening Citizen News* noted that "you may hear plenty of him before the California Intercollegiate Baseball Association schedule is completed. He has a contract to handle the Trojan nine this season, and if all goes well, he may continue to coach it for many a season to come."

His name is Rod Dedeaux. Dedeaux coached solo from 1943 to 1945. The next year, he teamed with Sam Barry and they celebrated the Trojan's first NCAA title in 1948. He took over the program two years later after Barry died.

Dedeaux built a dynasty with NCAA titles in 1958, 1961, 1963, 1968, 1970 to 1974, and 1978. He developed more than 50 major league players including Tom Seaver, Randy Johnson, Fred Lynn, Mark McGwire, Dave Kingman, Ron Fairly, and many more.

USC honored their coach on March 30, 1974 with the opening of Dedeaux Field. Pitcher Russ McQueen made it extra special with his no-hitter versus California 7-0 as the Trojans swept a doubleheader from the Golden Bears. Dedeaux retired from USC in 1986 after a career spanning 45 years.

In 1999 he was named Coach of the Century by both *Baseball America* and *Collegiate Baseball*. Seven years later, Dedeaux was honored as a charter inductee to the College Baseball Hall of Fame. He also made significant contributions to amateur baseball as an ambassador and coach of the United States Olympic baseball team in 1964 and 1984.

Q: What was Rod Dedeaux's salary as coach of the Trojans?

For more baseball, visit www.californiasportsastounding.com

A: Dedeaux, who wore the #1 jersey, was paid an annual salary of $1. He already had a fulltime job as president of Dart Transportation, Inc., a million-dollar trucking firm he founded in 1938 with $500.

CALIFORNIA SPORTS BIRTHDAYS
More Fun for March 5

Q: Kiley Neushul, born in 1993, won a 2016 Olympic gold medal in what women's sport: water polo, softball, or swimming?

....

Did You Know?

USC left fielder Mike Gillespie won an NCAA title at the College World Series in 1961. He returned as head coach in 1998 and managed the Trojans to their 12th title. Second baseman Wes Rachels was named most outstanding player.

A: The Isla Vista native won an Olympic gold medal in water polo for Team USA.

NOTABLE EVENT
March 5, 1997

Los Angeles Dodgers manager Tommy Lasorda was inducted into the National Baseball Hall of Fame. Lasorda, who bled blue for the Dodgers from 1976 to 1996, took them to World Series titles in 1981 and 1988. The Dodgers retired his number 2 jersey on August 16, 1997. Three years later, he came out of retirement to represent America as the Olympic baseball coach. Lasorda made history as the first manager to win a World Series and Olympic gold as he guided Team USA to victory over defending champion Cuba.

Six Pockets in the 1800s
March 6, 1870

The Monterey-based *Californian*, the state's first newspaper, mentioned billiards in the October 3, 1846 issue. "People may have their fun as much as they please; they may play their billiards, their cards and all other games of amusements."

Three years later, the *Placer Times* advertised "Billiard Saloon on K, between First and Second streets, next door to the North American Hotel. Billiards, pool, and other games played every evening."

Only two months before statehood in 1850, the San Francisco-based *Daily Alta California* proclaimed "Billiards! Set the Balls in Motion!! Just put up in B. F. Williams' Parker House Saloon, our magnificent billiard tables, Bassford's patent air cushions, of the most approved style. These tables are entirely new, just arrived from New York, and surpass in beauty and accuracy of workmanship, anything of the kind ever brought to this city. The public are respectfully invited to examine and satisfy themselves."

California's first big billiard event happened in 1870 at the Mechanics Pavilion in San Francisco. "The Great Billiard Match—The Championship of America" blared the headline of the *Daily Alta California*. A reporter noted "the event engaged the interest and attention, not only of a large number of our own citizens, but also that of thousands of others in Chicago, New York, and other cities of the Union, and in England also, for the wires were in the Pavilion, and in direct connection with the Atlantic cable."

Pavilion manager Mr. M.E. Hughes organized the event and raised all 2,800 seats for superb viewing around the elegant rosewood table. The contestants for the $1,000 prize and golden cue were Mr. Deery of San Francisco and Chicagoan Mr. Rudolph. Deery induced Rudolph to play the match in San Francisco with the claim that "in no other city in America would the money taken at the door be so large." The match lasted several hours, until 1:30 a.m., when Rudolph finally prevailed 1,500 to 1,327.

The newspaper concluded with "It is said that Mr. Rudolph intends to take up his residence in San Francisco and to practice his skill amongst us. If so, this city will certainly have reason to feel proud of having as residents the two greatest players in the United States. Billiards will doubtless increase in public favor.

Q: The Pacific Coast Championships were held two months later at what famous billiard hall in San Francisco: McCormick's Billiards, Dave & Busters, or Deery & Little's Billiard Hall?

For more billiards, visit www.californiasportsastounding.com

A: Deery & Little's Billiard Hall located on Bush Street.

CALIFORNIA SPORTS BIRTHDAYS
More Fun for March 6

Q: Ann Curtis, born in 1926, first woman and first swimmer to win the 1948 Sullivan Award as outstanding American amateur athlete of the year, was honored in with a parade in what California city? Hint: A huge Billiard tournament happened there in 1870.

· ·

Did You Know?

Jose Parica of La Puente was the first Californian inducted into the Billiard Congress of America Hall of Fame. He was honored in 2014.

A: A mile-long parade was held on Market Street in her hometown of San Francisco.

NOTABLE BIRTHDAY
March 6, 1871

Solomon Garcia Smith, born in Los Angeles, 1897 World Featherweight champion, was the first world champion of Hispanic ancestry. He had a Mexican mother and an Irish father.

Sactown Pro Hoops
March 14, 1913

Professional basketball may have arrived in Sacramento as early as 1913. The *Stockton Independent* announced, "A professional basketball league has been organized in San Francisco to include several interior cities and towns. The circuit consists of two San Francisco teams and fives from Livermore, Petaluma, Vallejo, Sacramento and Lodi."

Over 70 years later, in 1985, the National Basketball Association approved the move of the Kansas City Kings to Sacramento. This team had started in Rochester, NY in 1923 and endured several changes as it moved to Cincinnati and Kansas City. The Sacramento Kings started NBA play October 25, 1985 with a season opening loss to the Los Angeles Clippers 108-104 at the Arco Arena. Six days later, the Kings conquered the Houston Rockets 122-116 for their first home win.

The Kings enjoyed their best season in 2002 when they won the Pacific Division and home court advantage in the playoffs. They ended up losing game six in the playoffs to the Los Angeles Lakers on May 31. A fourth quarter nightmare of several questionable officiating calls against the Kings and 21 free throws made by the Lakers didn't help. Sacramento's playoff run ended with a game seven loss on June 2.

The Kings moved into their new downtown arena, the Golden 1 Center in 2016. Their new home has hosted opening rounds of the NCAA Basketball men's tournament and the California Interscholastic Federation High School Basketball State Championship.

Q: Which Sacramento Kings head coach hold the franchise record for most regular season wins? Hint: He also coached four other NBA teams.

For more basketball, visit www.californiasportsastounding.com

A: Rick Adelman won 395 games as head coach from 1998 to 2006.

CALIFORNIA SPORTS BIRTHDAYS
More Fun for March 14

Q: Gordon Mallatratt, born in 1914, second baseman, played for the Team USA demonstration baseball team at what Olympics: 1936 or 1948?

....

Did You Know?

On November 15, 2013 Sacramento Kings fans set a Guinness World record for the loudest crowd roar at an indoor stadium. 17,317 fans at the Sleep Train Arena registered a peak reading of 126 decibels. Painful! The Detroit Pistons spoiled the fun with a 97-90 win.

A: Gordon, a San Francisco native and Stanford graduate, played baseball at the 1936 Olympics in Berlin, Germany.

NOTABLE BIRTHDAY
March 14, 1983

Amber Stachowski, born in Mission Viejo, water polo player, 2003 World Champion, 2004 Olympic bronze medalist.

CIF Start
March 28, 1914

California's population at statehood in 1850 was 92,597. The state grew rapidly, and by 1914 had over 2,377,549 residents, an increase of slightly over 60 percent. California had sprawling high school athletic programs with no statewide guidance. This growth necessitated a formal organization to govern high school sports.

The founding of the California Interscholastic Federation in Berkeley on March 28 filled that void. CIF leaders adopted a Constitution that same day. Their first official Federation meeting was held on July 4, 1914. It was decided to have several geographical sections to provided local control of the sports programs. The *San Francisco Call* gave this description: "It was announced that lower San Joaquin valley had formed a branch section of the federation. The objects of the federation are to divide the state into sections wherein the control of athletics will come under the faculty of the schools."

CIF has grown to 10 sections covering every region in the state. Their recent sports survey shows participation is at an all-time high of over 1600 member schools with over 815,000 student-athletes competing, nine times the population of the entire state in 1850.

Q: What are the CIF's two fastest growing sports for boys and girls?

For more high school sports, visit www.californiasportsastounding.com

A: Boys are joining lacrosse and volleyball, while girls are wrestling and playing lacrosse.

CALIFORNIA SPORTS BIRTHDAYS
More Fun for March 28

Q: Ronald "Ronnie" Ray Smith, born in 1949, sprinter, won a gold medal in what relay at the 1968 Olympics: 4 x 100-meters or the 4 x 400-meters?

· ·

Did You Know?

Marie Ishida was the CIF's first female executive director. She served from 2001 to 2012. Ishida's career in education lasted 40 years, including positions at Artesia High School, Carmel High School, and Santa Cruz High School.

A: Smith, a native of Los Angeles, was a sprinter at San Jose State College. Smith won a gold medal in the 4 x 100-meter relay.

NOTABLE BIRTHDAYS

March 28

1964: Mike Batesole, born in Anaheim, baseball coach, 1998 National Coach of the Year with Cal State Northridge, 2008 College World Series champion with Fresno State.

1968: Teee Sanders Williams, native of Los Angeles, volleyball player, 1992 Olympic bronze medalist for Team USA.

1991: Derek Carr, born in Fresno, NFL quarterback for the Oakland Raiders from 2017 to 2019, NCAA leader in 2013 in passing yards and touchdowns for the Fresno State Bulldogs.

Native Americans
March 30, 1854

The Kitanemuk, Yokuts, and Chumash indigenous people of California played one of America's most popular sports at Tejon Pass as early as 1854. The first reference to this sport appeared in the *San Joaquin Republican* on March 30, 1854. The newspaper reported that "Captain P. E. Connor, who left Tejon Pass some fifteen days ago, arrived in this city yesterday morning. He has kindly furnished the following interesting particulars in that region. One hundred Native Americans, from the other side of the mountains, arrived the day before he left. They occupy their leisure time in various kinds of amusements, the game they most delight in being football."

Q: What Native American from California played college and professional football with the "Athlete of the Century" Jim Thorpe?

For more football, visit www.californiasportsastounding.com

A: Pedro "Pete" Calac, born in Valley Center and member of the Rincon Band of Luiseño Indians. Calac played running back and was a teammate of Thorpe with the NFL's Canton Bulldogs from 1916 to 1920 and the Oorang Indians from 1922 to 1923.

CALIFORNIA SPORTS BIRTHDAYS
More Fun for March 30

Q: Olympic skier William Johnson, born in 1960, made history in what event: slalom, downhill, or cross country skiing?

Did You Know?

The California Indian Education website at www.calie.org honors the greatest Native American Indian athletes of recorded history. CIE is a 501(c)(3) non-profit American Indian Organization.

Among the California born honorees are NFL linebacker Brandon Chillar, judoka Ben Nighthorse Campbell, PGA tour golfer Rod Curl, MLB pitcher Kyle Lohse, and mixed martial artist Virgil Zwicker.

John Tortes "Chief" Meyers, from the Cahuilla, was born in Riverside. He was a Major League Baseball catcher from 1909 to 1917 for the New York Giants. In 1912 Meyers hit .358, finished third in the National League MVP award voting, and was the primary catcher for Hall of Fame pitcher Christy Mathewson.

. . . .

Did You Know?

The California Indian Education website at www.calie.org honors the greatest Native American Indian athletes of recorded history. CIE is a 501(c)(3) non-profit American Indian Organization.

Among the California born honorees are NFL linebacker Brandon Chillar, judoka Ben Nighthorse Campbell, PGA tour golfer Rod Curl, MLB pitcher Kyle Lohse, and mixed martial artist Virgil Zwicker.

John Tortes "Chief" Meyers, from the Cahuilla, was born in Riverside. He was a Major League Baseball catcher from 1909 to 1917 for the New York Giants. In 1912 Meyers hit .358, finished third in the National League MVP award voting, and was the primary catcher for Hall of Fame pitcher Christy Mathewson.

A: The Los Angeles native won the downhill event at the 1984 Winter Olympics and became the first American male to win a gold medal in alpine skiing.

NOTABLE BIRTHDAY
March 30, 1909

Alan Morgan, born in Los Angeles, sailor, 1932 Olympic gold medalist in the eight-meter event. Crew member for fellow Angeleno Owen Churchill aboard his boat the *Angelita*.

Norton Breaking Jaws
March 31, 1973

Heavyweight boxer Ken Howard Norton was facing Muhammad Ali at the San Diego Sports Arena. He was in the best shape of his life, his trainer Eddie Futch had already helped Joe Frazier beat Ali, and he even had a hypnotist who boosted his self-confidence. Even though he was a 5-1 underdog, he had a great chance to topple a legend.

Ali arrived in San Diego overweight by five pounds, overconfident, and undertrained. He also spent too much time on the golf course, where he injured his right ankle after horsing around with friends.

Norton, a self-described "ham and eggs" fighter wanted to eat more steak. He fought aggressively from round one, and stunned Ali by breaking his jaw. A California State Athletic Commission ringside physician told Angelo Dundee, Ali's trainer, that Ali's jaw was broken in the first round. Dundee wanted to stop the fight, but Ali refused and continued the bout. The remaining 11 rounds were dominated by Norton, who landed more punches and controlled the pace. Ali courageously hung on and endured the pain, but didn't score enough points. Norton won by split decision and became the North American Boxing Federation heavyweight champion.

After the fight, a frustrated Ali hit his head and fists against the wall in his dressing room before he was taken to Clairemont General Hospital. A 90-minute surgery wired together his left jawbone, which was broken three quarters of an inch apart. After surgery, he was placed on a liquid diet for six weeks. Ali had at least one visitor. Two days later, Norton drove up in his one indulgence, the car he owned before the fight, his $13,000 silver Lincoln Mark IV with initials on the door. Norton visited Ali briefly and then drove north to his home in Carson.

Q: How many more times did Ali and Norton fight?

For more boxing, visit www.californiasportsastounding.com

A: Two. Ali beat Norton in a split decision at the Forum in Inglewood on September 10, 1973. Their last fight was on September 28, 1976 at Yankee Stadium when Ali won a unanimous decision.

CALIFORNIA SPORTS BIRTHDAYS
More Fun for March 31

Q: Donald Barksdale, born in 1923, basketball player, was the first African American to play for Team USA at which Olympics: 1948, 1952, or 1956?

....

Did You Know?

Los Angeles boxing promoter Tom McCarey staged the first heavyweight title fight in California. The bout was held on February 23, 1906 at the Pacific Athletic Club in Los Angeles. Canada's Tommy Burns won a unanimous decision over Marvin Hart of Kentucky after 20 grueling rounds. Burns defended his title 13 times before losing to America's Jack Johnson in 1908.

A: Barksdale, a native of Oakland, won a gold medal at the 1948 Olympics.

NOTABLE BIRTHDAY
March 31, 1984

James Jones, San Jose native, NFL wide receiver from 2007 to 2015, caught five passes as the Green Bay Packers won Super Bowl XLV over the Pittsburgh Steelers 31-25.

The Wizard's Farewell
March 31, 1975

He coached his first basketball season in California and ended with a 22-7 record, but lost to the Oregon State Beavers in the Pacific Coast Conference final in March of 1949. His teams improved in the 1950's, but were over-shadowed by national title teams from the University of San Francisco Dons 1955 and 1956, plus the University of California Golden Bears in 1959.

The turning point came in the 1963-1964 season. His team finished un-defeated at 30-0 and won the NCAA title. His guard, Walt Hazzard, was the Most Outstanding Player in the tournament. One of his assistant coaches was a former player of his, Jerry Norman. Norman expanded recruiting nation-wide and was a defensive specialist who implemented a full court zone press.

UCLA would repeat as champions in the 1964-1965 season. There was a down year in 1965-1966, but starting with the 1966 season his teams dom-inated college basketball. Bruin superstars Lew Alcindor, Sidney Wicks, and Bill Walton peaked with their best play at the NCAA tournament.

Coach guided the Bruins to one final tournament in 1975. John Wood-en was ready for a farewell. Wooden announced his retirement after beating Louisville 75-74, coached by his former assistant Denny Crum in the NCAA semifinal. Two days later, he used only six players in the final. Tournament MOP Richard Washington scored 28 points as the Bruins ran away from the taller Kentucky Wildcats 92-85 at the San Diego Sports Arena. The "Wiz-ard of Westwood" finished his coaching career with a remarkable tally of 10 NCAA titles in just 12 years from 1964 to 1975.

Q: Who was the first California team to win the NCAA title?

For more basketball, visit www.californiasportsastounding.com

A: The Stanford Indians defeated the Dartmouth Big Green 53-38 to win the 1942 NCAA title. Stanford forward Howie Dallmar won Most Out-standing Player honors.

CALIFORNIA SPORTS BIRTHDAYS
More Fun for March 31

Q: Ron "Speedball" Brown, born in 1961, helped set a world record of 37.83 seconds as part of which track and field relay event at the 1984 Olympics: 4 x 100-meters or the 4 x 400-meters?

··

Did You Know?

The first NCAA Division I men's basketball tournament final played in California was on March 19, 1960 at the Cow Palace in Daly City. The Cal Golden Bears coached by Pete Newell were the defending national champions. They had an All-American center in Darrall Imhoff, but it wasn't enough as the Ohio State Buckeyes won the title 75-55.

California's first NCAA Division I women's final was held on April 1, 1984 at Pauley Pavilion on the campus of UCLA. USC defended their title with a 72-61 win over the Tennessee Volunteers. Trojans Cheryl Miller, Pam McGee, and Paula McGee were named to the all-tournament team.

A: Brown, a Los Angeles native, led off the men's 4 x 100 meters relay for Team USA.

NOTABLE BIRTHDAY
March 31, 1985

Patty Fendick, Sacramento native, 1986 and 1987 NCAA singles champion at Stanford. 1991 Australian Open doubles champion with Mary Joe Fernandez.

APRIL
AMAZING

CC in CA
April 1, 1929

A little known event took place on this date when Lucius Ergatz high-jumped 10 feet for the first time ever but was disqualified when the line judge called a foot fault. Then 10 seconds later, yelled, "April Fools!" He was beaten to death by the crowd. April Fools! None of this actually happened, but please continue reading.

California's rapid growth in the modern era spurred the creation of several community colleges and in turn many sports associations. For example, at one point there was the Central California, Northern Junior College, and Southern California Athletic Associations. In 1929, these were unified into the California Junior College Federation, now known as the California Community College Athletic Association. (CCCAA)

The CCCAA manages 110 schools and over 24,000 student-athletes. It sponsors 24 sports, with men and women competing in 12 each. The CCCAA oversees nine all-sports conferences, two football only conferences, and four wrestling only alliances.

Men's state championships were held for the first time in 1948. Jimmy Smith coached the Fullerton College Hornets to the swimming crown. Women started competing nearly 30 years later in 1977, with cross country, track, and volleyball. De Anza and Glendale took the large and small division cross country titles, Santa Barbara City College won track and field honors, while Santa Ana College and Monterey Peninsula College captured the large and small division volleyball championships.

California baseball lost one of its great coaches on January 26, 2020. John Altobelli, coach of the Orange Coast College Pirates, Altobelli coached the Pirates from 1993-2019 and won four CCCAA titles in 2009, 2014, 2015, and 2019. On that date eight other people died including his wife Keri, daughter Alyssa, NBA superstar Kobe Bryant and his daughter Gianna, 13-year-old Mamba basketball player Payton Chester, her mother Sarah Chester, Mamba assistant basketball coach Christina Mauser, and pilot Ara Zobayan.

Q: What were the last men's and women's sports added by the CCCAA?

For CCCAA and other college conferences, visit www.californiasportsastounding.com

A: Men started playing volleyball in 1991. The women added beach volleyball in 2015.

CALIFORNIA SPORTS BIRTHDAYS
More Fun for April 1

Q: Nick "The Greek" Peters, born in 1939, sportswriter, covered which Major League baseball team from 1961 to 2007: Los Angeles Dodgers, Oakland Athletics, or the San Francisco Giants?

Did You Know?

California's community colleges have produced some of America's greatest athletes. Among the many are baseball's Jackie Robinson, Tom Seaver, and Duke Snider, football's Frank Gifford, Hugh McElhenny, Ollie Matson, Warren Moon, and Keyshawn Johnson, tennis players Rosie Casals and Brad Gilbert, volleyball's Steve Timmons, track and field's Bob Seagren, Lee Evans, and Ruth Wysocki, Olympic swimming and diving legends Debbie Meyer, Pat McCormick, Shirley Babashoff, and Susie Atwood. And don't forget Pete Rozelle, NFL commissioner 1960 to 1989.

A: Peters was a baseball writer who covered the San Francisco Giants. He wrote for the *Oakland Tribune* and the *Sacramento Bee*.

NOTABLE BIRTHDAYS
April 1

1910: Robert "Bob" Van Osdel, born in Selma, high jumper, 1932 Olympic silver medalist in Los Angeles.

1976: David Gilliland, born in Riverside, stock car racing driver and team owner of David Gilliland Racing.

Barnyard Golf and a Near Riot
April 4, 1885

Barnyard golf made its first appearance in the town of Jackson, CA as early as 1885. The Sierra Nevada based newspaper *Amador Ledger* declared it is "the ruling game here. It has discounted skating as a popular amusement." This sport had the second name of "Horseshoe pitching."

The sport headed south and in 1900 the Long Beach Tourists' Horseshoe club was founded. Membership grew rapidly and by 1919 club President W.A. Hoyt managed the largest club in America with 500 members. Their home courts were at Pacific Park in Long Beach.

California's first state championship was held at Glendale High School on November 25-26, 1921. The event drew nearly 200 entries. W. R Bradfield of Long Beach won top honors. He scored 328 ringers, 122 of which were tossed two at a time. The successful tournament inspired UC Berkeley to add horseshoe pitching as a student sport and construction of a venue was started the same week.

California hosted the World Championship tournament for the first time in 1934. The event was held at the Goodyear athletic field in Los Angeles. Alhambra's Ted Allen won the crown with victories in all of his 23 matches. A near riot started when the promoter claimed he didn't have the $1,600 total prize money, which was promised to the top three finishers. He offered only a paltry $300 to Mr. Allen and $150 to Catherine Schultz, the women's winner. Two police cars were called as the promoter and the pitchers tried to punch each other. The pitchers were forced to go to civil court and collect their winnings. Deputy District Attorney Harry Johnston decided that the horseshoe hurlers could file civil suits to obtain the $1,600 in prize money advertised by the promoter, but that no basis for criminal prosecution existed. The result was unclear.

Q: Horseshoe courts are available at which Northern California Park: Golden Gate Park in San Francisco, Columbus Park in San Jose, or City Park in Vallejo?

> For more horseshoe pitching, visit www.
> californiasportsastounding.com

A: All three. San Jose has 21 courts, Vallejo has 20 courts, and San Francisco has 16.

CALIFORNIA SPORTS BIRTHDAYS
More Fun for April 4

Q: Jim Fregosi, born in 1942, was MLB shortstop and manager for which California team: the Oakland Athletics, Los Angeles Dodgers, or the California Angels?

. . . .

Did You Know?

California's largest horseshoe venue is Beach Park in Bakersfield with 26 courts. Bakersfield hosted the 2005 World Championships at the Kern County Fairgrounds.

Walter Ray Williams Jr. of San Jose—yes, that same Hall of Fame professional bowler—won six World Championships from 1978 to 1994. "Deadeye" was the first pitcher to enter a World Tournament with a 90 percent average.

A: The San Francisco native played shortstop for the Los Angeles and California Angels from 1961 to 1971. He managed the California Angels from 1978 to 1981. Fregosi was a six-time All-Star and was inducted into the Angels Hall of Fame in 1989.

NOTABLE BIRTHDAY
April 4, 1947

Ed White, born in San Diego, NFL offensive lineman, 1968 All-American at UC Berkeley, College Football Hall of Fame inductee 1999, Los Angeles Chargers Hall of Fame inductee 2004.

Soccer Clash
April 6, 1996

San Jose's entry to Major League Soccer involved an unusual looking logo and a dramatic first game win. The San Jose organization was established on June 15, 1994, when San Jose became a charter member of Major League Soccer. Their nickname was revealed a year later: the Clash. Team President Peter Bridgwater said, "It's an exciting, innovative, non-traditional and provocative nickname, exactly the kind of thing we want in a league. That the name fit the type of team he wanted—an aggressive, attacking team…winning by scores like 4-3, not 1-0."

Nike was Major League Soccer's financial partner and designer. They were tasked with branding, creating team colors, and a logo. The colors seemed to clash! San Jose wore celery green (is that a color?), forest green, red, and teal. The logo? Fans were unsure. Was it a Scorpion? A lobster? A coat hanger?

With colors and logo completed, the Clash were ready for the league's inaugural game. A sellout crowd of 31,683 fans loved it. Eric Wynalda scored the first goal in MLS history with only two minutes left in regulation as the Clash shutout D.C. United 1-0, not 4-3.

General Manager Dick Berg changed the team name to the Earthquakes three years later. New team colors were blue, black, white, and silver. San Jose shook off the Los Angeles Galaxy 2-1 in their California Clásico rivalry and claimed the 2001 MLS Cup. This was the first MLS Cup to match two teams from both the same conference and state against each other. San Jose won another title two years later with a 4-2 win over the Chicago Fire at the Home Depot Center in Carson. Almost 4-3.

Q: Who was the top goal-scorer for San Jose during the 1996 season?

To see the San Jose Clash logo and colors, visit www.californiasportsastounding.com

A: Former Santa Clara University star Paul Bravo scored 13 goals for the Clash that season.

CALIFORNIA SPORTS BIRTHDAYS
More Fun for April 6

Q: John Huarte, born in 1944, Notre Dame quarterback, won what college football award in 1964: Heisman or Oscar?

....

Did You Know?

Landon Donovan is one of over 25 players who have switched teams between the San Jose Earthquakes and Los Angeles Galaxy since the California Clásico started in 1996.

A: The Anaheim native won the Heisman Trophy.

==

NOTABLE BIRTHDAYS
April 6

1908: Ernesto "Schnozz" Lombardi, Oakland native, MLB catcher, eight time All-Star, National Baseball Hall of Fame inductee 1986.

1969: Bret Boone, born in El Cajon, MLB second baseman, All-Star 1998, 2001, 2003, first ever third generation player in MLB history, son of Bob Boone (born in 1947, catcher), brother Aaron (born in 1973, third baseman), and grandfather Ray (born 1923, infielder).

Galaxy on Top
April 13, 1996

The crowd was the largest ever for a non-World Cup or non-Olympic game in Los Angeles. Late arriving fans purchased tickets with only three minutes left in the game! Major League Soccer had arrived in Los Angeles as the LA Galaxy defeated the New York MetroStars 2-1 in their inaugural match in front of 69,225 fans at the Rose Bowl.

Team cofounder and president Danny Villanueva Jr. chose the name Galaxy because, "We're the city of the stars." Villanueva was known as "El Kickador" to sports fans as the placekicker and punter for the Los Angeles Rams from 1960 to 1964.

The Galaxy claimed a record five MLS Cups in 2002, 2005, 2011, 2012, and 2014. California's Landon Donovan was the team leader, elite goal scorer and part of four cups during his career from 2005 to 2014. The Galaxy also brought in European stars David Beckham from 2007 to 2012, and Zlatan Ibrahimović from 2018 to 2019 who were the most popular players in the league.

After playing in the Rose Bowl from 1996 to 2002, and selected U.S. Open Cup games at Cal State Fullerton's Titan Stadium from 1999 to 2011, the Galaxy moved to a new venue. Galaxy home games are played at Carson's Dignity Health Sports Park, the largest soccer specific stadium in America. The 27,000 seat stadium is located on the campus of California State University, Dominguez Hills.

Q: Who scored the first LA Galaxy goal in franchise history: El Kickador, Cobi Jones, or Landon Donovan?

For more soccer, visit www.californiasportsastounding.com

A: Cobi Jones scored in the 37th minute with an assist from Eduardo Hurtado.

CALIFORNIA SPORTS BIRTHDAYS
More Fun for April 13

Q: Brent Hilliard, born in 1970, led what college to their first NCAA men's volleyball title: The Pepperdine Waves, Long Beach State, or the San Diego State Aztecs?

....

Did You Know?

According to *Forbes*, the LA Galaxy franchise is worth more than 480 million dollars. The team generates over 60 million dollars a year in revenue.

A: Hilliard, a native of Dana Point, was the NCAA Player of the Year as the Long Beach State 49ers beat USC 3-1 for the 1991 championship. Hilliard won a bronze medal at the Olympics with Team USA the following year.

NOTABLE BIRTHDAYS
April 13

1913: Charles "The Bald Eagle" Whittingham, thoroughbred racehorse trainer from Chula Vista, 2,534 career wins, all-time leading trainer at Santa Anita Park, trained 20 horses who earned at least $1 million.

1933: Ben Nighthorse Campbell, born in Auburn, judoka, 1961-1963 U.S. Champion, 1963 Pan American Champion, 1964 Olympian, first Native American on the U.S. Olympic Judo Team.

1974: Chad Carvin, native of Laguna Hills, swimmer, 2000 Olympic silver medalist 4 x 200-meter freestyle relay.

Great Giants
April 15, 1958

Major League Baseball came to California in April of 1958. New York's Giants moved to San Francisco and the Brooklyn Dodgers relocated to Los Angeles. Both teams kept their nicknames.

At the time, no one knew for sure how the locals would respond to the new teams. National League President Warren Giles welcomed both teams and made this prediction:

As I see it our new fans in Los Angeles and San Francisco are going to be treated to a 'ding-dong' pennant race the kind that fans in the other cities have become accustomed to in the National League. Certainly, we are going to find new enthusiasm in California—the kind of enthusiasm which will permeate the entire league. The good news is that opening day would be a sell out at Seals Stadium.

San Francisco decided to give the Giants a welcome on the eve of opening day. Manager Bill Rigney, outfielder Willie Mays and dignitaries rode in convertibles over a four-mile route from Seals Stadium to the Sheraton-Palace Hotel. The biggest crowds were on the wide Market Street and in the financial district where thousands and thousands of workers came out of the sky scrapers to witness the event. Fans blanketed the motorcade with over 500 pounds of confetti and 2,000 balloons. After that came a character known as James A. 'Foghorn' Murphy, riding a horse, and announcing the baseball game tomorrow, just as he did for the Seals here 30 and 40 years ago.

The *Napa Valley Register* reported that "San Francisco welcomed the Giants to the Golden West today with the biggest parade since General Douglas MacArthur returned from his victorious campaign in the Pacific. An estimated one million fans lined the major streets for a 45-minute parade honoring the team that will carry the first San Francisco name in a major league."

In their first game, Giants pitcher Ruben Gomez shutout the Dodgers 8-0 before 23,448 fans. The Giants claimed their first pennant in 1962, but it was not until 2010 that they were crowned World Series Champions. Former San Diego Padre manager Bruce Bochy directed the Giants to World Series titles in 2010, 2012, and 2014.

Q: What 1958 Giants coach previously managed the San Francisco Seals of the Pacific Coast League and had a famous restaurant on Geary Street in Union Square: Salty Parker or Lefty O'Doul?

For more baseball, visit www.californiasportsastounding.com

A: Lefty O'Doul managed the San Francisco Seals from 1935 to 1951. He owned Lefty O'Doul's Restaurant and Cocktail Lounge, a hofbrau that served Bloody Marys.

CALIFORNIA SPORTS BIRTHDAYS
More Fun for April 15

Q: Dara "DT" Torres, born in 1967, swimmer, competed in how many Olympics: two, four, or five?

Did You Know? Part 1

Wilbur "Bill" King was part of the Giants original broadcasting team with Russ Hodges and Lon Simmons. He would eventually announce Oakland Athletics, Oakland Raiders, and San Francisco Warriors games.

Did You Know? Part 2

Dodgers' announcer Vin Scully called the game at Seals Stadium on April 15, 1958 for KMPC radio. Scully, who already had eight years with the team, continued his career in California and retired in 2016. His 66 years of service is the longest tenure of any broadcaster with a single team in professional sports history. The address to Dodger Stadium was renamed 1000 Vin Scully Avenue in 2016.

A: Five. Torres is the first swimmer to represent the USA in five Olympic Games: 1984, 1988, 1992, 2000, and 2008. She won 12 Olympic medals in the butterfly and freestyle events.

Blue Diamond Gala
April 16, 2015

Former team owner Peter O'Malley began the Los Angeles Dodgers Foundation in 1995. In 2012, Guggenheim Baseball Management led by Earvin "Magic" Johnson, and several other investors including Mark Walter, bought the Dodgers. Walter grew the foundation substantially as it became one of the leading sports charities nationwide. The foundation has invested more than $32 million in programs and grants to non-profits. Dodgers RBI, their baseball and softball youth development program, has more than 10,000 participants annually. Over 50 Dreamfields were built citywide providing over 368,000 youth with a field in their neighborhood. The Our LA Reads program develops reading skills for thousands of students with a goal of one million minutes annually.

The Blue Diamond Gala at Dodger Stadium started in 2015. This annual fundraiser draws over 2,000 attendees and generates millions in donations that provide youth with expanded access to education, health care, and sports. In 2020, the Dodgers were honored as the ESPN Sports Humanitarian Team of the Year.

In response to the COVID-19 pandemic, the foundation provided over $2.2 million in donations to over 6,000 families and a continued push for social justice.

Q: The Dodger Foundation awards how many grants to local organizations annually: 75, 100, or over 110?

For more baseball, visit www.californiasportsastounding.com

A: Over 110 grants are awarded annually.

CALIFORNIA SPORTS BIRTHDAYS
More Fun for April 16

Q: Anne Kursinski, born in 1959, showjumper, won two Olympic silver medals. She represented Team USA in how many Olympics: two, four, or five?

· ·

Did You Know?

In 2016 the San Francisco Giants became the first California team to win the ESPN Humanitarian of the Year Award. The team created Junior Giants in 1995 to help end the cycle of violence in impoverished areas around the city. Over the years, the program has served more than 275,000 children statewide.

The San Francisco 49ers won the award the following year. The 49ers committed over $4 million to local non-profits. Their STEAM (science, technology, engineering, art, and mathematics) education program is housed at the Denise DeBartolo York Education Center at Levi's Stadium.

A: The Pasadena native was a member of five Olympic teams from 1984 to 2008.

NOTABLE BIRTHDAY

April, 1993

Mirai Nagasu, born in Montebello, figure skater, first American ladies' singles skater to land a triple Axel, an edge jump at the 2018 Olympics. She was a bronze medalist in the 2018 team competition.

Smashing a Shuttlecock
April 17, 1933

California would host America's premier tournament for smashing a shuttle-cock, but not until the sport worked its way from New York in 1878 to the West Coast. Californians started using their racquets for informal competition by the early 1930s.

The first California state badminton championship was held at the Monterey High School gymnasium in 1933. California State Badminton Association members organized the event. Over 100 players from California and Washington participated.

Pasadena's Robert Ford and George McConk battled for the men's singles crown, with Ford prevailing 18-13, 15-7. McConk teamed with W.H. Joyce, also of Pasadena, to win the men's doubles event 15-6, 15-10 over visiting Seattle players Kurt Bet and Richard Peers.

Lois Beckman of Seattle won the women's singles title. Sally Cameron and Miss V. Jones of Pasadena claimed second in the women's doubles. The Old Monterey Polo Club, the local center of badminton, was used as a practice venue leading up to the tournament.

In 1947, California hosted the U.S. National Championships for the first time. The event was held at the Pan Pacific Auditorium in Los Angeles. Over 400 players nationwide participated. Several Californians won events. Among the winners were Pasadena's Dave Freeman in men's singles, San Francisco's Janet Wright in women's doubles, and Burbank's Wynn Rogers and Virginia Hill in mixed doubles. Over 4,000 spectators attended the tournament at the classic landmark building in the Fairfax District.

Q: Badminton exhibitions were given at what famous downtown Los Angeles theatre in 1936: Pantages or Paramount?

For more badminton, visit www.californiasportsastounding.com

A: The exhibitions were held on the stage of the Paramount Theatre. Blanche Brough, runner-up in the state tournament, and Velma Dunn, California junior women's champion, teamed with men's champions Bill Hurley and Jess Willard. They gave four exhibitions daily to sold out audiences at the 3,400-seat theatre.

CALIFORNIA SPORTS BIRTHDAYS
More Fun for April 17

Q: Bill Redell, born in 1941, was inducted into the College Football Hall of Fame and was honored for playing how many positions: two, four, or five?

....

Did You Know?

Dave Freeman of Pasadena was the 1949 World Champion in singles and a seven-time national champion in singles and doubles between 1939 and 1953. He is the first Californian inducted into both the U.S. and World Badminton Halls of Fame.

San Diego's Joseph Alston was a five-time national champion in singles and doubles from 1951 to 1953. In 1955 he became the first badminton player featured on the cover of *Sports Illustrated*. Two years later, he was the World Champion in doubles with Malaysia's Johnny Heah.

A: Redell, a native of Red Bluff, played quarterback, punter, placekicker, and cornerback for the Occidental College Tigers from 1962 to 1963.

NOTABLE BIRTHDAY
April 17, 1952

Thomas Bruce, born in Red Bluff, swimmer, 1972 Olympic gold medalist and world record in the 4 x 100-meter relay. California teammates Mark Spitz and Mike Stamm also earned medals.

Dodger Fence
April 18, 1958

Los Angeles welcomed Major League baseball with a parade for the Dodgers from City Hall to the Coliseum. There were two Dodgers per convertible, and all cars were placarded to help fans identify the players. What about the team's nickname? Dodgers President Walter F. O'Malley was flexible since "nicknames spring up locally, so whatever the Los Angeles fans want to call us is fine." Los Angeles fans continued to call the team "Dodgers."

The weather forecast was sunny leading a local paper to predict that "the Dodgers will get a taste of their new home's most notorious product—smog."

The Dodgers played their first home game against the San Francisco Giants at the Memorial Coliseum. There was concern about configuring the oval shaped Coliseum for baseball. The result were very short dimensions in left field, only 250 feet down the line, but center field was a distant 425 feet and right-center 440 feet. Five days before the game, the *San Bernardino Sun* reported "that an amateur team from the University of Southern California had taken batting practice in Memorial Coliseum and hit 13 home runs."

78,672 fans arrived and set a major league record for a single regular season game. Luckily, the stadium workers installed a 40-foot-high by 140-foot wire mesh screen in left field to challenge the home run hitters. Everyone celebrated the result as the Dodgers beat their rivals 6-5. Four years later, the team moved into Dodger Stadium.

Los Angeles won their first World Series title in 1959 by defeating the Chicago White Sox. The Sandy Koufax-led Dodgers added a four-game sweep of the New York Yankees in 1963 and a title over the Minnesota Twins in 1965. Los Angeles topped the Yankees again in 1981. Kirk Gibson's pinch-hit home run in the 1988 World Series against the Oakland Athletics is probably the most famous moment in team history. The dramatic home run ignited a 4-1 rout of the A's. Los Angeles added another title in 2020 by edging the Tampa Bay Rays 4-2 as teams played a shortened season to avoid the deadly coronavirus that has killed thousands of Americans.

Q: What Dodger outfielder reconfigured his swing to hit high flies over the left field screen?

For more baseball, visit www.californiasportsastounding.com

A: Wally Moon. The outfielder's towering home runs over the left field barrier were called "Moon shots."

CALIFORNIA SPORTS BIRTHDAYS
More Fun for April 18

Q: Brenda Villa, born in 1980, water polo player, won how many Olympic medals: two, three, or four?

. . . .

Did You Know?

Duke Snider was the first Californi-born Dodger to hit over 300 home runs and have over 1,000 runs batted in. The Los Angeles native played center field and was an 8-time All-Star from 1947 to 1962.

A: The Los Angeles native won a gold, two silvers, and a bronze between 2004 and 2012. Female Water Polo Player of the Decade for 2000 to 2009 by the FINA *Aquatics World Magazine*.

NOTABLE BIRTHDAYS
April 18

1888: George "Duffy" Lewis, born in San Francisco, MLB left fielder, World Series champion with the Boston Red Sox 1912, 1915 and 1916.

1937: Fred Newman, world record free throw basketball shooter from Santa Monica, attended California Institute of Technology, in 24 hours made 20,371 free throws from a total of 22,049 taken (92.39 percent) at Caltech on September 29-30, 1990.

Jawing with Joey
April 23, 2005

Joseph "Jaws" Chestnut, better known as Joey, has chomped through the competitive eating world. The Vallejo native graduated from San Jose State University with a degree in engineering and construction management, but changed careers to become a fulltime gurgitator.

His first notable win was at the 2005 Stockton Asparagus Festival when he ate 6.3 pounds of the veggie in 11.5 minutes and earned $1,000. The 240-pound Chestnut trained by fasting and stretching his stomach with milk, water, and protein supplements. He improved his breath control by running at least three times a week.

Joey set world records from Stockton to San Diego. In 2016, he gobbled up 14.5 pounds of boysenberry pie in eight minutes. Doughnuts? In 2017, he took only eight minutes to inhale 55 glazed doughnuts. The next year, he devoured 25.5 ice cream sandwiches in only six minutes. Shrimp? How about swallowing seven pounds of shrimp in eight minutes. He won the Nathan's Hot Dog Eating Contest in New York several times starting in 2007. In 2021, Joey ate 76 hot dogs and buns in 10 minutes to set a new world record and claim the mustard belt.

San Jose is also home to Matthew "Megatoad" Stonie. He won the 2015 Nathan's Contest and was ranked as high as number four by Major League Eating. The 134-pound Stonie's records include gorging on 20 pounds and 13 ounces of pumpkin pie in eight minutes at Elk Grove and ingesting 113 one-ounce silver dollar pancakes in eight minutes at the Silver Dollar Fair in Chico.

Q: What are Joey Chestnut's least favorite foods? Hint: One is raw, and one causes bloating.

For more competitive eating, visit www.californiasportsastounding.com

A: Kimchi and raw oysters.

CALIFORNIA SPORTS BIRTHDAYS
More Fun for April 23

Q: Adolph Camilli, born in 1907, National League first baseman from 1933 to 1945, recorded the last out of what hall of famer's career in 1935? Hint: He was a two-time 20 game winner.

....

Did You Know?

Major League Eating is the world body that oversees all professional eating contests. The organization holds about 70 events annually, with several in California.

A: The native of San Francisco played for the Philadelphia Phillies in 1935 and recorded the last out of Babe Ruth's career, a ground out.

NOTABLE BIRTHDAYS
April 23

1959: Marcella "Marcy" Place, born in Long Beach, field hockey player, bronze medalist at the 1984 Summer Olympics in Los Angeles. Teammate and Palo Alto native Sheryl Ann Johnson also medaled.

2000: Chloe Kim, Long Beach native, snowboarder, trained at both the Mountain High resort in the San Gabriel Mountains and Mammoth Mountain. 2018 and 2022 Olympic champion in the halfpipe. First snowboarder to win the Olympic, World, Youth Olympic, and X Games.

A Trio of Buds
April 27, 1969

This racquet sport needed a trio of Buds to build it towards a world championship. Californians discovered racquetball in 1969 and led the way in developing America's elite players. That year, El Cajon's Dr. Bud Muehleisen beat San Diego's Charlie Brumfield to win the singles title at the U.S. National Racquetball Tournament in St. Louis. That's one "Bud."

Racquetball grew tremendously during the 1970s and San Diego was the California hub. The city hosted several national tournaments and had over 200 courts. Two of America's leading manufacturers of racquetball equipment were in San Diego. Franklin Wesley "Bud" Held started Ektelon and was the first American to hold the world javelin record. (That's two Buds.) Leach Industries was owned by Bud Leach, was a National Slalom Water Ski Champion. ("Bud" number three.)

Los Angeles had several racquetball clubs and organized the 1972 National Championships at the Westside YMCA which drew 184 entries.

Santa Clara's Decathlon Club hosted the 1981 World Championships, the first held in California. USA's Ed Andrews won the men's singles title, while Cindy Baxter captured the women' crown. Sacramento's Gleneagles Racquetball and Athletic Club staged the tournament in 1984. The USA swept the men's and women's team titles.

Q: San Diego based pro racquetball player Marty Hogan could serve up to speeds of 109 mph, 131 mph, or 142 mph?

For more racquetball, visit www.californiasportsastounding.com

A: National Racquetball Hall of Fame inductee Marty Hogan could smack his serve up to 142 mph.

CALIFORNIA SPORTS BIRTHDAYS
More Fun for April 27

Q: Patricia "PattiSue" Plumer, born in 1962, Olympic distance runner, set the American record in 1989 in which event: 1,500 meters, 5,000 meters, or 10,000 meters?

....

Did You Know?

The Sacramento State University Hornets women's team won the United States Racquetball Association titles from 1986 to 1989.

Orange Coast College student Lynn Adams turned pro and was eight-time player of the year from 1982 to 1990. She was inducted into the National Racquetball Hall of Fame in 1997.

San Francisco's Fran Davis was inducted in 2004. She has coached the U.S. National Team, conducted successful racquetball camps, and was the U.S. Olympic Committee Coach of the Year in 1987.

Rocky Carson of Newport Beach won a record five International Racquetball Federation World Championships men's singles between 2008-2016.

A: The Covina native ran 14:59.99 in the 5,000 meters on July 3, 1989.

NOTABLE BIRTHDAYS
April 27

1911: Robert Sutton, Los Angeles native, sailor, 1932 Olympic gold medalist in the 8 meter class aboard the boat Angelita.

1935: Ron Morris, born in Glendale, pole vaulter, 1952 and 1953 CIF State Champion at Burroughs High School in Burbank, All-American at USC, 1960 Olympic silver medalist.

1983: Donald Penn, born in Los Angeles, NFL offensive tackle, three-time Pro Bowler, played for the Oakland Raiders from 2014 to 2018.

Kicking it with LAFC
April 29, 2018

The Los Angeles Football Club, or LAFC, gave Southern California another franchise in Major League Soccer. Though the team was founded in 2014, the official name was decided a year later. Vice-Chairman and owner Henry Nguyen said, "The name that we chose is true to Los Angeles, authentic to world football and speaks to our global ambitions."

Their first MLS home game was on April 29, 2018 with a dramatic 1-0 shutout over the Seattle Sounders at the new Banc of California Stadium. The 22,000 seat venue, built next to the Los Angeles Memorial Coliseum, is the first open air stadium built in Los Angeles since Dodger Stadium in 1962.

The LAFC enjoy a friendly rivalry with the LA Galaxy. Their rivalry is called El Tráfico. Soccer fans voted for the name after sports blogging Network SB Nation conducted polls on blogs LAG Confidential and Angels on Parade. El Tráfico, (the traffic in Spanish) refers to the well-known traffic congestion in Los Angeles. Finishing behind in the voting were the names Battle of the 110, Battle of Los Angeles, and LA/Hollywood Derby. LAFC is the gritty upstart team, is inner city, based in downtown, wears black and gold, and their fans refer to their rivals as the Carson Galaxy, a team from the suburbs. Galaxy fans have responded by calling LAFC "Chivas 2.0" after the defunct pro soccer team from 2014.

The young franchise already has a devoted following. LAFC has sold out its home games and is developing relationships with the community. In 2018, the club opened their new $30 million dollar headquarters and performance center at the campus of California State University, Los Angeles. LAFC renovated the campus stadium field and has supported Cal State students through internships and collaborations with university educational programs. The club has pledged over $1.5 million to the University.

LAFC fans will see Olympic soccer at their home stadium. The Banc of California Stadium is the venue for the men's and women's soccer tournament at the 2028 Summer Olympics.

Q: Who was the first captain in club history: "General" Ciman or "Captain" Mervel?

For more soccer, visit www.californiasportsastounding.com

A: Laurent "The General" Ciman.

CALIFORNIA SPORTS BIRTHDAYS
More Fun April 29

Q: Johnny Miller, born in 1947, 1973 U.S. Open champion, and 1976 British Open winner, is a member of what hall of fame?

. . . .

Did You Know?

The LAFC established the Academy in 2016 to provide greater access to the game for the community and a professional pathway for elite players in the region. In 2020 the LAFC signed Academy products Erick Duenas, Tony Leone, and Christian Torres as the first three homegrown players in club history.

A: The San Francisco native was inducted into the World Golf Hall of Fame in 1998. Miller developed his golfing skills at San Francisco's Olympic Club.

NOTABLE BIRTHDAYS
April 29

1978: Michael "Mike" Bryan, Camarillo native, professional tennis player, teamed with identical twin brother Robert to be the #1 doubles team in the world 10 times between 2003 and 2014. Mike is six foot three and plays right-handed.

1978: Robert "Bob" Bryan, born in Camarillo, professional tennis player, teamed with identical twin brother Mike. Only doubles team to win Olympic gold medal plus four consecutive Grand Slams starting with the 2012 Olympics in London, followed by 2012 US Open, 2013 Australian Open, 2013 French Open, and Wimbledon 2013—known as the Bryan Golden Slam. Bob is six foot four and plays left-handed.

MAY
NIFICENT

Splashing into a Cove
May 1, 2000

You know you're doing well when a body of water is named after you. McCovey Cove is the unofficial name of a section of San Francisco Bay beyond the right field wall. It was named after Giants' hall of fame first baseman Willie McCovey who hit 521 home runs in his career.

San Francisco outfielder Barry Bonds became the first player to launch a regular season home run into McCovey Cove as the Giants crushed the New York Mets 10-3 at Pacific Bell Park on May 1. Bonds hit the home run off Rich Rodriguez, a native of Downey, CA who was a former Giants pitcher. Joseph Figone, a member of the grounds crew the previous year at Candlestick Park, steered his motorized raft quickly to snare the souvenir. There are no plans yet to rename the cove after Figone.

Q: Who proposed the name "McCovey Cove"?

For more baseball, visit www.californiasportsastounding.com

A: Sportswriters Mark Purdy of the *San Jose Mercury News* and Leonard Koppett of the *Oakland Tribune*.

CALIFORNIA SPORTS BIRTHDAYS
More Fun for May 1

Q: Archibald "Archie" Williams, born in 1915, set a track and field world record and won Olympic gold in 1936. What was his event: the high jump, 400 meters, or long jump?

Did You Know?

Relief pitcher Trevor Hoffman set a Major League record for saves with one team as the San Diego Padres beat the Chicago Cubs 4-3 at Qualcomm Stadium on May 1, 2002. His 321 saves broke the record of 320 set by Dennis Eckersley of the Oakland Athletics.

A: The Oakland native ran the 400-meters. He set a world record of 46.1 seconds on June 19, then followed with his Olympic win on August 7. UCLA sprinter Jimmy LuValle won the bronze medal.

NOTABLE EVENT
May of 1850

Apparently, the first newspaper reference to bullfighting appeared in the *Daily Alta California* four months before statehood. On May 16, 1850, the paper reported, "The Olympic Circus, in Kearney street, we perceive by a Card, has been released to a company for the purpose of giving exhibitions and sports of various kinds, among which stands most prominent the favorite Spanish recreation of Bull-fighting (spelled as two words). A company of professional bullfighters from Mexico have been engaged. Senor Jose M. Aguella, the most expert and celebrated fighter in Mexico, is among the number to appear tonight."

NOTABLE BIRTHDAY
May 1, 1914

John Henry Lewis, born in Los Angeles, boxer, World Light Heavyweight champion 1935-1938, fought at San Francisco's Dreamland Auditorium, Civic Auditorium, and Olympic Auditorium.

OC in SFO
May 6, 1860

America's oldest athletic club was established in the backyard of leader Arthur Nahl's home on Broadway near Montgomery Street in San Francisco. Members exercised on parallel and horizontal bars, climbing ropes, and swinging rings. On May 29, the *Daily National Democrat* reported: "A New Club—Some twenty or thirty gentlemen have organized a club to train themselves in fencing, boxing and gymnastics generally. They call themselves the San Francisco Olympic Club."

The club was renamed on September 8, 1873, and the *Oakland Daily Transcript* noted "R.H. Lloyd has been installed as President of the Olympic Club."

Among the club's famous athletes were Shasta native Scott Leary, swimmer and medalist in the 50 and 100-yard freestyle at the 1904 Olympics. On July 18, 1905, he became the first American to swim 100 yards in 60 seconds flat. Shot putter Ralph Rose won six Olympic medals between 1904-1912. Boxer "Gentleman Jim" Corbett won the world heavyweight championship in 1892.

What started with 23 members has now grown to over 5,000 men and women, plus several hundred junior members. Olympians compete in over 19 sports and enjoy two historic clubhouses in San Francisco: City Clubhouse, near Union Square, and Lakeside, at the Pacific Ocean. Golfers can choose from three courses: the 9 hole par 3 Cliffs Course, the 18 hole Ocean Course, or the 18 hole Lake Course called "Best in the West" by Hall of Famer Bobby Jones.

The club has hosted several major golf tournaments including the U.S. Open five times between 1955 and 2012. Californians Billy Casper and Scott Simpson won the 1966 and 1987 titles respectively. The U.S. Women's Open was held at the Olympic Club for the first time in 2021.

Q: What open water swim relay is sponsored by the Olympic Club?

For a variety of sports, visit www.californiasportsastounding.com

A: The Trans Tahoe relay is one of the largest open water swims in the world and covers about 10 miles across the width of Lake Tahoe. Swimmers race from Sand Harbor Beach in New Washoe City, NV to Skylandia Beach in Tahoe City, CA.

....

Did You Know?

Olympic Club member Maureen "Mo" O'Toole won a silver medal in women's water polo at the 2000 Olympics. Maureen was honored as World Water Polo Female Athlete of the Year six times. She was MVP of the U.S. Women's National Team 15 times. O'Toole is a 2003 USA Water Polo Hall of Fame inductee.

NOTABLE EVENT
May 6, 1968

San Francisco Giants relief pitcher Lindy McDaniel sets a National League record of playing 225 games without committing an error.

CPC
May 11, 1876

A horseback mounted team sport rode into California the same year the sport made its American debut in New York. A sport of braided tails, bumps, chukkas, and stomping the divots.

The *San Jose Mercury-News* provided the first newspaper reference. The paper described the San Jose based California Polo Club and their planned trip to Chicago, Philadelphia, and New York with "seven daring riders and fourteen pure blood California horses." San Jose's contingent was headed by rider Captain Nell H. Mowry and horse owner T.K. Reed.

The article continued, "This game is simply shinny on horseback, and those who have seen the excited group, with canes reversed, barking at each other's shins, in the wild strife to knock a small block out of bounds, can imagine the wilder work when spirited horses lake part in the game, and the block is a ball which bounds so easily, when struck, as men with such advantages for hard striking, strike. The dangers to both horses and riders are greater than can be imagined.

Our San Jose horsemen will most likely carry the crowds in the East. Their horses under Spanish bridle and saddle are tractable to a degree unknown west of the Mississippi.

Here in California, where boys and girls, even, ride bareback, and professional horsemen defy the law of gravitation like flies, we don't think so much of these feats. When Mowry throws himself under his horse and into the saddle on the opposite side—won't those Quakers stare! We bid our Polo Club bon voyage, and hope they will bring home lots of honors, and not a bone broken."

Q: What other polo club started in the Bay Area by Navy officers less than three months later?

For more polo, visit www.californiasportsastounding.com

A: The Pacific Tournament and Polo Club was organized August 2 by Navy officers at Mare Island Naval Shipyard and private citizens of Vallejo.

CALIFORNIA SPORTS BIRTHDAYS
More Fun for May 11

Q: Montague "Monte" Upshaw, born in 1936, set a national scholastic long jump record in 1954 of 25 feet 4.5 inches. What famous sprinter held the record for 21 years?

· ·

Did You Know?

California has over 25 polo clubs sanctioned by the U.S. Polo Association. The clubs range from Yuba City in Sutter County to Lakeside in San Diego County.

The first Californian inducted into the Museum of Polo and Hall of Fame was Riverside native Eric Pedley in 1991. Eric won U.S. Open Championships in 1924, 1926, and 1930. He had a nine goal handicap rating in 1930, the second highest possible.

California hosted the World Polo Championships for the first time in 1998 at the Santa Barbara Polo & Racquet Club. The tournament returns to California in 2022 at Indio's Empire Polo Club.

A: Olympic gold medalist Jesse Owens.

NOTABLE BIRTHDAY
May 11, 1983

Matt Leinart, native of Santa Ana, USC quarterback, 2004 Heisman Trophy winner, NFL quarterback 2006-2012, College Football Hall of Fame inductee 2017.

Diggin it at the YMCA
May 11, 1897

This sport's first exhibition was in 1896, but it took a year for it to travel from Massachusetts to California. Among the many elements of this sport are the serve, pass, set, spike, block, and dig.

The first volley ball [originally spelled as two words] game was described in the *San Francisco Call*. "A new game called volley ball was played for the first time on the Pacific Coast last Tuesday evening at the gymnasium of the YMCA 'Volley ball' is the invention of Mr. Morgan of Holyoke, Mass., who has been instructor in gymnastics and athletics for a number of years.

Volley ball has the following advantages over basket-ball, handball and lawn tennis: It is not so rough as basket-ball, accidents are almost impossible; it is not liable to be so one-sided as handball and tennis usually are for the average player and the expenses for court and outfit are very small. The game is fully described in the 'Association Athletic Handbook for 1897,' where also the rules are given in detail.

The game played Tuesday evening was a practice game between two teams from the Mission Young Men's Christian Association and from the German Branch YMCA Four men played on a side with the following line-up: Mission team—Lamont, Tayler, Smith, Sankey, McCloud. German team—Herrings, J. Tonjes, Homer, H. Tonjes. The score of the volley ball game stood 40 to 31 points in favor of the Mission team."

Q: What was the original volleyball net height? Hint: Less than seven feet.

For more volleyball, visit www.californiasportsastounding.com

A: The first net height was six feet six inches. Current net heights are seven feet 11 5/8 inches for men and seven feet 4 1/8 inches for women.

CALIFORNIA SPORTS BIRTHDAYS
More Fun for May 11

Q: Donald "Don" McKenzie, Jr., born in 1947, won two gold medals in swimming at the 1968 Olympics in which events: medley relay and the backstroke or breaststroke?

. . . .

Did You Know?

Flo Hyman and Eugene "Gene" Selznick were the first two Californians honored as inductees to the International Volleyball Hall of Fame. Hyman played indoor volleyball and won a silver medal for Team USA at the 1984 Olympics. She died suddenly at the age of 31 due to Marfan syndrome, a genetic disorder she never knew she had.

Selznick played indoor and beach volleyball. In 1956 he became the first American to be selected All-World following the World Championships in Paris. Selznick was a 10-time USVBA first team All-American between 1951 and 1965.

A: McKenzie, a native of Hollywood, won the 100-meter breaststroke and the 4 x 100-meter medley relay. He was the only Californian on the relay team.

NOTABLE BIRTHDAY
May 11, 1950

Dane Iorg, born in Eureka, MLB first baseman and outfielder, World Series champion with the St. Louis Cardinals in 1982 and the Kansas City Royals in 1985.

Kicking at Konko
May 11, 1956

A new martial art from the Ryukyu Islands south of mainland Japan was brought to California before 1960. This striking art frequently uses punching, kicking, knee strikes, elbow strikes, and open-handed techniques to subdue an opponent.

Tsutomu Ohshima introduced karate to California in 1955. The Japanese native was the first person to teach the sport in America. In May of 1956 he opened America's first karate dojo (practice room) at Konko Church in Los Angeles. The following year in Little Tokyo, he gave the first public demonstration of karate, and on March 7 started the first university karate club at Caltech. Ohshima founded the Southern California Karate Association in 1959.

California's first major tournament was the Long Beach International Karate Championships organized by Ed Parker and held in 1964. Bruce Lee introduced himself to fans by demonstrating his one-inch punch, where he held his fist no more than one inch from his target and used an explosive burst for punching power. Lee also demonstrated one arm, two-finger push-ups. Long Beach attracted notable fighters through the years such as Chuck Norris, Mike Stone, Jerry Piddington, and Billy Blanks. The tournament is still in existence but has been renamed the Long Beach International Martial Arts Expo.

Q: Who pioneered full contact karate in 1974?

For more karate, visit www.californiasportsastounding.com

A: Tarzana native Benny "The Jet" Urquidez.

CALIFORNIA SPORTS BIRTHDAYS
More Fun for May 11

Q: Terri Stickles, born in 1946, won a bronze medal in which swimming event at the 1964 Olympics: 100-meter freestyle or 400-meter freestyle?

. . . .

Did You Know?

USA National Karate-do Federation is the national governing body of karate for the United States Olympic Committee. California's registered clubs are based in Granite Bay, Orange, and San Pablo.

The Martial Arts History Museum is located in Burbank. The museum is designed as an Asian educational, cultural, and artistic experience, it is a place in which visitors can learn about each of the different Asian countries (China, Japan, Korea, Thailand, the Philippines, etc.) and how martial arts played a significant role in their culture, history, and traditions.

A: The San Mateo native won a bronze medal in the 400-meter freestyle as the USA swept the top three places.

NOTABLE EVENT
May 11, 1963

Sandy Koufax of the Los Angeles Dodgers pitched the second no-hitter of his career as he beat Juan Marichal and the San Francisco Giants 8-0 at Dodger Stadium. Koufax threw 111 pitches, but delivered just enough breaking balls to finish the game. Koufax threw a total of four no-no's and was inducted into the National Baseball Hall of Fame.

San Francisco Hoisting
May 14, 1858

Athletes with weight plates hoisted the sport as early as 1858 according to this account from the *Daily Alta California*: "Mr. Frank Wheeler, proprietor of the Pioneer Gymnasium on Battery between California and Pine Streets, accomplished his great feat, of raising, without cessation, two 14.5-pound weights, 58,617 times, in ten consecutive hours. As the feat is probably unparalleled in this or any other country, the leading facts are worthy to be preserved as a matter of reference. The object was simply to illustrate, what an amount of physical endurance the human frame is capable of sustaining under the effects of long continued exercise.

During the performance, Mr. Wheeler partook sparingly of broiled beef, which was put into his month by his friends, and towards the close, drank a wine glass or two of champagne. He was seated the whole time. The aggregate weight raised was 821,638 pounds, or 410 tons lifted four feet from the ground. This would more than ballast a clipper ship."

The modern era produced three of California's greatest weightlifters, Tommy Kono, Mario Martinez, and Sarah Robles. Kono was born in Sacramento. He learned to weight lift after his family was sent to the Tule Lake internment camp in 1942 during World War II. Kono set seven Olympic and 26 world records, won two Olympic gold medals, and was a six-time World Champion. The International Weightlifting Federation named Kono the "Lifter of the Century." Soledad's Mario Martinez won an Olympic silver medal in 1984, plus ten national titles. Sara Robles, a native of San Diego, won bronze medals at the 2016 and 2020 Olympics and a gold medal at the 2017 World Championships.

Q: Tommy Kono set world records in how many weight classes: four, five or all of them?

For more weightlifting, visit www.californiasportsastounding.com

A: Kono set world records in four different weight classes: lightweight (149 pounds), middleweight (165 pounds), light-heavyweight (182 pounds), and middle-heavyweight (198 pounds).

CALIFORNIA SPORTS BIRTHDAYS
More Fun for May 14

Q: William Clay Matthews III, born in 1986, NFL linebacker, Super Bowl XLV champion, six-time Pro Bowl Selection, played for what college team: UCLA Bruins or USC Trojans?

....

Did You Know?

The Los Angeles Athletic Club produced two national weightlifting champions in 1928. Al Bevan, a light-heavyweight at 182 pounds, lifted 605 pounds in the press, snatch, clean, and jerk. Tom Tyler, a heavyweight, hoisted 760 pounds.

A: Matthews, a Northridge native, played for the USC Trojans from 2004 to 2008. He was the first Trojan to be awarded three consecutive Special Teams Player of the Year awards.

NOTABLE BIRTHDAY
May 14, 1994

Tony Gonsolin, born in Vacaville, MLB pitcher, 2020 World Series champion with the Los Angeles Dodgers.

CCAA Champions
May 18, 1938

The first reference to the California Collegiate Athletic Association appeared in the *Fresno Bee*, which the Fresno State College board "approved the entry of Fresno State in the newly organized California Collegiate Athletic Association." San Diego State, San Jose State, and UC Santa Barbara joined Fresno as charter members.

There have been several changes in membership through the years, but the CCAA has adapted to become America's most successful NCAA Division II conference. All 12 members belong to the California State University system. The conference has won over 150 NCAA titles.

Cameron "Scotty" Deeds coached the California State College, Los Angeles Golden Eagles tennis team to the first national title in CCAA history, a NCAA Division II championship in 1963. Gil Rodriguez won the singles title. Deeds added team titles in 1964 and 1965, with Gary Johnson as singles champion.

In 2019, the Cal State San Bernardino women's volleyball team, coached by Kim Cherniss, won their first national title. The Coyotes finished their undefeated season with a 3-1 win over Nebraska-Kearney.

The conference sponsors six men's and seven women's sports.

Q: Cal Poly Humboldt is the northern most member of the conference. What is their "choppy" nickname?

For more about the CCAA, visit www.californiasportsastounding.com

A: Lumberjacks. Their school colors are green and gold.

CALIFORNIA SPORTS BIRTHDAYS
More Fun for May 18

Q: Michael Whitmarsh, born in 1962, volleyball player, won a silver medal with partner Mike Dodd at the inaugural beach volleyball tournament in which Olympics: 1992, 1996, or 2000?

. . . .

Did You Know?

The California State Monterey men's golf team coached by Jason Owen won the 150th NCAA title in conference history on May 20, 2011. The Otters defeated Lynn University 3-2 in the title match at the Robert Trent Jones Golf Trail at The Shoals in Florence, Alabama. Monterey's Dylan Jackson aced the 178-yard, par-3 13th hole. His six under par 66 tied the lowest score of the tournament.

A: The San Diego native medaled at the 1996 Summer Olympics in Atlanta.

NOTABLE EVENTS

May 18

1978: The International Olympic Committee selected Los Angeles to host the 1984 Summer Olympic Games. The event was formally known as the Games of the XXIII Olympiad.

1997: Arcata's Christa Johnson won the Women's Professional Golf Association Championship. Christa finished her career with 15 wins on the LPGA Tour.

Squashed
May 19, 1905

A racket and ball sport played in 185 countries debuted in California just after 1900. The sport is played by two players in a four-walled court with a small hollow rubber ball. After New Hampshire claimed America's first court in 1884, the sport moved west and in 1902 landed on the west coast. San Francisco's Olympic Club made plans for courts in March of 1902, "which will only take place when the funds of the club warrant." Courts were also planned at the Potter Hotel in Santa Barbara. The *Morning Press* on June 25, 1902 noted that "Mr. Potter's idea being to make the gardens of the hotel a special feature of the place, and to provide amusement for his guests about the grounds. Plans are being made for a number of tennis courts, croquet grounds, squash courts, bowling alleys and other features essential to the needs of a modern resort."

The first reference to a squash tournament appeared in 1905. The *Morning Press* wrote "SQUASH BOOM AT COUNTRY CLUB interesting Round Robin Handicap Now Being Played—Tourney with Los Angeles. The game of squash is having a great boom at the present time among the players who use the courts at the Country club, and some good games have been played during the last few weeks. Both tennis and golf are being neglected for the newer and more strenuous pastime, and there is talk of a tournament in the near future in which all the players in the club have promised to compete. At the present time an interesting round robin handicap is in progress, for a handsome sweepstake cup put up by the four men who are entered. Several matches have been played already, but as several are still to be played it is impossible to tell who will carry off first honors."

There is a possibility that a squash tournament will be arranged with the players of the Los Angeles Country club, to take place sometime during the summer months. The Santa Barbara Country Club could put out a four-man team which would make a good showing against any four players in the south."

Q: Where is California's largest squash facility? Hint: It's located in Southern California.

For more squash, visit www.californiasportsastounding.com

A: The Access Youth Academy in San Diego has seven singles and one doubles court.

CALIFORNIA SPORTS BIRTHDAYS
More Fun for May 19

Q: Gilbert McDougald, born in 1928, MLB infielder, won how many World Series titles with the New York Yankees: three, four, or five?

....

Did You Know?

UC Berkeley has both men's and women's squash teams. The men were ranked as America's #1 club team in 2020. The women's team was established in 2008 as the first women's squash club team at a public university on the West Coast. They are a member of the College Squash Association and compete in the CSA National Team Championship annually.

The Arroyo Seco Racquet Club with five courts, and the Los Angeles Athletic Club which has over 300 players, are among the best-known venues for squash in Southern California.

Berkeley resident Alex Eichmann was California's first national champion. He played for the Pacific Coast team, which won the 1974 U.S. National Team Championships.

A: The San Francisco native won five World Series between 1951 and 1958.

NOTABLE BIRTHDAY
May 19, 1959

Paul Cayard, born in San Francisco, 1988 US Sailing Rolex Yachtsman of the Year, 2011 National Sailing Hall of Fame charter inductee, and 2020 Bay Area Sports Hall of Fame inductee.

Lefty
May 23, 2021

His first win in his home state as a professional golfer came at the 1993 Buick Invitational of California at the Torrey Pines Golf Course. The victory was by four strokes while his parents Phil and Mary watched from the gallery. Tournament officials gave him a first place check of $180,000 and a Buick Avenue Ultra automobile, which he gave to his dad.

"Lefty" was ranked 26 in the top 50 of the Official World Golf Rankings from 1993-2019, the only golfer in history with that accomplishment. He won six majors along the way, including the 2021 PGA Championship at age 50 years, 11 months, and 7 days, the oldest major champion in history. His brother Tim caddied for him.

Phil Mickelson is also a philanthropist and entrepreneur. In 2004 he established the Phil and Amy Mickelson Foundation, which supports several youth and family initiatives. He also founded Birdies for the Brave, the PGA Tour's national military outreach initiative, which raises money for a variety of charities supporting the veterans and military families. In 2019 The Phil and Amy Mickelson Foundation became the host organization of The American Express PGA Tour event held each January in Palm Springs. The first year of the event was a massive success as $1 million was raised for charities in the Coachella Valley. When not playing on the pro tour or giving back to communities, Mickelson designs and builds golf properties.

Q: Which was the first golf hall of fame to welcome Mickelson as an inductee?

For more golf, visit www.californiasportsastounding.com

A: He was inducted into the World Golf Hall of Fame near St. Augustine, Florida in 2012.

CALIFORNIA SPORTS BIRTHDAYS
More Fun for May 23

Q: Louis Balbach, born in 1896, diver, won a bronze medal in at the 1920

Olympics in which diving event: springboard or platform?

....

Did You Know?

The first Junior World Golf Championship was held August 26-30, 1968 at the Torrey Pines Golf Course in San Diego. La Jolla's Bob Martin won the boys age 15-17 division, while Susan Rapp of San Diego crushed the girls 15-17 field by 10 strokes.

The tournament started with 475 junior golfers from seven countries and 20 states has grown to 1,250 participants from 56 countries and 42 states. San Diego's Junior Golf Association organizes the event. Notable California winners include Phil Mickelson, Corey Pavin, Craig Stadler, and Tiger Woods. 1989 girls champion Brandie Burton of San Bernardino went on to the LPGA Tour where she became the youngest female golfer to surpass over $1 million in career earnings. She was inducted into the Southern California Golf Association Hall of Fame in 2019.

A: The San Jose native won a bronze medal in the three-meter springboard event. Clarence "Bud" Pinkston, who attended San Diego High School, won the silver medal. Pinkston added a gold medal in the 10-meter platform event.

NOTABLE BIRTHDAY
May 23, 1969

Pat Hurst, born in San Leandro, professional golfer on the LPGA Tour, 1998 ANA Inspiration champion, tournament was played at the Mission Hills Country Club in Rancho Mirage.

Fantastic Fresno
May 25, 1998

Fresno State's softball team coached by Margie Wright entered the 1998 NCAA Division I Tournament underappreciated and seeded only 7th out of 32 teams. The Bulldogs certainly didn't play like it, as they chewed up #2 Michigan, #4 Washington, and #5 Nebraska. Their reward was a matchup with powerful Arizona in the title game.

Arizona waited with their NCAA record of 67 victories. The Wildcats had not been scored on in the tournament, had won five of the last seven NCAA titles and bested Fresno State three times during the regular season, outscoring them 16-6.

The Bulldogs didn't care. Amanda Scott pitched a three hit shutout and second baseman Nina Lindenberg hit a home run to give Fresno State its first NCAA title in any sport. Amanda was named the Women's College World Series Most Outstanding Player. She finished her career with All-American honors along with Lindenberg, centerfielder Laura Berg, and leftfielder Becky Witt.

Fresno honored the team with a parade as they rode on a fire truck from Fashion Fair Mall along Shaw Avenue, and ended with a capacity crowd at Bulldog Diamond.

Q: Fresno State renamed Bulldog Diamond on May 3, 2014. What is the new name?

For more softball, visit www.californiasportsastounding.com

A: Margie Wright Diamond in honor of the retired Fresno softball coach.

CALIFORNIA SPORTS BIRTHDAYS
More Fun for May 25

Q: Paul Hait, born in 1940, swimmer, won a 1960 Olympic gold medal in what medley relay: 4 x 100-meters or 4 x 200-meter freestyle?

. . . .

Fresno Did You Know? Part 1

Ranked just #21 in pre-season baseball polls, the Fresno State baseball team shocked everyone but themselves by winning the 2008 NCAA Division I title. Coach Mike Batesole's team defeated another Bulldog team, this one from Georgia 6-1. Fresno pitcher Justin Wilson allowed only six hits and outfielder Steve Detwiler smashed two homes runs in the victory. Sophomore third baseman Tommy Mendonca was voted the Most Outstanding Player of the tournament.

A: The Pasadena native won a gold medal in the 4 x 100-meter medley relay. Hait and California teammate Lance Larson powered the team to a world record of 4:05.4 in the final.

. . . .

Fresno Did You Know? Part 2

The Student Horse Center, located on the Fresno State campus, is the site of all Fresno State equestrian home shows. Sponsored by the Department of Animal Science, the Student Horse Center is run and operated by students. Animal Science students are responsible for the care, exercise, and feeding of all university and privately owned horses housed at the center. The facility features 20 stalls in a main barn, 20 more in an adjacent pipe barn and four additional turnout pens.

NOTABLE BIRTHDAY
May 25, 1979

Carlos Bocanegra, born in Alta Loma, soccer player, captain of the U.S. Men's National Team six years between 2001 and 2012.

The Ice is Fine
May 26, 1916

The fastest team sport in the world has players moving up to 29 mph and shooting an object at over 100 mph. The sport gradually expanded from America's northeastern states in 1892 to the west coast.

San Francisco and San Diego helped introduce hockey to California in May of 1916. On May 10th *The San Francisco Call* announced that "The first chance local sport followers will have of seeing the much-discussed game of ice hockey will be given them this afternoon by Manager A. C. Morrison of the Techau Tavern Ice Palace. The first-and second-string teams of the newly organized San Francisco Hockey Club will have their initial tryout. This club will enter a team in the proposed California Amateur Hockey League. The game today is a club practice."

Three days later, the *San Diego Union and Daily Bee* published this account: "The Ice Rink Hockey Game Tonight First Time in California. Fast Teams. San Diego vs. Canada. Don't Miss It! Come on up the ice is fine! Admission 10 cents. The ice hockey teams to play first game here in the Exposition tonight. Ice hockey will be introduced in California tonight when two teams stage an exhibition game at the ice rink at the Exposition. The game tonight may be regarded as the preliminary to a series." The venue referred to in the article was the Panama-California Exposition at San Diego's Balboa Park.

San Francisco's Techau Tavern Ice Palace hosted the first official game on May 26. The San Francisco Call hyped the event one last time describing hockey as "even faster and harder than the ordinary boxing bout, and it requires a man in excellent training to up against the awful pace of the game." A near sellout crowd saw the Polo Hockey Club captained by Corbett Moody edge the San Francisco Hockey Club 10-9.

Q: What was the first California city to host the NCAA Division I Men's Ice Hockey Tournament known as the Frozen Four: San Jose, Los Angeles, or Anaheim?

For more hockey, visit www.californiasportsastounding.com

A: The Frozen Four was played at the Arrowhead Pond of Anaheim in 1999.

CALIFORNIA SPORTS BIRTHDAYS
More Fun for May 26

Q: Darrell "Howdy Doody" Evans, born in 1947, MLB first baseman, was a California junior college state champion in baseball and basketball for what school? Hint: Baseball Hall of Famer Jackie Robinson and his brother Olympic 200-meter silver medalist Mack Robinson also attended the school.

· ·

Did You Know?

Frank Zamboni, the inventor of the ice resurfacing machine that bears his name, built the Iceland Skating Rink in 1939. The rink in Paramount is located just a few blocks from the Zamboni® factory. Iceland has what may be the only pipe organ currently playing regularly in any ice skating arena in the country. The Wurlitzer organ was first installed in 1941.

A: Evans attended Pasadena City College from 1966 to 1967. He was an All-Star first baseman for the San Francisco Giants in 1983. Evans was inducted into the Giants Wall of Fame in 2008.

NOTABLE BIRTHDAY
May 26, 1949

Dante "Dan" Pastorini, born in Sonora, Oakland Raiders quarterback in 1980, also won several races in the 1980s as a National Hot Rod Association Top Fuel dragster driver.

Deadpan 61
May 28, 1933

The San Francisco Seals were finishing the last three games of their 1932 Pacific Coast League baseball season when they were short a shortstop. An outfielder named Vince suggested to manager Ike Caveney that his 17-year-old younger brother who was playing semi-pro ball, could fill in. The younger brother did okay. He had two hits in nine at bats for a .222 average. The youngster had a wild, but powerful arm that was more suited to the outfield. In 1933 Caveney invited the young man to spring training and joined the team as a right fielder. He started his first game on April 9 and had two hits as the Seals outslugged the Portland Beavers 11-10.

California newspapers kept misspelling his name as "DeMaggio," but the shy player who was nicknamed "Deadpan" by his teammates for his stoic demeanor would soon get proper media attention statewide.

On May 28, Joe DiMaggio embarked on a 61-game hitting streak, breaking the old league mark by 12 games. The streak tested his endurance. He played 61 games in 56 days, including 13 doubleheaders. DiMaggio responded to the grind by batting .405 and played superb defense. He crushed the pitching of rival California teams such as the Hollywood Stars, Los Angeles Angels, and the Sacramento Senators. DiMaggio's streak finally ended on July 24 against pitcher Ed Walsh of the Oakland Oaks.

Joe would go on to a Hall of Fame career with the New York Yankees. He won nine World Series between 1936 and 1951 and was a 13-time All-Star. DiMaggio set the Major League Baseball record 56-game hitting streak in 1941. He could have padded his statistics but joined the military to serve during World War II, just like Ted Williams and many other major leaguers. He was named to the Major League Baseball All-Century Team in 1999.

Q: Who were Joe DiMaggio's baseball-playing brothers?

For more baseball, visit www.californiasportsastounding.com

A: Dom and Vince. Dom was a seven-time All-Star center fielder with the Boston Red Sox from 1940-1953. Vince played center field for the Pittsburgh Pirates from 1940 to 1944 and was a two-time All Star.

CALIFORNIA SPORTS BIRTHDAYS
More Fun for May 28

Q: Shelley Hamlin, born in 1949, professional golfer, three LPGA victories, won how many California Women's Amateur Championships: three, four, or five?

. . . .

Did You Know?

Joe DiMaggio was not the Pacific Coast League's Most Valuable Player during his record breaking 1933 season. The honor went to his teammate and shortstop Augie Galan. His batting average of .356 was 16 points higher than Joe's.

Augie played 189 games, two more than DiMaggio. He had six more hits, six more doubles, and nine more triples. The Berkeley native went on to a career in the Major Leagues. Galan was a three-time All-Star with the Chicago Cubs and Brooklyn Dodgers from 1934 to 1946.

A: Shelley, a native of San Mateo, won four consecutive California Women's Amateur Championships from 1967 to 1970. She attended Stanford and was the 1971 AIAW National Champion.

NOTABLE EVENT
May 28, 1957

California gained two Major League Baseball franchises as the National League approved the proposed moves of the Brooklyn Dodgers and the New York Giants.

Brisk Breed
May 29, 1920

Owen Patrick "O.P." Smith and friend George Sawyer of the Blue Star Amusement Company opened the first commercial greyhound racetrack in Emeryville. The oval track featured Smith's invention: the one-pound mechanical rabbit, a more humane alternative to live lures. Heavy machinery weighing 1,600 pounds carried the tiny rabbit. Emeryville had the first mechanical lure oval circuit in the world! The track was located on Park Avenue between Horton and Holden Streets. It was constructed of wood from Sawyer's closed boxing arena in Oakland. Smith spent over $40,000 on the track, which attracted 500 fans for the inaugural races.

The *San Francisco Call* exaggerated the greyhounds speed when it wrote, "Coursing, one of the most popular of sports a decade ago, will be revived this afternoon at the new coursing park in Emeryville, when thirty of the fastest greyhounds in America start stepping at ninety miles an hour, after the elusive mechanical hares. Races will be staged every Saturday and Sunday afternoon. Because of the many prizes offered, some of the fastest greyhounds in the West will be seen in action."

Q: How fast can a greyhound run?

For more greyhound racing, visit www.californiasportsastounding.com

A: Greyhounds, dogs that hunt primarily by sight and speed instead of scent, can reach a maximum race speed of about 45 miles per hour.

CALIFORNIA SPORTS BIRTHDAYS
More Fun for May 29

Q: Lavone "Pepper" Paire Davis, born in 1924, a professional baseball catcher, was a National Women's Baseball Hall of Fame inductee in 2013. What is the name of her rhyming autobiography?

. . . .

Did You Know?

Southern California discovered greyhound racing as early as November of 1920. The *Los Angeles Times* reported of five races held at Maier Park in Vernon, just five miles south of downtown Los Angeles.

The first racing plant in Los Angeles opened at Culver City on June 22, 1932. Over $150,000 was spent by the Culver City Kennel Club to build the venue. Nearly 500 dogs were kenneled in Southern California for the opening. Organizers set up a 25-day season so not to interfere with opening of the Summer Olympics on July 30.

A: Lavone, a Los Angeles native, wrote *Dirt in the Skirt.*

NOTABLE BIRTHDAYS

May 29

1954: John Hencken, Culver City native, 100 and 200-meter breaststroke swimmer, 5-time Olympic medalist, including three golds between 1972-1976, Stanford University graduate, swam for the Santa Clara Swim Club, International Swimming Hall of Fame inductee 1988.

1962: Eric Davis, born in Los Angeles, MLB outfielder from 1984 to 2001, All-Star with the Cincinnati Reds 1987 and 1989, and World Series champion in 1990.

NOTABLE EVENT

May 29, 1990

Oakland Athletics left fielder Rickey Henderson stole his 893rd base breaking Ty Cobb's American League record. Rickey set his record in front of a home crowd at the Oakland-Alameda County Coliseum in a 2-1 loss to the Toronto Blue Jays.

JUNE
TASTIC

Stockton Speed
June 1, 1957

He had taken his final economics exam at UC Berkeley that afternoon, then drove to Stockton, with barely any time to warm up before the evening meet. No American had ever done what he was about to do. The race would be held on the clay track at Baxter Stadium at the University of Pacific. His coach Brutus Hamilton had the lanky six-foot-three-inch 150-pound runner well prepared.

He had only four competitors but challenged himself to a very fast pace. University of California's Don Bowden became the first American to run a sub four-minute mile when he ran 3:58.7 that night in the Pacific Association Amateur Athletic Union track meet. The 20-year-old also became the youngest runner to accomplish that feat. A plaque honoring his race is on display at the UOP student dining hall.

Q: When was the next sub-4 minute mile run in California: 1959, 1960, or 1961?

For more track and field, visit www.californiasportsastounding.com

A: Jim Beatty, representing the Santa Clara Youth Village, ran 3:58.0 at the California Relays in Modesto on May 28, 1960.

CALIFORNIA SPORTS BIRTHDAYS

More Fun for June 1

Q: Russell "Russ" Webb, born in 1945, water polo player, 1972 Olympic bronze medalist. Who was his coach? Hint: He competed in two sports.

Did You Know?

In 1958 Don Bowden and his California teammates set a world record of 7:20.9 in the 4 x 880-yard relay. The record was broken at the Coliseum Relays in Los Angeles with 34,656 fans in attendance. Don and his California teammates Maynara Orme, Jerry Siebert and Jack Yerman broke the old mark of 7:22.7 set by Occidental College the previous year.

A: Kenneth "Monte" Nitzkowski, a Pasadena native, swam in the 1952 Olympics and coached water polo in the 1972, 1980, and 1984 games.

NOTABLE BIRTHDAYS
June 1

1937: Charles "Charlie" Rogers, from National City, sailing in the Dragon class (one design keelboat), won a bronze medal at the 1964 Olympics. His teammate was Huntington Park native Richard "Dick" Deaver. The helmsman was 1968 Olympic gold medalist Lowell North.

1999: Richard Torrez, born in Tulare, boxer, member of the Tulare Athletic Boxing Club, 2017 and 2018 U.S. Champion in the super heavyweight division, 2020 Olympic silver medalist in the super heavyweight division.

NOTABLE EVENT
June 1, 1975

Nolan Ryan of the California Angels pitched the fourth no-hitter of his career to defeat the Baltimore Orioles 1-0 at Anaheim Stadium.

World's Greatest Ski Race
June 2, 1926

This surface water sport was invented in America's Midwest in 1922 and reached the Golden State four years later. Miss Dorothy Mathews of New York introduced the sport on her visit to Southern California. The *Los Angeles Times* revealed: "More difficult than aquaplaning, and therefore more dangerous, is the latest sport of water skiing introduced to the Southland. Miss Mathews possesses the only pair of skis on the Pacific Coast, and is the only woman on the coast capable of using them."

Dorothy went to Oakland the next day where the *Oakland Tribune* touted the sport "Sport for Water Sprites. Miss Mathews is introducing the sport of water skiing to the Pacific Coast beach resorts. She is seen skiing on one foot."

Water skiing spread to a variety of locales statewide including Oakland's Lake Merritt and Coronado. Even the Mojave Desert community of Baker had water skiing on Silver Lake in 1938 thanks to heavy rains and floods. The first race on San Francisco Bay, a 64 mile event, was held at the St. Francis Yacht Club in 1940.

The World's Greatest Ski Race inaugural event was held in 1949 as part of the El Redondo Aqua Fiesta. Ed Stanley finished first in 1 hour, 41 minutes, and 31 seconds in his trip to Catalina Island and return.

Today, the start and finish of the race are near the Queen Mary, the retired British ocean liner. Racing fans board the ship for the best views of the start and finish. Organized by the Long Beach Boat & Ski Club, the 62 mile event has over 100 boats and is the world's only recurring open-ocean ski race. Skiers range in age from 12 to almost 80 and represent the USA, Australia, Great Britain, and several other countries. Boats range from 19 to 43 feet tow skiers at speeds up to 90 miles per hour. Competition is in 19 different classes from novice to open division.

The modern era has featured Bellflower's Chuck Stearns and Riverside's Todd Haig. Stearns won 11 titles in four decades from 1955 to 1982. Haig has dominated the event with over 15 wins since 2000 and a personal best time of 46:36 in 2014. The first woman to break the one hour mark was hall of famer Debbie Nordblad with her time of 59:08 in 1996.

Q: Chuck Stearns opened a water ski school where in California: Long Beach, Lake Perris in Riverside County, or the Salton Sea Beach Resort?

For more water skiing, visit www.californiasportsastounding.com

A: Salton Sea Beach Resort. Chuck started skiing there as a 17-year-old in 1956.

CALIFORNIA SPORTS BIRTHDAYS
More Fun for June 2

Q: Craig Stadler, born in 1953, professional golfer, 1982 Masters Tournament champion, set what Master's record in 2014: lowest score, most bogeys, or father-son combo?

....

Did You Know?

Long Beach's Marine Stadium was the first California venue to host national and world water ski championships. The stadium hosted the 1953 National Water Skiing Championships and the 1961 World Championships.

The San Diego State Aztecs won the first National Intercollegiate Water Ski Championships, which were held in Monroe, Louisiana on October 14, 1979. Mark Scharosch and Lisa Nock were the top men's and women's finishers for the Aztecs.

A: The San Diego native and his son Kevin were the first father and son to play in the same Masters Tournament together.

NOTABLE BIRTHDAY
June 2, 1940

Jim Maloney, born in Fresno, MLB pitcher, attended Fresno High School, Fresno City College, and UC Berkeley, 1965 All-Star with the Cincinnati Reds, pitched no-hitters in 1965 and 1969. Finished career with the California Angels in 1971.

King Ducks
June 6, 2007

The Mighty Ducks of Anaheim, the National Hockey League franchise founded by the Walt Disney Company in 1993, were under new ownership for the 2006-2007 season. Several changes were made including renaming the team, arena, and uniform colors. The team was renamed the Anaheim Ducks. Their home rink known as the Arrowhead Pond of Anaheim became the Honda Center. Black, metallic gold, and orange became the new uniform colors, with white replacing black for road jerseys.

That first year, the Ducks won their first Pacific Division title ahead of the San Jose Sharks and Los Angeles Kings in 2007. They advanced to the Stanley Cup Finals and routed the Ottawa Senators 6-2 at the Honda Center to win the series four games to one. California had welcomed its first Stanley Cup winner.

Q: Who were the new owners of the Ducks?

For more hockey, visit www.californiasportsastounding.com

A: Orange County philanthropists Henry and Susan Samueli.

CALIFORNIA SPORTS BIRTHDAYS
More Fun for June 6

Q: John "The Reckless Russian" Rudometkin, born in 1940 in Santa Maria, NBA forward, All-American at USC. Who gave him his nickname?

Did You Know?

The Ducks held an online contest to name their rivalry series with the Los Angeles Kings. Over 12,000 votes were submitted. "Freeway Face-Off" received the most votes ahead of three other finalists: "Freezeway Series," "Ice-5 Series," and "Crosstown Showdown."

A: Chick Hearn, who announced USC football and basketball games from 1956 to 1961. Hearn then became the first broadcaster for the Los Angeles Lakers in 1961. His hall of fame career included play-by-play of a record 3,338 consecutive Los Angeles Lakers games from 1965 to 2001.

NOTABLE BIRTHDAY

June 6

1871: William "Bill" Lange, born in San Francisco, MLB centerfielder 1893 to 1899 for the Chicago Colts and 1897 National League stolen base leader with 73. He played for the California minor league Oakland Colonels in 1892 with games at Piedmont Baths Ball Park on the north end of Lake Merritt.

1939: Dave Grayson, San Diego native, pro football cornerback, 6-time American Football League All-Star 1962-1969, played for the Oakland Raiders 1965-1970, all-time AFL leader in interceptions with 47.

NOTABLE EVENTS

June 6

1992: First baseman Eddie Murray drove in two runs and became the all time RBI leader among switch hitters as the New York Mets sunk the Pittsburgh Pirates 15-1. The Los Angeles native's new record of 1,510 was one ahead of Mickey Mantle. Eddie was inducted into the National Baseball Hall of Fame in 2003.

2007: San Diego Padres reliever Trevor Hoffman recorded his 500th career save as the Padres beat the Los Angeles Dodgers 5-2 at Petco Park.

San Francisco Steam Wagon
June 9, 1860

California's first automobile, or "steam wagon," appeared in San Francisco. The vehicle was imported from England and assembled by the Vulcan Foundry on First Street. *Daily Alta California* reported "the engine, with tender attached, containing coal, wood, and attaches of the foundry, started for a trip to the Mission Dolores." The trip consumed just one bag of coal and a few arms full of firewood. About two hundred fifty gallons of water was needed for the boiler. Running time was less than three quarters of an hour. "Throngs of persons, of all ages and both texts, crowded the streets, and expressed astonishment at the huge machine." Lewis Blanding, pilot or helmsman, steered the successful trip, which ended back at the Foundry.

Let the races begin. The Golden State's first noteworthy races were held in Los Angeles, Santa Monica, and Oakland. Barney Oldfield broke the world record in Los Angeles on November 21, 1903 by racing the Agricultural Park one mile oval in 55 seconds—just over 60 miles per hour. In July of 1909 the Apperson "Jackrabbit" driven by Harris Hanshue, won the Santa Monica automobile road race covering 202 miles in three hours eight minutes and three seconds. His speed of 64.44 mph hour set a new world record. Three months later Jack Fleming guided his four-cylinder 40 horsepower car to win the 258-mile Oakland Portola Road Race. Fleming's original time of 64.51 mph was corrected to 63.11 by the A.A.A. and Harris Honshue still kept his record.

Q: How many fans attended the Oakland Portola Road Race?

For more auto racing, visit www.californiasportsastounding.com

A: Over 250,000 fans attended the 15-car race as part of the larger Portola Festival.

CALIFORNIA SPORTS BIRTHDAYS
More Fun for June 9

Q: Tedy Bruschi, born in 1973, NFL linebacker, won how many Super Bowls with the New England Patriots: three, four, or five?

....

Did You Know?

The Portola Festival featured an auto show in San Francisco's Emporium basement. Over 160 automobiles were displayed ranging from monster six-cylinder road runners, rated at 70 horsepower or more to the plodding two-cylinder delivery trucks.

The four-day festival celebrated the rebuilding of San Francisco from the earthquake in 1906 and honored Gaspar de Portolá, the first governor of the California's, Alta and Baja.

A: The native of San Francisco won Super Bowls XXXVI, XXXVIII, and XXXIX.

NOTABLE BIRTHDAY
June 9, 1983

Erin Cafaro, born in Modesto, rower, won Olympic gold medals in women's eight at the 2008 and 2012 Olympics.

NOTABLE EVENT
June 9, 1985

The Los Angeles Lakers, led by MVP Kareem Abdul-Jabbar, defeated the Boston Celtics 111-100 to win the NBA Finals four games to two. The victory over the Celtics was the first in Laker history in the NBA Finals.

A Racket at Horticultural Hall
June 15, 1880

Cooper's Store on Sixth and J Street in Sacramento advertised equipment for this racket sport as early as 1879. Formal competition swung into California the following year. The *Sacramento Daily Union* proclaimed: "The game which for five years has been engaged in with so much enthusiasm in Great Britain found its way to California this summer, and lawn tennis is now fairly installed on this coast.

Like archery, it is a pastime in which both sexes can obtain as much or as little exercise as they please, and one also which requires constant practice to become expert in the game. The first lawn tennis club in San Francisco originated with a party of young Englishmen, who imported a tennis set, and hired Horticultural Hall for a court. Here they are found every afternoon working most energetically with racket and ball."

One month later the newspaper followed up with a more critical viewpoint: "Although the present season is just opened, more than ten thousand tennis sets have already been sold in this city this year. Tennis is a weak and silly game, uninteresting, flat and unprofitable, if the players do not play to win first, last and always, and if they do not fully comprehend and appreciate what the initiated call points. As the variable restrictions, privileges and conditions of the game are many and not simply and accurately set forth in the published rules, it is natural that novices should at first fall into errors in playing the game, even if they have been prudent enough to examine it."

Q: When was the first lawn tennis club formed in Southern California?

For more tennis, visit www.californiasportsastounding.com

A: A lawn tennis club was organized in San Gabriel by Mrs. General Stoneman in 1882.

CALIFORNIA SPORTS BIRTHDAYS
More Fun for June 15

Q: Ellsworth "Babe" Dahlgren, born in 1912, first baseman, played 621 consecutive games in the minors for which Pacific Coast League baseball team: Sacramento Solons, Hollywood Stars, or Mission Reds?

....

Did You Know?

The first California tennis team to win the NCAA Division I Men's Tournament was the USC Trojans who topped William & Mary 9-6 in 1946. California hosted the NCAA Divison I Tournament for the first time in 1947 when matches were held at the UCLA courts. William & Mary cooked Rice 10-4. UC Berkeley player Edward Chandler claimed the first singles titles by a Californian in 1925 and 1926. Several California schools have won the tournament including USC, Stanford, UCLA, Pepperdine and the University of San Francisco.

Stanford, with over 20 titles, has dominated NCAA women's tennis. The Cardinal won the inaugural tournament in 1982 over UCLA 6-3. Stanford's Alycia Moulton won the singles title.

A: The San Francisco native played first base for the Mission Reds from 1931 to 1934. He was a 1939 World Series champion with the New York Yankees.

NOTABLE BIRTHDAY
June 15, 1948

Michael Holmgren, born in San Francisco, quarterbacks coach and offensive coordinator for the San Francisco 49ers from 1986 to 1991, winning Super Bowls XXIII and XXIV. Won Super Bowl XXXI as head coach of the Green Bay Packers.

Bugbee's Cold Idea
June 17, 1871

San Francisco architect Sumner Bugbee had a sports invention in 1871. The *San Francisco Chronicle* reported, "Bugbee has another scheme on foot of a very novel nature. He proposes to have constructed a large rink, with a floor of real ice, which can be made artificially, and kept frozen by means of a newly invented and very ingenious machine. With such a rink, where ice skates could be used, the town would be sure to become skating mad, and rollers would be at a discount."

Despite this early idea, it appears that California's first ice skating rink didn't open until 1889. San Francisco socialite James Brett Stokes opened a rink in town and introduced afternoon teas and prizes for skating matches. The *San Francisco Call* noted that "someone threw a piece of iron in the machinery one day and we came near not having any more ice skating. It only lasted through one season, but was a great success. Unfortunately, the club melted away at the end of the year."

Southern California's first large ice skating rink opened in Los Angeles on February 10, 1925. Melrose Avenue was the site of the coolest place in town, the Palais de Glace. The *Los Angeles Times* joyfully observed that "Thousands of ardent devotees in gala attire furnished a picturesque background for the premier of the king of winter sports —ice skating—in Los Angeles' newest amusement arena, the Palais de Glace." Selected attendees, all expert exponents of the art of ice skating, gave exhibitions which were enthusiastically received. 4,500 fans filled the seats.

Q: What was the first competition held at the Palais de Glace: Ice Follies, Golden State Skating Championship, or the Southern California Skating Championship?

For more ice skating, visit www.californiasportsastounding.com

A: One month later, the Palais de Glace hosted the first Southern California Skating Championship. Johnny Micko, a visitor from St. Paul, Minnesota, timed three minutes and 27 seconds to win the mile race.

CALIFORNIA SPORTS BIRTHDAYS
More Fun for June 17

Q: Venus Williams, born in 1980, tennis player, winner of 23 Grand Slam Events, won how many Grand Slam doubles events with sister Serena: 10, 14, or 15?

. . . .

Did You Know?

In 1978, Charlie Tickner became the first Californian to win the World Figure Skating Championship in men's singles. The Lafayette native won a bronze medal two years later in the same event.

San Jose's Peggy Fleming was the first women's World Champion from the Golden State, winning titles from 1966-1968. She also won a gold medal in ladies singles at the 1968 Olympics.

A: The Lynwood native won 14 Grand Slam doubles events with Serena from 1999-2016. Serena Williams has her own astounding career with 39 Grand Slam titles and over 1,000 matches played!

NOTABLE BIRTHDAY
June 17, 1943

Steve Clark, born in Oakland, swimmer, won three gold medals at the 1964 Olympics; 4 x 100 and 4 x 200 freestyle relays, and 4 x 100 medley relay.

NOTABLE EVENT
June 17, 1973

San Francisco's Johnny Miller scorched the Oakmont Country Club Course in Pennsylvania with an eight-under-par 63 in the final round to win the 1973 U.S. Open. Miller won his first major and defeated four hall of famers: Jack Nicklaus, Arnold Palmer, Lee Trevino, and Gary Player.

Pebble Beach Pulverized
June 18, 2000

Fog invaded the first round of the U.S. Open Golf Tournament at Pebble Beach, but this California golfer had an early start and missed most of it. He finished the day with a six-under-par 65. The ugly weather continued for round two, but he was the only golfer to ignore it as he stretched his lead to six strokes. Super windy conditions and the unforgiving rough made round three a disaster for most, but he finished at par and stretched his lead to 10 strokes, the largest 54 hole lead in Open history. The final round was bogey free and his competitors crumbled behind him.

Tiger Woods won the 100th U.S. Open by a record 15 shots at the Pebble Beach Golf Links with a 12-under-par 272. His score equaled the U.S. Open scoring record set by Jack Nicklaus, Lee Janzen, and Jim Furyk, all achieved on par-70 courses. Nicklaus played in this, his final U.S. Open, but shot 73-82 and did not make the cut. Tiger's first U.S. Open win was a classic. His 15-stroke margin of victory remains the largest in a major championship. Tiger's payday for conquering Pebble Beach was a check for $800,000. Woods continued on that year and early 2001 to a create a "Tiger Slam." He held all four major championships simultaneously—the U.S. Open, Open Championship, PGA Championship, and the 2001 Masters—though not in the same calendar year.

Q: Where was the first U.S. Open played in California?

For more golf, visit www.californiasportsastounding.com

A: The Riviera Country Club in Pacific Palisades hosted the 1948 U.S. Open. Hall of Fame golfer Ben Hogan won the tournament by two strokes.

CALIFORNIA SPORTS BIRTHDAYS
More Fun for June 18

Q: Jason Castro, born in 1987, MLB catcher, in 2009 won a gold medal in what international amateur baseball tournament: Baseball World Cup or World Baseball Classic?

. . . .

Did You Know?

Pebble Beach, CA is home to the first United States Pony Club on the West Coast. The club was formed in 1954 by expert horseback rider Dick Collins. He developed summer day camps and monthly horse trials for local youth. Collins helped organize the 1960 U.S. Olympic Team Trials at the Pebble Beach Equestrian Center. In 2003 he was inducted into the U.S. Eventing Association Hall of Fame.

A: The Castro Valley native played for the USA in the Baseball World Cup held in Nettuno, Italy.

NOTABLE EVENT
June 18, 2014

Clayton Kershaw pitched a no-hitter as the Los Angeles Dodgers crushed the Colorado Rockies 8-0 at Dodger Stadium. Kershaw struck out 15 and did not allow a walk. This was the shortest interval between no-hitters in franchise history. Less than a month ago on May 25, Dodger pitcher Josh Beckett threw a no-hitter as Los Angeles beat the Philadelphia Phillies 6-0.

Stupendous Staples
June 19, 2000

They had moved in the Staples Center in downtown Los Angeles on November 3, 1999. Their record during the National Basketball Association regular season was an impressive 67-15, good enough for first place in the Pacific Division. The team had two All-Stars, center Shaquille O'Neal and a 21-year-old shooting guard named Kobe Bryant. The playoffs were a lot more challenging than the regular season. An opening round series against the Sacramento Kings went to the five game limit, but this Los Angeles team prevailed. The Western Conference Finals series went the full seven games, but they closed out the Portland Trailblazers 89-84 playing before their home fans.

The Los Angeles Lakers were ready for the NBA Finals. They disposed of the Indiana Pacers 116-111 to win the series in six games. This win at the Staples Center gave the Lakers their first National Basketball Association title since 1988. First year Lakers coach Phil Jackson would win four more NBA championships in Los Angeles.

Q: Who was the lone Californian on the Lakers roster? Hint: he played guard.

For more basketball, visit www.californiasportsastounding.com

A: Oakland native Brian Shaw. The point guard won five NBA titles with the Lakers, three as a player from 2000 to 2002, and two as an assistant coach from 2009 to 2010.

CALIFORNIA SPORTS BIRTHDAYS

More Fun for June 19

Q: John "Johnny" Gray, born in 1960, set an American outdoor 800-meter record of 1:42.60 in 1985. How long did the record last: 24, 34, or 35 years?

. . . .

Did You Know?

The first girls high school state basketball championship tournament was held in 2005. Oakland Tech rallied from a 12 point deficit with 6:38 to play and edged Canyon Springs 64-63 in the Division I title game at the Arco Arena in Sacramento. Winners of divisions II through V were Troy (Fullerton), Bishop Amat (La Puente), Piedmont, and Pinewood (Los Altos).

A: Gray, a native of Los Angeles, enjoyed his record for 34 years until Donovan Brazier ran 1:42.34 at the 2019 World Championships.

NOTABLE EVENT
June 19, 1955

In perhaps the greatest upset in California golf history, Iowa's Jack Fleck defeated hall of famer Ben Hogan in an 18 hole playoff to win the U.S. Open at the Olympic Club. This was the first U.S. Open held at the Lake Course of the Olympic Club.

NOTABLE BIRTHDAY
June 19, 1968

Jud Buechler, born in San Diego, NBA small forward won three titles with the Chicago Bulls from 1996 to 1998. He also excelled as an All-American volleyball player at the University of Arizona.

Bows and Arrows
June 20, 1879

The sport of bows and arrows landed in California before 1880. California's first archery tournament was held at the Oakland Cricket Grounds near Emery station on the line of the Berkeley Railroad. Archers competed in teams of five and shot at targets up to 50 yards. One individual prize went to Frank C. Havens of Oakland's Bow Club. Miss Bessie Craig of San Francisco's Pacific Archery Club won the ladies prize. The other individual prize went to H.E. Button of Santa Cruz.

Sacramento archers were also busy in 1879. They organized the first clubs in the Central Valley. One article in the *Sacramento Bee* described the sport as "Generally regarded as one of the most enjoyable outdoor amusements, and is confined exclusively to neither sex. Unlike croquet, there is no monotony to archery."

Six months later, in January of 1880, archers proposed the formation of a Pacific Coast Archery Association, similar in purpose and methods to the National Archery Association.

Q: Northern California towns San Rafael, Mill Valley, and Sausalito organized clubs and helped the sport grow in the early 1880's. How old is archery?

For more archery, visit www.californiasportsastounding.com

A: Although archery probably dates back to the Stone Age—around 20,000 BC—the earliest people known to have regularly used bows and arrows were the Ancient Egyptians, who adopted archery around 3,000 BC for hunting and warfare.

CALIFORNIA SPORTS BIRTHDAYS
More Fun for June 20

Q: Robert "Bob" King, born in 1906, 1928 Olympic gold medalist in what track and field event: triple jump, high jump, or discus?

· ·

Did You Know?

The first archery club in Southern California was formed in September of 1879. The *Los Angeles Herald* announced: "A Meeting of the Archery Club will be held in the parlor of the Cosmopolitan Hotel for the purpose of electing officers."

Archery Hall of Fame inductee Jim Easton organized the 1983 World Archery Championships in Long Beach. He has also donated the funds to build the largest archery training range in North America, the Easton Archery Center of Excellence in Chula Vista. The center hosts the SoCal Showdown, an annual outdoor target archery tournament first organized by the Roadrunner Archery Club. Easton Archery is located within the Chula Vista Elite Athlete Training Center.

In 2014, the first United States Intercollegiate Archery Championships were held at El Dorado Park in Long Beach. This was the same venue used for the 1984 Summer Olympics.

The largest archery clubs in Northern California are the Black Mountain Bowmen in San Jose, the Redwood Bowmen in Oakland, and the San Francisco Archers in Pacifica.

A: King, a native of Los Angeles, was president of his senior class at Stanford University. He cleared six foot four ¼ inch to win the high jump gold medal in a competition that lasted over three hours.

NOTABLE BIRTHDAY

June 20, 1978

Nichole "Nikki" Serlenga, San Diego native, soccer midfielder, silver medalist for Team USA at the 2000 Olympics.

Summer in San Diego
June 20, 1997

Some people called it the "Olympics of Alternative Sports." Others gave it the nickname the "Punk Olympics." This was a new event in California. The real name was the Summer X Games III, which opened for competition in San Diego and Oceanside from June 20 to 28. ESPN televised the event. Over 221,000 fans attended and watched 10 sports.

Oceanside hosted the street luge and the new event of downhill inline skating, while San Diego staged skateboarding, wakeboarding, skysurfing, and the remaining events at Mission Bay.

Wakeboarding and inline skating for men and women were some of the new sports added for the event. Those joined such popular sports as skateboarding, skysurfing, and street luge.

California's winners were led by Carlsbad's Tony Hawk who rolled to victory in the vertical skateboard competition. Two years later he landed the world's first two and a half revolution 900 degree aerial spin on a vertical ramp at the X Games in San Francisco. His spectacular achievement overcame 10 years of concussions and injuries to his ribs, back, and teeth to experience the greatest moment of his competitive career.

It was Summertime in San Diego, but the snowboarders were not left out. Organizers provided 185 tons of snow for the final event. Snowboard Big Air contestants jumped off a 90-foot tower and a 250-foot-long ramp. Over 15,000 spectators crammed into Mariner's Point Park and enjoyed the view. Truckee native Kevin Jones was the top California finisher in second place.

Q: San Diego was the first California city to host the X Games. What city was next?

For more X Games, visit www.californiasportsastounding.com

A: The X Games returned to San Diego in 1998 before moving to San Francisco's Pier 30 and 32 in 1999. Over 265,000 fans set an X Games attendance record.

CALIFORNIA SPORTS BIRTHDAYS
More Fun for June 20

Q: Ronald Hornaday Jr., born in 1958, professional stock car racing driver, won which NASCAR series four times: NASCAR Cup Series or NASCAR Camping World Truck Series?

. . . .

Did You Know?

Alphonse Hamann caught a California record 692 pound striped blue marlin off of Balboa, CA in 1931. The fish weighed 692 pounds and was 13.5 feet long. Hamann landed the marlin after a one hour and 52 minute battle.

A: Hornaday, a native of Palmdale, won the NASCAR Camping World Truck Series in 1996, 1998, 2007, and 2009.

NOTABLE BIRTHDAYS
June 20

1982: April Ross, born in Costa Mesa, beach volleyball player, 2012 Olympic silver medalist, 2016 Olympic bronze medalist, and 2020 Olympic gold medalist.

1999: Cory Juneau, San Diego native, skateboarder, 2020 Olympic bronze medalist in the skate park event.

SCIAC Beginnings
June 21, 1915

The Southern California Intercollegiate Athletic Conference was founded by some of the Golden State's leading academic institutions. Charter members were the Occidental College Tigers, Pomona College Sagehens, University of Redlands Bulldogs, Whittier College Poets, and the Throop College of Technology, which was renamed the California Institute of Technology in 1920. Caltech's teams were named the Beavers. All five schools are still members.

The SCIAC described their conference history as "Five Southern California institutions combined for the purpose of promoting and governing competition in intercollegiate sports with the fundamental principle of the conference being to encourage the highest ideals of amateur sports in an environment of high academic standards."

Four more schools eventually joined the conference. Additions included the California Lutheran Kingsmen and Regals, the Chapman University Panthers, the Claremont-Mudd-Scripps Stags and Athenas, and the University of LaVerne Leopards. Charter member Pomona College now has become Pomona-Pitzer Colleges for athletics.

All nine SCIAC teams compete in the NCAA Division III, which are athletic programs at colleges and universities that don't offer scholarships to their students.

Q: What three former member schools now compete in the NCAA Division I? Hint: One school's nickname is the Gauchos.

For more SCIAC and other college conferences, visit www. californiasportsastounding.com

A: San Diego State Aztecs, UCLA Bruins, and UC Santa Barbara Gauchos.

CALIFORNIA SPORTS BIRTHDAYS
More Fun for June 21

Q: Robert Svihus, born in 1943, played what position for the USC Trojans football team in 1962: defensive tackle, tight end, or offensive tackle?

．．．

Did You Know?

Art Ingels, a fabricator and race car builder for Kurtis Kraft, built the first go-kart in the garage of this home at Echo Park in 1956. He used a West Bend 2-cycle 750 lawnmower engine strong enough to power the 60 pound kart and support his 200 pound frame. The first organized races were held in 1957 at the Rose Bowl parking lot in Pasadena. Racing eventually branched out to the Eastland Shopping Center in West Covina and the Carpinteria Thunderbowl Racetrack.

Adams Motorsports Park in Riverside opened for go-kart racing in 1959. Their venue is the longest continuously running kart racing facility in the world. Owner Troy Adams has retained the original layout from 1959, but the track has been upgraded to become one of the most challenging racing circuits in the world.

A: The Los Angeles native played offensive tackle. USC finished the 1962 season undefeated and won the Rose Bowl 42-37 over #2 ranked Wisconsin.

NOTABLE BIRTHDAY
June 21, 1961

Jeanne Beauprey, born in Anaheim, volleyball player, and 1984 Olympic silver medalist, played for the Major League Volleyball champion Los Angeles Starlites in 1987.

Shooting Sparks
June 21, 1997

Women's professional basketball arrived in Los Angeles with the formation of the Women's National Basketball Association. League executives announced nicknames on February 13, 1997 and Los Angeles was given the "Sparks." The first game was held on June 21 at the Forum, but the Sparks flamed out against the New York Liberty and lost 67-57. A record crowd of 14,284 showed up, the largest to see a women's basketball game in Los Angeles since the 1984 Olympics. Sparks guard Penny Toler scored the first basket in league history on a 12-foot baseline jumper one minute into the game. The Sparks and the Sacramento Monarchs were the two California charter members of the WNBA. Sacramento won the 2005 title but folded in 2009.

Los Angeles claimed WNBA titles in 2001, 2002, and 2016. The Sparks defeated Sacramento for the Western Conference title in 2001 before beating the Charlotte Sting 2-0 in the finals. Los Angeles was the first WNBA team to finish the season undefeated at home with a record of 16-0 at Staples Center. Sparks coach Michael Cooper became the first person to claim NBA and WNBA titles, having won five championships as a player with the Lakers between 1980 and 1988. Lisa Leslie finished 2001 by becoming the first WNBA player to capture all three MVP awards in the same season.

Q: Who was the first owner of the Sparks? Hint: he also owned tennis and soccer teams.

For more basketball, visit www.californiasportsastounding.com

A: Los Angeles Lakers owner Jerry Buss owned the Sparks from 1997 to 2006. Buss had previously owned the now-defunct Los Angeles Strings of World Team Tennis and the Los Angeles Lazers' soccer team.

CALIFORNIA SPORTS BIRTHDAYS
More Fun June 21

Q: Richard Jefferson, born in 1980, basketball forward, won a bronze medal playing for Team USA at which Olympics: 2004, 2008, or 2012?

....

Did You Know?

Six-foot-five-center Lisa Leslie became the first WNBA player to dunk in a game during the Los Angeles Sparks 82-73 loss to the Miami Sol at the Staples Center on July 30, 2002. She scored on a one-handed dunk in the second quarter. Only eight days earlier Leslie was the first player in league history to score 3,000 points.

A: The Los Angeles native won a bronze medal at the 2004 Olympics in Athens, Greece.

===

NOTABLE EVENT
June 21, 1988

Guard Michael Cooper contributed 12 points as the Los Angeles Lakers hung on to defeat the Detroit Pistons 108-105 and clinch the NBA title 4-3 at the Forum in Inglewood. The win stopped a five-game losing streak in game seven of the finals since moving from Minneapolis to Los Angeles in 1960.

OTL
June 24, 1938

"Over the Line," is the name of a game related to baseball and usually played on the beach, originated in the late 1930s. The sport is named after its objective, to hit an orange rubber softball "over the line" in the sand 55 feet away from home plate. Only three players are needed per team.

The Whittier City Recreation Department conducted an OTL league in June of 1938. Games were also played that September at Wilmington Park in Los Angeles. The *San Pedro News Pilot* reported "The team of Hironi Shinji, Roy Spencer, and Louis Rodriguez holds the championship for over-the-line, a variation of softball."

OTL spread throughout California's beach communities and found a home in San Diego. Mike Curren of the Old Mission Beach Athletic Club introduced the sport to members in the summer of 1954. Beach volleyball players were bored waiting for courts to open and decided to try it. Mike, along with the help of his brother Terry, Delmar Miller, Mike Moore, Philip Prather, and Fred Thompson launched the annual World Championship Over-the-Line® Tournament. First at South Mission Beach, then Mariner's Point, and now Fiesta Island, the two-day tournament attracts over 1,000 teams and 50,000 spectators.

Q: What Southern California racetrack held an over-the-line tournament in the 1940s: Del Mar, Hollywood Park, or Santa Anita?

For more Over the Line, visit www.californiasportsastounding.com

A: Santa Anita Park staged a tournament in 1944.

CALIFORNIA SPORTS BIRTHDAYS
More Fun for June 24

Q: William "Buffalo Bill" Casper Jr., born in 1931, professional golfer, won the 1970 Masters Tournament in a playoff with which San Diego golfer?

. . . .

Did You Know?

Oakland's Jack Delinger was the first Californian to win the Mr. Universe bodybuilding competition. Delinger won the 1956 crown against a world class lineup in London. He returned home and operated a gym on Broadway at College Avenue in downtown Oakland.

A: Casper, a San Diego native, won the Masters by five strokes by carding a 69 in an 18-hole playoff against Gene Littler.

NOTABLE BIRTHDAYS

June 24

1960: Juli Inkster, born in Santa Cruz, professional golfer on LPGA tour, first LPGA golfer to win two majors in a decade for three decades. She won three majors in the 1980s, two in the 1990s, and two in the 2000s.

1963: Pamela Healy, a native of San Francisco, sailor, at age 13 was invited to become one of the first female members of the St. Francis Yacht Club, 1992 Olympic bronze medalist in the 470 class with Jennifer Isler.

50 Years of Volleyball
June 30, 2012

UCLA men's volleyball coach Al Scates retired after a remarkable 50-year career that started in 1963. He was an All-American player at UCLA before taking over the program at the age of 24. That first year he founded the Southern California Volleyball Association and was commissioner till 1972. The SCVA eventually became the Mountain Pacific Sports Federation.

Scates was hired as a part time coach at UCLA, so to make ends meet he worked 35 years as an elementary school teacher in Santa Monica. After winning 16 NCAA titles, the Bruins upgraded him to fulltime coach in 1997. He juggled both jobs for years, but survived on four hours of sleep per night. All he needed was one night of deep sleep per week!

Scates was an innovator and exceptional tactician. His most famous innovation was the blue curtain separating the first team practice from the rest of the players. The curtain was an isolator and motivator. Second string players were sent behind the curtain to practice with the assistant coaches. Scates couldn't see them and thus they were forced to fight to come back, improve, and train with the first team.

Al finished his career with 19 NCAA titles and 1,239 wins, an NCAA record for Division I coaches. He was the first recipient of USA Volleyball's All-Time Great Volleyball Coaches Award. He is an inductee of several organizations including the California Beach Volleyball, UCLA Athletics, and Volleyball Hall of Fame. Scates coached over 25 Olympians and over 50 NCAA All-Americans.

He developed many elite players, but especially Frederick "Karch" Kiraly who led the Bruins to three NCAA titles from 1979 to 1982. The FIVB named him the greatest volleyball player of the 20th century. Kiraly was the first male volleyball player to win three Olympic gold medals. Karch led the USA indoor team to victory in 1984 and 1988. He won the inaugural Olympic Beach Volleyball competition in 1996 with partner Kent Steffes.

After retiring from competition Karch became coach of the USA Women's National Team in 2012. He guided the team to their first Olympic gold medal in 2020. Kiraly became the first American to win a gold medal as a player and a coach.

Q: Who was the first volleyball player inducted into the UCLA Athletic Hall of Fame: Karch Kiraly or Kirk Kilgour?

For more volleyball, visit www.californiasportsastounding.com

A: Kirk Kilgour was voted a charter member of the hall of fame in 1984. He was a 1970 and 1971 NCAA Champion and All-American from 1970 to 1973. In 1986, his number 13 jersey became the first UCLA volleyball uniform to be retired.

CALIFORNIA SPORTS BIRTHDAYS
More Fun for June 30

Q: Burke "Buck" Deadrich, born in 1945, Olympic Greco-Roman wrestler was a 2012 inductee to what Northern California sports hall of fame: San Mateo or Castro Valley?

Did You Know?

Ruby Fox won a silver medal in the women's 25-meter pistol competition at the 1984 Olympics held in Los Angeles. This was the first time the event had been held for women at the Olympics. Shooters competed at the Prado Recreational Area in Chino.

A: The Oakland native was inducted into the Castro Valley Sports Hall of Fame.

NOTABLE EVENT
June 30, 1950

Bob Mathias set a decathlon world record with 8,042 points at the National AAU Meet in Tulare. The graduate of Tulare Union High School had won the 1948 Olympic decathlon two years earlier at the age of 17, the youngest gold medalist in a track and field event.

JULY
CAN'T
BELIEVE IT

Big West Beginnings
July 1, 1969

Many colleges have come and gone, while California dominates the Big West Conference. The BWC had meetings in June of 1968 to establish governance according to the *San Bernardino Sun* and the *Eagle Rock Sentinel*. It was officially founded as the Pacific Coast Athletic Association on July 1, 1969. The PCAA was renamed the Big West Conference in 1988 as a "simpler and more accurate description of its institutions."

Members compete in the NCAA Division I. Long Beach State and UC Santa Barbara are the only charter members remaining, though Long Beach State is the only school to keep continuous membership.

Long Beach State and rookie coach Jim Stangeland kicked off the inaugural conference football season on September 20, 1969 with a 32-16 road win over the UC Santa Barbara Gauchos.

Membership fluctuated over the years and stretched as far as Idaho, Louisiana, and Illinois, but has settled mostly in the Golden State.

The Big West has 11 members, with 10 in California and one in Hawaii. California's members are split between the California State University and the University of California systems. The California State Bakersfield Roadrunners and UC San Diego Tritons are the newest members, having officially joined on July 1, 2020. The conference sponsors 18 sports—eight for men, and 10 for women.

Q: Which baseball program won NCAA Division I titles in 1979, 1984, 1995, and 2004: The Cal State Northridge Matadors, UC Riverside Highlanders, or the Cal State Fullerton Titans?

For the Big West and other college conferences, visit www. californiasportsastounding.com

A: Augie Garrido coached Cal State Fullerton to championships in 1979, 1984, and 1995. George Horton led the Titans to another title in 2004.

CALIFORNIA SPORTS BIRTHDAYS
More Fun for July 1

Q: Lee "Rubberlegs" Guttero, born in 1913, basketball center, earned what recognition as a USC Trojan?

....

Did You Know?

The first Big West women's team to win a national title was the 1985 University of the Pacific Tigers volleyball squad coached by John Dunning. Pacific defeated Stanford 3-1 and repeated as champions the next year. Dunning coached 16 All-Americans for the Tigers, including Olympic medalists Elaina Oden and Jennifer Joines.

The Long Beach State women's volleyball team won NCAA titles in 1989, 1993, and 1998. Brian Gimmillaro was head coach for 32 years and developed over 20 All-Americans including Olympic medalists Misty May, Tara Cross-Battle, and Danielle Scott-Aruda.

Alan Knipe of Long Beach State won NCAA men's volleyball titles as a player and coach. He played for coach Ray Ratelle in 1991 and guided the 49ers to championships in 2018 and 2019.

A: Guttero, a native of Torrance, was USC's first two-time NCAA All-American.

NOTABLE EVENT
July 1, 1893

The San Francisco Bay City Club opened a wooden bicycle racetrack in Central Park. Three days of bicycle races were organized by the Bay City Wheelman. The *San Francisco Call* described it as "The greatest gathering of cyclists the Pacific Coast has seen, and the new track will be the fastest in America beyond doubt." Bay City Wheelman members raved about "the most perfect cycling grounds in California."

Ted the Pitcher
July 3, 1936

Seventeen-year-old Ted pitched and played left field, but his San Diego Padres lost to the Los Angles Angels 14-9 in a Pacific Coast League game at Wrigley Field. He entered the game as a pinch hitter in the seventh inning against Angels pitcher Glen Gabler and singled, his first hit in professional baseball. Ted pitched the bottom of the seventh, but gave up two home runs. His pitching career with the Padres was over. Among his teammates that season were future baseball hall of famer second baseman Bobby Doerr and All-Star centerfielder Vince DiMaggio. Ted Williams played one more season with the Padres, but by 1939 Major League Baseball was ready to see him start a hall of fame career. His first All-Star appearance was 1940 and his last, 1960.

Q: What other Pacific Coast League baseball team played at Wrigley Field in Los Angeles?

For more baseball, visit www.californiasportsastounding.com

A: The Hollywood Stars played at Wrigley Field from 1926 to 1935, and in 1938.

CALIFORNIA SPORTS BIRTHDAYS
More Fun for July 3

Q: Gregory Vaughn, born in 1965, MLB left fielder, four-time All-Star, played for which California team from 1996 to 1998?

Did You Know?

The World Underwater Hockey Championships were held in California for the first time in 1998. Teams from a record 14 nations participated in the tournament at the San Jose State University pool.

The Underwater Society of America based in Fremont, CA is the sanctioning body for underwater sports in the USA.

A: Vaughn, a Sacramento native, played for the San Diego Padres from 1996 to 1998.

NOTABLE BIRTHDAYS

July 3

1940: Lance Larson, born in Monterey Park, swimmer, attended USC, 1960 Olympic gold medalist 4 x 100-meter medley relay, silver medalist in the 100-meter freestyle.

1963: Christopher "Cle" Kooiman, born in Ontario, soccer defender, played for the U.S. team at the 1994 World Cup.

NOTABLE EVENT

July 3, 1970

Clyde Wright of the California Angels pitched the first no-hitter at Anaheim Stadium as the Halos beat the Oakland Athletics 4-0. Angels third baseman Ken McMullen hit a three run homer to seal the win.

A Full Contact Team Sport
July 7, 1877

Though it appears that this full contact team sport existed in San Francisco as early as 1872, the first newspaper reference to rugby didn't emerge until five years later. *The Placer Argus* gave this description from the town of Iowa Hill in Placer County: "Two or three lively football games in the evening relieved the monotony of life to the boys, and filled the minds of shopkeepers— the plate-glass owners—with apprehensions. Among the boys who enjoyed a kick at the ball were, if I am not mistaken, John Bisbee, John Butler, Doc. Petterson (usually miscalled Peterson), Prof. Hartson, J.F. Brown, and your humble servant. The rugby rules were not followed, but, anyway, it is a good, healthful kind of exercise."

California hosted the first ever Rugby World Cup Sevens on American soil with 52 matches during July of 2018. Matches were held at San Francisco's AT&T Park and drew over 100,000 fans. Rugby World Cup, the premier international competition outside the Olympic Games, featured teams from 24 nations. New Zealand claimed the men's and women's titles. In this competition, they did play by the rules.

Q: Rugby became UC Berkeley's first sport played against an outside opponent. What year did the program start?

For more rugby, visit www.californiasportsastounding.com

A: 1882. The California Golden Bears finished the year 2-1-1, their only loss to the Phoenix Club of San Francisco 7-4.

CALIFORNIA SPORTS BIRTHDAYS
More Fun for July 7

Q: Michelle Kwan, born in 1980, five-time World Champion figure skater from 1996 to 2003, trained in what Southern California town?

· ·

Did You Know?

The University of California, Berkeley rugby program has won over 30 collegiate championships since 1980. Coach Jack Clark has developed over 135 All-Americans.

A: Kwan, a native of Torrance, trained at the Ice Castle International Training Center in Lake Arrowhead.

NOTABLE BIRTHDAY
July 7, 1954

Randy Smyth, born in Pasadena, sailor, 1984 Olympic silver medalist in the multihull event with Santa Monica teammate Jay Glaser, 1992 Olympic silver medalist in the multihull event.

NOTABLE EVENTS
July 7

1982: Steve Scott, an Upland native, ran 3:47.69 to set an American record in the mile. Scott's record was achieved at Bislett Stadium in Oslo, Norway.

2019: Redding's Megan Rapinoe converted a tie-breaking penalty kick in the second half to help the USA to its fourth Women's World Cup with a 2-0 shutout of the Netherlands. Rapinoe won the Golden Ball award as the best player in the tournament.

Pasadena Heat
July 10, 1999

Coach Tony DiCicco didn't need this in February. His World Cup roster had lost 2-1 to the "World All-Stars," a group who had only practiced one hour together. His hall of fame midfielder Michelle Akers suffered a fractured cheekbone in the game. All of this in just the first exhibition of the year played at Spartan Stadium in San Jose, but local newspapers had already declared his team as "vulnerable."

He had 14 more exhibitions to get everyone ready to compete with the world's best. Four years earlier his team had lost to Norway 1-0 in the semi-finals of the FIFA Women's World Cup. His team wanted redemption. California would host the World Cup final for the first time.

The U.S. women national soccer team zipped through the competition with wins over Denmark, Nigeria, North Korea, and Germany. Their next test was a semifinal match on July 4 at Stanford Stadium. 73,123 soccer fans roared their approval as the U.S. shutout Brazil 2-0.

America had reached the final against China at the Rose Bowl. A world attendance record for a women's sporting event was set as 90,185 fans crammed into the stadium despite temperatures of over 90 degrees. The Pasadena heat drained the players and dictated a more deliberate strategy. A scoreless 90-minute regulation and 30-minute extra time forced a penalty kick shootout. U.S. soccer stars did their part as Carla Overbeck, Joy Fawcett, Kristine Lilly, and Mia Hamm scored on their attempts. With the score tied 4-4 Brandi Chastain booted the winning goal and the exhausted USA team celebrated their historic win.

Q: Which California-born player has played in the most international matches for the U.S. Women's National Team?

For more soccer, visit www.californiasportsastounding.com

A: Julie Foudy. She played in 274 matches from 1987 to 2004. Foudy won Olympic gold medals in 1996 and 2004, plus World Cups in 1991 and 1999.

CALIFORNIA SPORTS BIRTHDAYS
More Fun for July 10

Q: Dana Shrader, born in 1956, swam to an Olympic gold medal in the women's 4 x 100-meter medley relay at which Olympics: 1972, 1980, or 1984?

....

Did You Know?

The Santa Clara Broncos were the first California team to win the NCAA Division I Women's Soccer Tournament. Santa Clara's Aly Wagner was voted the Most Outstanding Offensive Player, while teammate Danielle Slaton was named the Most Outstanding Defensive Player. Coach Jerry Smith's team defeated the defending national champion North Carolina Tar Heels 1-0 to claim the 2001 crown.

A: The Lynwood native swam in the preliminary heats of the relay at the 1972 Olympics. Her California teammates were Shirley Babashoff, Sandy Neilson, and Susie Atwood who swam in the preliminaries and finals.

NOTABLE BIRTHDAYS
July 10

1962: Michael Saxon, born in Whittier, NFL punter, Super Bowl XXVII champion with the Dallas Cowboys, Pasadena City College Sports Hall of Fame inductee 2018.

1985: Jared Dudley, San Diego native, NBA forward, 2020 NBA champion with the Los Angeles Lakers.

California State Games
July 14, 1988

USC graduate Sandi Mabry used her sports administration degree and two years of planning to organize the inaugural California State Games in San Diego. Opening ceremonies were held at San Diego State's Aztec Bowl. The games are an Olympic style multi-sport event for amateur athletes of all ages.

Olympians Pat McCormick, two-time diving gold medalist, and Brian Goodell, winner of two gold medals in freestyle swimming, gave the opening speeches. Over 3,000 athletes from across the state competed in 13 sports over the long weekend. Events were held at San Diego State, UC San Diego, and Balboa Park.

California is a member of the National Congress of State Games, an organization of 30 Summer State Games and 10 Winter State Games groups. Summer Games attract over 10,000 athletes in over 25 sports. San Diego hosts most of the events, but in the winter, ski races have been held at the June Mountain ski area in the Eastern Sierra Nevada Mountains.

Q: How many sports are offered at the Winter Games?

For more California State Games, visit www. californiasportsastounding.com

A: Four. Figure skating, ice hockey, gymnastics, and roller skating.

CALIFORNIA SPORTS BIRTHDAYS
More Fun for July 14

Q: William "Willie" Steele, born in 1923, won the 1948 Olympic gold in what track and field event: triple jump, decathlon, or long jump?

Did You Know?

California State Games alumni include Olympians, World Champions, players in the MLB, NBA, NFL, and WNBA, UFC Champions and X-Games

Gold Medalists. Two examples are skateboarder Brighton Zeuner and judoka Ronda Rousey. Brighton was the youngest girl to compete in the X Games at age 11. In 2014, she was named California State Games Sport Athlete of the Year. Rousey became the first American to win an Olympic medal in women's judo with her bronze in the middleweight divison at the 2008 Olympics. Four years later, she was the first UFC bantamweight champion.

A: Steele, who was born in El Centro, won gold in the long jump. He trained under coach Bud Winter at San Jose State, and was the 1947 and 1948 NCAA long jump champion at San Diego State.

NOTABLE BIRTHDAY
July 14, 1967

Robin Ventura, Santa Maria native, MLB third baseman, two-time All-Star (1992 and 2002), Olympic gold medalist for Team USA in 1988.

NOTABLE EVENTS
July 14, 1987

Major League Baseball held their All-Star game at the Oakland-Alameda County Coliseum. The National League team shutout the American League 2-0.

Five years later on July 14, 1992 the All-Stars returned to California. San Diego hosted the game at Jack Murphy Stadium. The American Leaguers routed the Nationals 13-6.

West Coast Winners
July 18, 1952

The West Coast Conference was established in 1952 as the California Basketball Association. WCC athletes have produced over 25 NCAA Division I individual or team champions. The first reference to the conference appeared in the *Santa Cruz Sentinel*, which noted "Formation of a new college basketball league comprised of five of the top Northern California independents was announced yesterday. The teams are the Santa Clara University Broncos, St. Mary's College of California Gaels, San Jose State Spartans, University of San Francisco Dons, and University of the Pacific Tigers.

Named the California Basketball Association, the league will begin formal competition with the 1952-53 season. The five schools, which have been meeting on an unofficial basis for five years, will adhere to Pacific Coast conference rules."

CBA competition started on January 2, 1953 when the University of the San Francisco Dons demolished the San Jose State Spartans 67-47 at Kezar Pavilion.

Name changes occurred along the way. It became the West Coast Athletic Conference in 1956, then the shortened West Coast Conference in 1989. After several membership changes through 2013 the WCC settled on 10 members, with seven in California. Southern California has the Loyola Marymount University Lions, Pepperdine University Waves, and the University of San Diego Toreros. Northern California has Saint Mary's College of California, Santa Clara University, University of San Francisco and the University of the Pacific.

Gloria Nevarez made history in 2018 as the first Latina to become an NCAA Division I conference commissioner. She oversees 15 men's and women's sports.

Q: What University of San Francisco Dons basketball duo won NCAA titles in 1955 and 1956?

For more WCC, visit www.californiasportsastounding.com

A: Center Bill Russell and point guard K.C. Jones. USF's Phil Woolpert won the UPI Coach of the Year award both seasons. They went on to win numerous NBA championships together with the Boston Celtics.

CALIFORNIA SPORTS BIRTHDAYS
More Fun for July 18

Q: Michael "Mike" Neel, born in 1951, cyclist, was the 1971 and 1973 U.S. track champion in what event: long distance, popping wheelies, or the pursuit?

. . . .

Did You Know?

The University of San Francisco athletic teams changed their nickname on December 11, 1931. USF's old nickname was the Gray Fog, but the San Francisco Junior Chamber of Commerce considered the name too chilly and hurtful to the city's advertising. Students and alumni proposed names included sea lions, seals, and seagulls, but the Dons tallied the most votes.

A: The Berkeley native won the individual pursuit event.

NOTABLE BIRTHDAY
July 18, 1972

Sean Nolan, born in Palo Alto, water polo goalie, 1991 and 1992 NCAA champion with the UC Berkeley Golden Bears.

San Lorenzo River Surf Scenes
July 19, 1885

This surface water sport began in a California river. Surfing was introduced to the Golden State by Hawaiian princes in July1885. Brothers David Kawananakoa, Edward Keli'iahonui and Jonah Kūhiō Kalaniana'ole studied at Saint Matthew's Episcopal Day School in San Mateo, but would travel to Santa Cruz for ocean fun. They surfed the mouth of the San Lorenzo River in Santa Cruz.

The Daily Surf (sounds appropriate) newspaper published an article "Beach Breezes: Some Scenes a Surf Reporter Saw on Sunday." The story noted that "The young Hawaiian princes were in the water, enjoying it hugely and giving interesting exhibitions of surf-board swimming as practiced in their native islands."

Q: When was the Santa Cruz Surf Museum founded?

For more surfing, visit www.californiasportsastounding.com

A: Santa Cruz, the world's first surfing museum, opened in 1986.

CALIFORNIA SPORTS BIRTHDAYS
More Fun for July 19

Q: Robert "Long Bob" Meusel, born in 1896, World Series champion in 1923, 1927, and 1928, played with which two New York Yankee hall of famers?

Did You Know?

California has four unique surf museums that preserve the sport's history. Three are based in Southern California. The California Surf Museum is located in Oceanside. Twenty two miles north in San Clemente is the Surfing Heritage and Culture Center. The Huntington Beach International Surfing Museum in based in Surf City, USA. Northern California offers the Santa Cruz Surfing Museum, which traces over 100 years of surfing history.

Malibu Surfrider Beach and Santa Cruz are California's first designated surf reserves, a program that protects exceptional surf spots. These two reserves are among only nine in the world.

A: Meusel, a native of San Jose, was a teammate of San Francisco native Tony Lazzeri. The California contingent was rounded out by pitcher Dutch Ruether of Alameda and shortstop Mark Koenig of San Francisco.

NOTABLE BIRTHDAYS
July 19

1908: William "Bill" Thompson, born in Napa, rower, 1928 Olympic gold medalist in the coxed eights. The Olympic crew were UC Berkeley rowers.

1923: Alex Hannum, native of Los Angeles, pro basketball player and coach, 1964 NBA Coach of the Year with the San Francisco Warriors, 1969 ABA Coach of the Year with the Oakland Oaks, Naismith Memorial Basketball Hall of Fame inductee 1998.

LA 84
July 28, 1984

The world's premier sports competition appeared in California for the third time. First held in the summer of 1932, then a winter edition in 1960, then the summer of 1984. Opening ceremonies for the 1984 Summer Olympics were held at the Los Angeles Memorial Coliseum. The Games of the XXIII Olympiad featured 21 sports. A record 140 nations competed for medals.

Peter Ueberroth and the Los Angeles Olympic Organizing Committee revolutionized the organization of the Games and achieved a $232.5 million surplus. Part of that money helped create the LA84 Foundation, a nationally recognized leader in support of youth sport programs and public education. The foundation advocates for the important role sports participation plays in positive youth development. LA84 began operations in 1985 as a grant making and educational foundation. The foundation supports hundreds of non-profit youth sports organizations throughout Southern California annually, trains coaches, commissions research, convenes conferences, and maintains the world's premier Olympic and sports library collection.

Casey Wasserman, president of the Los Angeles Olympic Organizing Committee, led the successful bid for Los Angeles to host the 2028 Summer Olympics. The forthcoming Games of the XXXIV Olympiad will also be promoted as LA28.

Q: The Olympic sports venues were spread throughout Southern California. How far south of the Los Angeles Memorial Coliseum were events held: 25, 50, or 100 miles?

For more Olympics, visit www.californiasportsastounding.com

A: Equestrian events were held at the Fairbanks Ranch Country Club in Rancho Santa Fe, about 107 miles south of the Los Angeles Memorial Coliseum.

CALIFORNIA SPORTS BIRTHDAYS
More Fun for July 28

Q: Monica Abbott, born in 1985, attended North Salinas High School, was Cal-Hi Softball Athlete of the Year in 2003. What position did she play?

....

Did You Know?

Owen Morse of Crestline, CA set a hang gliding world record of 222.22 miles over the Owens Valley in June of 2020. Morse launched just north of Owens Lake and soared as high as 17,000 feet over the 100-mile-long valley. His out and back trip landed close to the launching site. Morse's record culminated six years of training.

A: The Santa Cruz native was a pitcher. World Champion with Team USA 2006, 2010, and 2018. Olympic silver medalist 2008 and 2020. Six-time USA Softball International Cup champion between 2006 and 2019.

NOTABLE BIRTHDAY
July 28, 1972

Ed Templeton, born in Garden Grove, 1995 North American Skateboard Champion, started his career in Huntington Beach. Ed learned the sport from neighbor and professional skateboarder Mark "The Gonz" Gonzales.

Games of the X Olympiad
July 30 to August 14, 1932

The 1932 Summer Olympics were held during the Great Depression, but were still a marvelous success. Los Angeles was the only city to bid for the Games, and was selected by default. After winning the bid, organizers renamed 10th Street as Olympic Boulevard, a name still in use.

California's sports fans witnessed many firsts, including, the first podium. Medal winners stood on a victory stand and watched the raising of the flag of the winner's country. The photo-finish camera also made its debut.

For the first time, the Games lasted 16 days and spanned three weekends, no previous Summer Olympics had lasted less than 79 days. A record crowd of over 100,000 fans at the opening ceremony was the largest ever at an Olympic event. The first Olympic Village housed only the male athletes—female competitors were housed in the Chapman Park Hotel on Wilshire Boulevard. For the first time, the Games finished in the black financially. The Organizing Committee realized a surplus of more than $1 million. Another innovation was the introduction of timekeeping equipment accurate to the nearest hundredth of a second. A new maximum quota of three athletes per nation per event was introduced.

1,332 athletes from 37 countries participated, which included 126 women. Those numbers were impressive considering the world economy and limited commercial aviation at the time. 18 world records were broken or equaled.

USC high jumper Bob Van Osdel was the first California born medalist with his silver medal in the men's high jump on July 31.

Q: Oakland's Buster Crabbe set an Olympic record of 4:48.4 to win the gold medal in which swimming event?

For more Olympics, visit www.californiasportsastounding.com

A: Crabbe won the 400-meter freestyle. He later became a movie and television actor.

CALIFORNIA SPORTS BIRTHDAYS
More Fun for July 30

Q: Bill Cartwright, born in 1957, who was California High School State Basketball Player of the Year in 1974 and 1975, won how many NBA titles?

....

Did You Know?

On July 20, 1929, the *Los Angeles Times* reported that "Olympic Boulevard is the name proposed for the new Tenth Street, by the Tenth-Street District Improvement Association at a meeting Thursday evening in the Tenth-Street school. The selection will be sent to Council with a request that the change be made as soon as the entire street has been improved."

Tenth Street was renamed Olympic Boulevard, a name it retains today.

A: Lodi's Bill Cartwright won three NBA titles as the starting center of the Chicago Bulls from 1991 to 1993.

NOTABLE BIRTHDAYS
July 30

1910: Prentis Hale, San Francisco native, skier, hunter, and sportsman, Stanford graduate, president of the Organizing Committee for the 1960 Winter Olympic Games.

1977: Misty May-Treanor, born in Los Angeles, volleyball player, captain of 1998 NCAA champion Long Beach State, first women's team to finish season undefeated, three-time Olympic gold medalist in beach volleyball 2004, 2008, and 2012, Newport Harbor High School Hall of Fame inductee 2014, International Volleyball Hall of Fame inductee 2016.

AUGUST
ASTONISHERS

Wild West in CA
August 1, 1911

What started as an essential part of cattle ranching eventually became a sport. For some reason a law was passed that made it happen. The first reference to this sport appeared as a California state law on April 3, 1851, and applied to those who rode broncos, roped calves, wrestled steers, and rounded up cattle. The new law was called "An Act to Regulate Rodeos."

The law stated: "Every owner of a stock farm shall be obliged to give, yearly, one general Rodeo, within the limits of his farm, from the first day of April until the thirty-first day of July, in the counties of San Luis Obispo, Santa Barbara, and San Diego; and in the remaining counties, from the first day of March until the thirty-first day of August in order that parties interested may meet, for the purpose of separating their respective cattle."

WILD WEST DAYS

Competitive rodeos became commonplace when Salinas hosted Wild West Days in 1911. On August 1, the first rodeo was held at the Salinas racetrack grounds at Sherwood Park. However, it was advertised as a Wild West Show. Since it ran for a whole week, Iver "Red" Cornett called it "Big Week" and Frank Griffen wanted to call it "The California Rodeo." To this day, both names are still used to refer to the rodeo.

Among the pioneers of the Salinas Rodeo, in addition to the above, were H.E. Abbott, James E. Breen, Sam Matthews, Lawrence "Butch" Beevers, Arthur Hebbron, Julius Trescony, John Bryan, E.J. Redmond, Ed Bordieu, A.J. Zabala, P.E. Zabala, and H.W. Lynch.

The *San Francisco Call* published a detailed article and this long headline: "Salinas Ropes and Throws Care Wild West Show Is Home Grown. Women Victors Set Fast Pace in Horse Races. Men Conquer Wild Broncos and Plunging Bulls and Hold Lassoing Contests."

Q: Who preserves the Salinas rodeo history?

For more rodeo, visit www.californiasportsastounding.com

A: Staff of the California Rodeo Heritage Collection Museum, which is located on the rodeo grounds.

CALIFORNIA SPORTS BIRTHDAYS
More Fun for August 1

Q: Sammy Lee, born in 1920, was first to win consecutive Olympic gold medals in what event: freestyle swimming or platform diving?

....

Did You Know?

The Red Bluff Roundup started in 1921 and is a major stop on the professional rodeo circuit. It was inducted into the ProRodeo Hall Fame and Museum in 2015.

The inaugural National Intercollegiate Championship Rodeo was held at the Cow Palace in 1949. Sul Ross State College of Texas won the team title. The Cal Poly San Luis Obispo Mustangs were the runner-up by 45 points. Cotton Rosser of Cal Poly finished in second place in the all-around competition.

A: The Fresno native won consecutive 10-meter platform diving Olympic gold medals in 1948 and 1952. He graduated with a medical degree from USC and coached several elite divers including Olympic champion Greg Louganis.

NOTABLE BIRTHDAY
August 1, 1988

Sarah Robles, born in San Diego, 2016 and 2020 Olympic bronze medalist in the 75 kg. and 87 kg. divisions.

Southern California Bangers
August 2, 1975

This international professional co-ed sports league had teams like the Albuquerque Lazers, Denver Comets, and Salt Lake City Stingers, but most were based in California. Just one team was needed to claim itself as an international league, so organizers chose El Paso-Juarez, covering both sides of the twin town. California fielded the Los Angeles Stars, San Diego Breakers, San Jose Diablos, and Santa Barbara Spikers in the International Volleyball Association.

Retired Los Angeles Laker Hall of Famer Wilt Chamberlain was an owner/player for the Southern California Bangers. His first team practice was held at Santa Monica High School. Chamberlain made his debut five days later with 23 kills out of 50 spikes as the Bangers crushed El Paso in four games. Wilt's star power wasn't enough—the Bangers finished the season in last place with a record of 6-18. Los Angeles beat the Breakers for the inaugural championship in 1975. Wilt promoted the league and eventually became commissioner in 1978. The league disbanded after the 1979 season.

Q: Who introduced Wilt to the sport of volleyball: Los Angeles Lakers teammate Keith Erickson or Eugene Selznick?

For more volleyball, visit www.californiasportsastounding.com

A: Volleyball Hall of Famer Eugene Selznick.

CALIFORNIA SPORTS BIRTHDAYS
More Fun for August 2

Q: Linda Fratianne, born in 1960, Olympic and World champion medalist, is the first female skater to land what type of triple jumps?

· ·

Did You Know?

The first Windsurfer One Design Class National Championships were held at Mission Bay Park in San Diego on October 14, 1973. Mission Bay, the largest man-made aquatic park in America, is an ideal location for windsurfing with its channels and islands.

Californians took home the trophies. Bruce Matlack of Newport Beach won the men's division. Long Beach's Susie Swatek claimed the women's title.

A: The Northridge native landed a toe loop and salchow in her program at the 1976 U.S. Nationals.

NOTABLE BIRTHDAYS
August 2

1933: Matt Hazletine, born in Ross, played center for the UC Berkeley football team, NFL linebacker with the San Francisco 49ers 1955-1968, NFL Pro Bowl 1963 and 1965, College Football Hall of Fame inductee 1989.

2000: Hailey "Hails" Langland, born in Irvine, first female snowboarder to land a "cab 1080 double cork," a trick that spun her three times and inverted twice, and won a gold medal at the 2017 Winter X Games.

NOTABLE EVENT
August 2, 1959

San Francisco Giants rookie first baseman Willie McCovey hit his first major league home run in a 5-3 win over the Pittsburgh Pirates at Seals Stadium. He spent his entire career playing for teams in California; the Giants, San Diego Padres, and Oakland Athletics. Willie was inducted into the National Baseball Hall of Fame in 1986.

Early Whiff-Whaff
August 11, 1902

Early whiff-whaff, as it was called, paddled into California in the early part of the 20th century. Informal matches were held throughout the state in 1900 and 1901. The Los Angeles Country Club and San Francisco's Hotel Rafael held the state's earliest tournaments in 1902. California's first major competition was held in August of that year. The Southern California Ping Pong (table tennis) Championships were organized in conjunction with the 18th annual tournament of the Southern California Lawn Tennis Association. The matches were held at the Casino courts in Santa Monica. Frank Godfrey of Riverside defeated Miss May Sutton to win the overall singles title.

The first U.S. Open Table Tennis Championships west of Chicago was held at Inglewood's Morningside High School from March 13-15, 1959. Susie Hoshi of Los Angeles defended her women's singles title. She had made history the previous year as the first California woman to win the national title.

Q: Who was the first U.S. Open Table Tennis men's singles champion from California: Erwin Klein or Richard Miles?

For more table tennis, visit www.californiasportsastounding.com

A: 17-year-old Erwin Klein of Los Angeles won the 1956 men's singles division. That same year he teamed with Leah Neuberger to win the World Table Tennis Mixed Doubles Championship.

CALIFORNIA SPORTS BIRTHDAYS
More Fun for August 11

Q: Richard Moore, born in 1910, sailor, won an Olympic gold medal in which event at the 1932 games in Los Angeles?

· ·

Did You Know?

Kim Rhode, a double trap and skeet shooter, has set several Olympic firsts. The native of Whittier is the first Olympian to medal on five different continents, the first summer Olympian to win an individual medal at six consecutive summer games (1996, 2000, 2004, 2008, 2012, 2016), and the first woman to medal in six consecutive Olympics.

A: The San Bernardino native sailed in the 8 meter open event. He was a member of the Los Angeles based California Yacht Club.

NOTABLE BIRTHDAY

August 11, 1947

Jan Henne, born in Oakland, freestyle swimmer, won four medals at the 1968 Olympics, gold in the 100-meter freestyle and the 4 x 100-meter freestyle relay, silver in the 200-meter freestyle, bronze in the 200-meter individual medley.

NOTABLE EVENT

August 11, 1991

John "Wild Thing" Daly, a native of Carmichael, won the PGA Golf Championship held in Carmel, Indiana. The underdog Daly was only the ninth alternate entering the tournament, but finished with his first tour victory.

Neil Puncher
August 13, 1903

In this rematch, a scheduled 20 round fight lasted only two rounds as Francis James Neil, better known as Frankie Neil, knocked out Harry Forbes at the Mechanics' Pavilion in San Francisco to win the World Bantamweight Championship. Neil knocked down Forbes three times and ended it with a vicious punch to the stomach. Neil's win avenged a loss to Forbes nine months earlier at Oakland's Reliance Athletic Club.

Neil trained for the bout Croll's Gardens and Hotel in Alameda, which touted itself as "The West Coast's Premier Training Grounds for the Dedicated Pugilist" and housed several of America's elite boxers. The building is registered as a California Historical Landmark #954.

Q: What California born heavyweight boxer trained at Croll's: James Corbett or Jerry Quarry?

For more boxing, visit www.californiasportsastounding.com

A: James "Gentleman Jim" Corbett, heavyweight champion from 1892 to 1897.

CALIFORNIA SPORTS BIRTHDAYS
More Fun for August 13

Q: Gary Ilman, born in 1943, swimmer, won gold medals in which relays at the 1964 Olympics: medley relay or freestyle relay?

Did You Know?

Eric Medlen was a National Hot Rod Association fuel funny car driver and calf roper. He was honored after his tragic racetrack death in 2007.

Yorba Linda's John Force Racing started the Eric Medlen Project to build safer cars. The result are enhanced NHRA safety requirements that include padded roll bars with heavy foam insulation and seven layers of flame-resistant fabric. Sonoma Raceway holds an annual Eric Medlen Ice Cream Social benefit to help Bay Area racers with a scholarship fund.

A: The Glendale native won gold in the 4 x 100-meter freestyle and 4 x 200-meter freestyle. Teammate Steve Clark of Oakland also earned gold as Team USA set world records in both relays.

NOTABLE BIRTHDAYS
August 13

1909: Wilhelmina von Bremen, born in San Francisco, sprinter, 1932 Olympic gold medalist in the 4 x 100 meter relay, bronze medalist in the 100 meters.

1934: Gary Davidson, Garden Grove native, lawyer and businessman, founded the World Football League. He cofounded with Buena Park mayor Dennis Murphy the American Basketball Association and the World Hockey Association.

Larsen's Legacy—From Runner to Biographical Movie
August 16, 1958

San Diego's Balboa Park 8 Mile Run had a new champion. The 19-year-old effortlessly finished with a solid time of 44 minutes. This runner loved to race but injuries cut his career short. He chose San Diego State University to learn more about physical education and kinesiology, study of the mechanics of body movements. How can people run faster?

As coach of Monte Vista High School 12 miles east of San Diego, his teams were CIF San Diego section champions from 1963 to 1966. They also won their division of the 1965 Mt. San Antonio College Cross Country Invitational, America's largest cross country invitational.

The next stop was Grossmont College where his runners set 11 national community college records and won an unprecedented seven consecutive state titles from 1972 to 1978. On July 28, 1976, he helped merge San Diego's Toads Track Club and the Jamul Athletic Club to form the Jamul Toads. Just four months later the Toads won the 1976 AAU Championship by 18 points over the defending champion Colorado Track Club.

A promotion came his way in 1979 when he was named the UCLA cross country coach. He became the head track and field coach from 1984 to 1999 after succeeding Jim Bush. His teams won NCAA track titles in 1987 and 1988, and Pac-12 cross country titles in 1980 and 1981. UCLA's dual meet record was a remarkable 118-3-1.

Bob Larsen emphasized threshold training, where runners pushed to their limits and stayed at that pace as long as possible. Runners trained as a group, making the workouts competitive, and helping everyone improve. No one conquered each single practice, because there was always room for improvement.

One example was the test workout. Runners did one lap around the track at their top speed, rested for a precious 60 seconds, then repeated the process for a total of 12 laps. The test workout was a challenge for even the most gifted runners. Larsen had the ability to develop the total person and understand each runner from state champions to the slowest. He cared about the athletes' well-being. He did that by customizing training for each runner, which gave them the confidence to overcome any challenge.

After retiring from UCLA in 1999, Bob and coach Joe Vigil established the Running USA group, a high-altitude training center at Mammoth Mountain. They trained Meb Keflezighi and Deena Kastor at 8,000 feet. Their training paid off at the 2004 Olympic marathon as Meb won a silver medal in the men's race and Deena claimed a bronze in the women's race. The USA was the only country to win two medals in the marathon. Meb became the first runner in history to win the New York Marathon (2009), Boston Marathon (2014), and win an Olympic medal.

Larsen's legacy was covered in the entertaining movie, *City Slickers Can't Stay With Me: The Coach Bob Larsen Story* and the enjoyable book, *Running to the Edge*.

Q: Who was the first Grossmont College runner to win consecutive state cross country titles: Bob Lamorandier, Ed Mendoza, or Terry Cotton?

For more cross country, visit www.californiasportsastounding.com

A: Ed Mendoza won the California Community College State Championships in 1971 and 1972. He would go on to compete in the 10,000 meters at the 1976 Olympics.

··

Did You Know?

Bob Larsen never lost to USC in 15 years as UCLA head track and field coach from 1984-1999. Larsen also coached the San Diego Youth Team. In July of 1973 the team went to Sweden and Finland, the first time ever a U.S. Junior Track Team had traveled abroad. Bob, along with Santa Monica Track Club coach Tom Tellez are the first two Californians named as USA Track and Field Legend Coaches.

Kirk Pfeffer of Grossmont College ran 29:03 for 10,000 meters on March 28, 1976 at Irvine's Meet of Champions to set an American Community College record.

MW Ascent
August 18, 1873

California has 12 mountain peaks with an elevation of at least 14,000 feet. In the Sierra Nevada at 14,505 feet, Mount Whitney is the contiguous United States' highest summit. It was named after Josiah Whitney, the State Geologist of California nine years earlier.

The Inyo Independent published this article on September 13, 1873:

"The Highest Yet. A. H. Johnson, C. D. Begole and John Lucas, of Lone Pine, have demonstrated the fact that its summit can be attained. On the 17th of August these gentlemen were on the summit of Mount Whitney. The other peak was evidently the highest, and they resolved to go to its top. The next day they started, and passing over two deep canyons, spending the entire day in the labor, they finally succeeded in reaching its highest point, and have the honor of being the first to stand on the greatest elevation in the United States. They gave it the name of "Fisherman's Peak." The three men were on a fishing trip to nearby Kern Canyon...The summit is of granite and flat-topped. The party built a monument to commemorate what there is good reason to believe was the first visit ever made to the spot. The ascent was made from the southwest and the descent nearly west. Both routes were very steep and most laborious, as the party had to climb along the sharp, serrated crests of the rocky "ribs" on the mountain side. But the trip was made without accident, and is well worth recording."

The trio wrote the following letter to the *Inyo Independent* on October 25: "We left three half dollars, coined in 1871, upon which were carved names and dates. Lucas came away minus a boot sole, and Begole placed a four-foot stick in the monument, and thereon was fastened the top of a sardine box, also engraved with names and date."

Q: What is the name of California's second highest peak: North Palisade, Mount Williamson, or White Mountain Peak?

For more climbing, visit www.californiasportsastounding.com

A: Mount Williamson. The peak in the Sierra Nevada measures 14,379 feet, only 126 feet lower than Mount Whitney.

CALIFORNIA SPORTS BIRTHDAYS
More Fun for August 18

Q: Derryl Cousins, born in 1946, MLB umpire, served as umpire in the 1988 World Series between which two California teams?

· ·

Did You Know?

Mr. Elias Pierce was first to ascend Northern California's 14,179-foot Mount Shasta in 1854. Two years later Mrs. D.A. Lowrey of Scott's Valley and four others were the first women climbers to scale the mountain. The ladies planted the U.S. flag on the summit and then commenced their descent. The *Daily Evening Sentinel* noted "They have accomplished what was thought to be an impossibility."

A: The Fresno native umpired the series between the Los Angeles Dodgers and the Oakland Athletics. Los Angeles prevailed four games to one.

NOTABLE BIRTHDAY
August 18, 1984

Kimberly "Kim" Glass, born in Los Angeles, volleyball player, 2008 Olympic silver medalist.

Best Box Car
August 18, 1946

Who could race the fastest motorless vehicle on a downhill road? Over 100 of America's best young drivers would find out. 97,363 fans watched 14-year-old San Diegan Gilbert Klecan win the 1946 All-American Soap Box Derby in Akron, Ohio. Klecan, nicknamed the "Graphite Kid," topped 112 city champions from across America. Gilbert smeared graphite on the side of his racer to smooth out the big number nine officials had put on it before the race. The graphite also ended up on his face and feet, but he didn't mind. His mom greeted him at the finish line and wiped his face with a handkerchief. He steered his blue racer downhill to victory in 27.13 seconds, at 35 mph for the 953-foot course and was the first Californian to win the event.

Gilbert built the car himself in a Point Loma body shop and spent $9.70 for everything. He even got special permission to paint the car and put the newspaper *San Diego Journal* on the side. Klecan spent a lot of time on the little things such as springs, polishing, and streamlining. The result was a center lane win by six inches. His reward was a four-year college scholarship at the age of 18. He attended Fresno State College.

Q: Who was the first California girl to win the All-American Soap Box Derby: Faith Chavarria or Sally Sue Thornton?

For more box car racing, visit www.californiasportsastounding.com

A: 12-year-old Faith Chavarria representing the Tri-County areas of San Luis Obispo, Santa Barbara, and Ventura, won the 1989 masters division race.

CALIFORNIA SPORTS BIRTHDAYS
More Fun for August 18

Q: Sarah Hammer, born in 1983, cyclist, won four silver medals at the 2012 and 2016 Olympics in which events: road cycling or track cycling?

. . . .

Did You Know?

The Bill Speeg Memorial Scholarship Fund was established in 2016. The Fund honors the late Bill Speeg of Valley Center, CA who passed away in 2014 at the age of 46.

The top three finishers in the Local and Rally Divisions of the FirstEnergy All-American Soap Box Derby World Championship race annually receive scholarships from the fund.

Speeg became involved with the Soap Box Derby in 1999 when his daughter Ashley began to race. Bill quickly became involved in local Oceanside and statewide California Soap Box Derby activities, serving as a board member and in other official capacities. The Speeg family traveled to races throughout the country where he offered technical support, financial assistance and mentoring to many young racers. He had served as a Regional Director for nearly 10 years at the time of his passing.

A: The Redondo Beach native won silver medals in track cycling. Her events were team pursuit and omnium.

NOTABLE EVENT
August 18, 1977

Don Sutton of the Los Angeles Dodgers tied a National League record by pitching his fifth one-hitter as he shutout the San Francisco Giants 7-0 at Dodger Stadium. Sutton tied the record held by Fresno born pitchers Tom Seaver and Jim Maloney.

San Francisco Rolling
August 21, 1870

Roller skating wheeled into Califoria in August of 1870. San Francisco's *Daily Alta California* announced: "ROLLERSKATING, THE PUBLIC, PARTICULARLY the young people, will be delighted to bear that this fascinating exercise, so much indulged in in many of the Eastern cities, will be introduced here this week, at Union Hall."

A week later the paper advertised "Roller Skating at Union Hall, Howard Street, admission to evening assemblies 50 cents, day assemblies 25 cents. The Management reserve and enforce the privilege of excluding anyone disregarding the rules, and will refuse admittance to all not of genteel appearance."

Finally, one day later, on the 29th, a reporter noted, "The amusement of roller skating, introduced at Union Hall, has proved very popular, the participants entering into the spirit of the fun with great enthusiasm."

Q: When was the first reference to a roller skating contest: 1875, 1885, or 1895?

For more roller skating, visit www.californiasportsastounding.com

A: The *Sacramento Daily Union* described "A Race on Rollers" at the Old Pavilion on February 12, 1885.

CALIFORNIA SPORTS BIRTHDAYS
More Fun for August 21

Q: Nion Tucker, born in 1885, was a 1928 Olympic gold medalist in four-man bobsled, was a sports lobbyist for what Bay Area venue: Kezar Stadium or the Cow Palace?

Did You Know?

Brad Lackey of Berkeley became the first American to win the 500cc Motocross World Championship in 1982. Brad began riding motorcycles at the age of nine with his father through the mountains of the Bay Area. He was inducted into the Motorcycle Hall of Fame in 1999 and the Motorsports Hall of Fame of America in 2013.

Los Angeles native Danny LaPorte also made history at the 1982 World Championship. He was the first American to win the 250cc division. Danny spent his early days training in the California desert and in vacant lots near his home in Torrance. The Motorcycle Hall of Fame honored him as a 2000 inductee.

A: Tucker, a native of Suisun City, lobbied to hold sports events at the Cow Palace in Daly City.

NOTABLE BIRTHDAY
August 21, 1913

Cornelius "Corny" Johnson, born in Los Angeles, high jumper, 1932 and 1933 CIF State Champion, 1936 Olympic gold medalist.

NOTABLE EVENT
August 21, 1966

San Diego golfer Mickey Wright won her 13th and final major title at the Women's Western Open golf tournament. Mickey, who at 11 years old had her first lesson at the La Jolla Country Club, finished her career in 1969 as perhaps the greatest woman golfer in history.

The Ultimate Game Known by Another Name
August 25, 1974

Ultimate, originally known as Ultimate Frisbee—a name that was changed because Frisbee is a registered trademark—started throwing flying discs around in 1968 with a master qualification meet at the Rose Bowl. Six years later, the same venue hosted the World Frisbee Championships. The event was sanctioned by the International Frisbee Association. Academy Award winner Tatum O'Neal, honorary queen, tossed out the first Frisbee. The event program described Frisbees as a "registered trademark of Wham-O Manufacturing Company for flying saucers used in sports games." Wham-O founders Richard Knerr and Arthur "Spud" Melin marketed Frisbees worldwide and wanted it to be a sport, and not a toy.

California tournaments offer competition in five divisions: Club, College, Youth, Masters, and Beach. Stanford and UC Santa Barbara have won the most college titles.

The California Ultimate Association at calulti.org is a non-profit growing the sport by providing support and resources to local leagues. CUA has hosted the Open High School State Championships and the USA Southwest Club Regional Championships. Popular venues include the SilverLakes Equestrian and Sports Park in Norco, and the Fresno Regional Sports Complex.

Q: California's Irv Kalb, Tom "TK" Kennedy, and Dan "Stork" Roddick were charter inductees to the USA Ultimate Hall of Fame in which year: 1980, 2000, or 2004?

For more ultimate, visit www.californiasportsastounding.com

A: All three were inducted in 2004.

CALIFORNIA SPORTS BIRTHDAYS
More Fun for August 25

Q: James "Wally" O'Connor, born in 1903, Olympic freestyle swimmer and water polo player, competed in how many Olympics: three or four?

. . . .

Did You Know?

The United States Olympic Committee officially recognized USA Ultimate as a Recognized Sport Organization in 2014. This status allows the sport to position itself with the International Olympic Committee as a possible addition to the to the 2028 Olympics in Los Angeles.

A: The Madera native competed in water polo all four Olympics from 1924 to 1936.

NOTABLE BIRTHDAY
August 25, 1956

Thomas "Tommy" Martin, born in Stockton, U.S. Judo Champion, member of Olympic teams for 1976 and 1980.

NOTABLE EVENT
September 1, 1979

California Angels third baseman Carney Lansford hit three consecutive bases empty home runs as the Halos beat the Cleveland Indians 7-4 at Cleveland Stadium.

El Cajon LL
August 26, 1961

The Fletcher Hills Northern Little League produced California's first Little League World Champions. Co-managers Don Dolan and Jim Pursley had 12-year-old players from El Cajon and La Mesa. They guided the boys to 14 straight wins in the single elimination baseball tournament. The team won the western regional in San Bernardino, then headed to Williamsport, PA for the finals. Going to Pennsylvania was exciting, especially since this was the first airplane ride for most of the players. Williamsport officials called the team "El Cajon" during their five day stay.

El Cajon reached the final against El Campo, Texas. Surprise! A San Diegan was there to meet them. Hall of Famer Ted Williams threw out the ceremonial first pitch and gave the players new gloves. Pitchers Mike "Sal" Salvatore and Mickey Alesandro combined for a no-hitter, but El Cajon was losing 2-1 in the final inning. Salvatore then hit a three-run home run 200 feet over the centerfield fence and a 4-2 win.

The team flew to Los Angeles where manager Don Dolan, a pilot for Pacific Southwest Airlines, flew them home on a charter flight to El Cajon's Gillespie Field. Over 5,000 fans met their baseball heroes who celebrated with a ride on a fire truck and a parade through El Cajon and La Mesa.

Q: Which El Cajon reserve player became a National Football League MVP quarterback with the Cleveland Browns in 1980: Bernie Kosar or Brian Sipe?

For more Little League history, visit www.californiasportsastounding.com

A: Brian Sipe, who played quarterback for the San Diego State Aztecs from 1969 to 1971.

CALIFORNIA SPORTS BIRTHDAYS
More Fun for August 26

Q: What race car driver, born in 1946, with the nickname "Swede," raced at the Indianapolis 500 in 1972 and 1973?

....

Did You Know?

The first Northern California Little League World Champion team came from San Jose in 1962. Twelve-year-old pitcher Ted Campbell, who at six foot one was the tallest player in Little League history, threw a no-hitter as San Jose beat Kankakee, Illinois 3-0. Campbell struck out 11 batters in the shutout.

California made it a three peat in 1963 as Granada Hills edged Stratford, CT 2-1. In extra innings, Jimmy Walker hit a bloop single to right field to drive in teammate Fred Seibly with the winning run. Granada Hills pitcher Dave Sehnem struck out 13 hitters to earn the win.

Golden State teams have added several more titles. Long Beach won the 1992 and 1993 tournaments, followed by Chula Vista in 2009 and Huntington Beach in 2011.

A: David "Swede" Savage, Jr. from San Bernardino. He died at the age of 26 from injuries he suffered during a crash at the 1973 Indianapolis 500.

NOTABLE BIRTHDAY
August 26, 1985

Rachel Buehler Van Hollebeke, born in Del Mar, soccer defender, nicknamed "The Buehldozer," won Olympic gold medals in 2008 and 2012.

Wet Anteaters
August 28, 1885

This was a new sport played in water between teams of seven players each. The first reference to this sport appeared in Stockton's *Evening Mail* newspaper: "A polo game will be played in the water at the swimming baths tomorrow evening. A band of music will be in attendance."

Five years later the *San Francisco Examiner* published the article "A Brand New Game for the Swimmers Called Water Polo." The writer described it as "Everybody except the referee is sure to get wet. A wrinkle of English origin that should catch on here. All you need is a good pair of lungs. If it is one peculiarly suited to this coast, its popularity is a foregone conclusion. Such a sport is water polo. The splendid opportunity the game gives an expert swimmer to show his skill in the water must have a tendency to make it, if introduced here, one of the most popular sports this coming summer at Monterey, Santa Cruz, and here in this city."

WATER POLO EXTRAS

America made a huge breakthrough in water polo at the 1924 Olympics thanks to the Californians who made up half the team. Stanford's Arthur Austin and Wally O'Connor, UC Berkeley's George Mitchell, and St. Mary's George Schroth led Team USA to a bronze medal. Charles Collett, a reserve who attended Stanford, made the trip to Paris but did not play.

California teams have dominated men's and women's intercollegiate water polo. UC Berkeley, UCLA, Stanford, and USC have won the majority of NCAA men's titles. Stanford, UCLA, and USC have won the most NCAA women's championships.

Brenda Villa, a Stanford graduate, won four Olympic medals in her career and was named Female Water Polo Player of the Decade by FINA Aquatics World Magazine.

Irvine is home to the USA Water Polo Hall of Fame. The Hall was established in 1976 and honors players, coaches, and officials.

Q: Which California school won their first NCAA Division I Men's Water Polo Championships over UCLA in 1979: San Diego State or UC Santa Barbara?

For more water polo, visit www.californiasportsastounding.com

A: The UC Santa Barbara Gauchos coached by Pete Snyder and led by Most Outstanding Player Greg Boyer routed UCLA 11-3. The win marked the first NCAA title in any sport for the Gauchos.

CALIFORNIA SPORTS BIRTHDAYS
More Fun for August 28

Q: David "Rags" Righetti, born in 1958, MLB pitcher, was the first player in MLB history to pitch a no-hitter and lead the American League in what category: shutouts or saves?

. . . .

Did You Know?

Ferdy Massimino's goal in the third overtime gave the UC Irvine Anteaters the 1970 NCAA Men's Water Polo Championship with a 7-6 win over the UCLA Bruins at the Belmont Plaza Olympic Pool in Long Beach. The UC Irvine win was its first NCAA Division I title in any sport. Mason Philpot made all four of his penalty shots to lead the team in scoring. Coach Ted Newland's team had six All-Americans: Massimino, Philpot, Mike Sherrill, Dale Hahn, Bruce Black, and Terry Klein.

A: The San Jose native pitched a no-hitter for the New York Yankees in 1983 and led the American League in career saves.

NOTABLE BIRTHDAY
August 28, 1919

Benjamin "The Toeless Wonder" Agajanian, born in Santa Ana, lost his toes in a freight elevator accident, ended up with a square right foot, NFL/AFL/AAFC placekicker, NFL champion in 1956 with the New York Giants, 1961 with the Green Bay Packers.

Mallets, Hoops, Balls, and a Poem
August 30, 1866

Californians started playing croquet as early as 1866. The *San Francisco Chronicle* published an ad for field and parlor croquet equipment: "Croquet! The New, Beautiful, and Fascinating Game of Field Croquet! A Delightful Outdoor Game! Parlor Croquet! A Charming Game for the Home Circle."

By year's end, the *Daily Alta California* and *Weekly Butte Record* reported of ladies "taking earnestly to the game of croquet." California's first formal club was organized three years later. The Young Ladies Croquet Club selected a ground on Aristocracy Hill in Nevada City.

The Sonoma Democrat published a poem three months later entitled "The Nicest Kind of Croquet."

"The evening was bright with the moon of May
And the lawn was light as though lit by day,
From the windows I looked—to see Croquet.
Of mallets and balls the usual display,
The hoops all stood in arch array,
And I said to myself, "Soon we'll see Croquet."
But the mallets and balls unheeded lay,
And the maid and the youth, side by aide sat they,
And I thought to myself, "Is *that* Croquet?"
I saw the scamp—it was light as day—
Put his arm round her waist in a loving way,
And he squeezed her hand. Was *that* Croquet?
While the red rover rolled forgotten away,
He whispered all that a lover should say,
And he kissed her lips —what a queer Croquet!
Silent they sat 'neath the moon of May,
But I knew by her blushes she said not nay,
And I thought in my heart, "Now *that's* Croquet."

Q: What are the two largest croquet clubs in the Bay Area: San Jose, San Francisco, or Oakland?

For more croquet, visit www.californiasportsastounding.com

A: The two largest clubs in the Bay Area are the San Francisco Croquet Club and Oakland Croquet Club.

CALIFORNIA SPORTS BIRTHDAYS
More Fun for August 30

Q: Robert "Bob" Kiesel, born in 1911, sprinter, won a gold medal and set a world record in what event at the 1932 Olympics: 400 meters, 100 meters, or the 4 x 100 relay?

. . . .

Did You Know?

Ben Rothman of Berkeley won the 2019 Golf Croquet World Championship singles title. He was the former resident croquet professional for the Mission Hills Croquet Club in Rancho Mirage.

The croquet facility at Mission Hills is one of the best in the world. This venue has hosted several tournaments including the U.S. Croquet Association National Championships every other year. In the spring of 2017 Mission Hills hosted the prestigious MacRobertson Shield competition, which is held every three and a half years, and is like the "Olympics" of croquet, a 17-day event involving competition between England, New Zealand, Australia, and the United States.

A: The Sacramento native ran the opening leg and won a gold medal in the 4 x 100-meter relay. Fellow Californian Hector "Hec" Dyer ran the third leg as the USA finished in 40 seconds to win the relay.

SEPTEMBER
SHOCKERS

A Sharp Combat Sport
September 1, 1850

The announcement of a combat sport was published just eight days before statehood. The San Francisco based *Daily Alta California* announced: "Fencing Exhibition"—On Sunday, the 1st of September next, at the Cafe de Paris, corner of Pike and Washington Streets. Monsieur Chabriel, Professor of Fencing at the National Academy of Paris, and Monsieur Chauvet, First Professor of Fencing in the First Regiment of Infantry, respectfully inform their friends and the public that they will give a Grand Fencing Exhibition as above. Several fencing masters and amateurs will fence on the occasion. Professors and amateurs wishing to join in the exhibition are politely invited to do so. Price of tickets $1—to be had at the place mentioned above." In today's currency that would be about $35. No mention of the eventual turnout.

Q: Fencing gradually spread that decade to what other Northern California cities? Hint: The two cities start with the letter S.

For more fencing, visit www.californiasportsastounding.com

A: Sacramento and Stockton opened fencing schools in the late 1850s.

CALIFORNIA SPORTS BIRTHDAYS
More Fun for September 1

Q: Al Geiberger Sr., born in 1937, professional golfer, set what scoring record in 1977?

Did You Know?

Francisco Webster Honeycutt, a native of San Francisco, was the first California fencer to medal at the Olympics. He won a bronze medal at the 1920 Olympics in the team foil competition.

Janice-Lee York Romary, born in Palo Alto, was the first woman to compete in six Olympic Games. She contended in women's individual foil starting at the 1948 London Olympics and ending in 1968 at Mexico City. Romary was honored at the 1968 Olympics as the first female flag bearer for America. She graduated from USC and was a member of the University of Southern California Fencing Club.

A: Geiberger, a native of Red Bluff, was the first golfer to shoot a 59 in a PGA Tour sanctioned event. Geiberger shot a round of one eagle, 11 birdies, and six pars at the Danny Thomas Memphis Classic.

NOTABLE BIRTHDAY
September 1, 1866

James "Gentleman Jim" Corbett, born in San Francisco, won the heavyweight title in 1892 with a technical knockout of John L. Sullivan in the 21st round. He was the only boxer to defeat the hall of famer Sullivan.

NOTABLE EVENT
September 1, 1960

Berkeley native George Harrison and Dick Blick from Los Angeles led Team USA to the gold medal in the men's 4 x 200-meter freestyle relay at the Olympics in Rome. The team swam 8:10.2 to set a world record.

Splendid Outdoor Pastime for Women
September 4, 1902

Field hockey became popular in California as early as 1902. The *Los Angeles Evening Express* displayed the headline: "Hockey for Los Angeles: Movement on Foot for the Introduction of This Splendid Outdoor Pastime for Women." The article noted, "English field hockey will be the next innovation in outdoor pastimes to be patronized in Los Angeles. Hockey has become quite a fad among the American women in the East, and what could be more natural than its being adopted on the Pacific Coast, particularly in Southern California?

There was a game held on May 1, 1903 at the San Diego Normal School (forerunner of San Diego State Teachers College). The *San Diego Union* announced a day earlier: "a game which is new on this coast will be played by the young ladies of the school, it is English field hockey, recently introduced into this country."

Q: Three Californians have won Olympic bronze medals in field hockey. How many years apart were their medals: 20, 36, or 52 years?

For more field hockey, visit www.californiasportsastounding.com

A: 52 years. Frederick Augustus "Fred" Wolters won a bronze medal as a member of the 1932 Olympic men's team. Sheryl Ann Johnson and Marcella Jeanette "Marcy" Place earned bronze medals representing the 1984 Olympic women's team.

CALIFORNIA SPORTS BIRTHDAYS
More Fun for September 4

Q: Charles "Charlie" Doe Jr., San Francisco native, born in 1898, rugby player, won how many Olympic medals: two or three?

. . . .

Did You Know?

Serra High School in San Diego, now known as Canyon Hills, has set many national high school records in girls field hockey. Barbara Hansen had eight assists in a game against Morse High in 1989. The previous record holder was Kori Jenkins, also of Canyon Hills who had seven assists against El Cajon Valley in 1996. Samantha Gallop played from 1980 to 1983 and ranks second all-time for most assists in a season with 42.

Canyon Hills went 87 games without a defeat from 1983 to 1986, which is tied for the second longest streak in the nation behind the 93 games by Walpole High of Massachusetts.

Santiago High School in Garden Grove holds the national record for most goals scored in a game with 24 against University High of Irvine in 1991.

A: The San Francisco native won gold medals at the 1920 and 1924 Olympics.

NOTABLE EVENT
September 4, 1972

Spitz Blitz! Mark Spitz won his seventh gold medal and set a seventh world record as the Team USA swam 3:48.16 to win the 400 x 100-meter medley relay race at the 1972 Olympics. California teammates Mike Stamm and Tom Bruce swam in the final and also earned gold. Spitz trained under hall of fame coaches Sherm Chavoor and George Haines. Chavoor led the Arden Hills Swim Club in Sacramento. Haines coached the Santa Clara Swim Club.

NOTABLE BIRTHDAY
September 4, 1984

Jason Donald, born in Fresno, infielder, 2008 Olympic bronze medalist, Jason homered to help the USA win the bronze medal game.

Oldest Organized Sport
September 8, 1868

A sport played as early as the 17th century was introduced to Californians in the second decade of statehood. This sport was first mentioned by the San Francisco based *Daily Alta California* which wrote: "Lacrosse, the new game, is said to be a modification of baseball. Quiggins says he has tried baseball, and he thinks the more it is modified the better it will be."

Southern California welcomed the sport in 1889 when the Los Angeles Lacrosse Club held their first meeting at the Young Men's Institute. The *Los Angeles Herald* happily announced: "We are unfeignedly glad to see the grand game of lacrosse introduced in our city. As a manly athletic game, we honestly believe that lacrosse has no superior."

College lacrosse was first mentioned on December 10, 1896 when the *San Francisco Call* reported, "An intercollegiate game of lacrosse will probably be played by the two universities next semester, and men are already in training for the event. It has long been the desire of lacrosse enthusiasts at both Stanford and Berkeley to put this fascinating sport on record as an intercollegiate contest."

MODERN LACROSSE

Many of California's men's teams compete in the Western Collegiate Lacrosse League. Cal Poly San Luis Obispo, Sonoma State, Stanford University, UC Santa Barbara, and UC Berkeley have won multiple titles since 1980. The Southwestern Lacrosse Conference was formed in 2009 and includes UCLA, USC, and several Division II schools from California. The leading collegiate women's programs are Stanford and USC, which have the greatest number of NCAA tournament appearances.

The National Lacrosse League is a men's professional indoor lacrosse league. In 2017, the San Diego Seals joined the NLL and began play in the 2018-2019 season.

San Diego also made history in 2022 as the first California city to be awarded the World Lacrosse Championships.

Q: The first Pacific Coast Lacrosse Championship was played in 1878 where: San Francisco's Recreation Grounds or UC Berkeley?

For more lacrosse, visit www.californiasportsastounding.com

A: The San Francisco Club and the Maple Club played on November 28, 1878 at San Francisco's Recreation Grounds.

CALIFORNIA SPORTS BIRTHDAYS
More Fun for September 8

Q: 18-year-old John Mykkanen, born in 1966, was the youngest male swimmer for Team USA at the 1984 Olympics held in Los Angeles. What was his event: freestyle or breaststroke?

....

Did You Know?

Miniature golf had several nicknames. The offshoot of the sport of golf was often referred to as mini golf, pee-wee golf, and midget golf. Inventor Garnet Carter of Georgia called it Tom Thumb golf, named for his Tom Thumb Golf Company, builder of miniature courses.

California's first Tom Thumb course opened in November of 1929. The course was laid out in the palm grove and tropical garden of the Jacob Stern estate adjoining the Hollywood Plaza Hotel. 400 golfers played at the grand opening, but only three equaled the par 43 at the 18-hole course. A month later, the *Long Beach Sun* described miniature golf as, "This new sport is one that puts new thrills in the game for veteran golfers."

The first regional titles in California were held two months apart in 1930. Long Beach hosted the Southern California Championships, while Santa Cruz conducted the first Northern California Championships at the El Recreo Course.

A: Mykkanen, a native of Anaheim, earned a silver medal in the 400-meter freestyle.

NOTABLE BIRTHDAY
September 8, 1977

Crystl "The Big Bruiser" Bustos, born in Canyon Country, softball player, 2000 and 2004 Olympic gold medalist, 2008 Olympic silver medalist, set an Olympic record with six home runs in the 2008 Games.

Marathon Success
September 9, 1908

California's original marathon was organized by the Los Angeles Athletic Club President Robert Rowan, and several members including referee Al Treloar, and clerk of course DeWitt C. Van Court. The 17-mile course started at club headquarters on Spring Street, traveled extensively on Washington Street (now known as Washington Boulevard), and finished at the club's annex on Windward Avenue in Venice. The race, dubbed the Southern California Marathon, was the first of its kind west of the Mississippi River.

Ten runners, all members of the Athletic Club, started the race. Edward Dietrich, whose longest training run was only six miles, ran 2:01.30 for top honors. He was awarded an exquisite 20-karat gold medal and a silver Herald Cup. Seven-year-old Harold Bailey, the official mascot of the Club, ran barefoot and hatless as he helped pace the runners for 10 miles.

The *Los Angeles Herald* offered praise: "The club is to be congratulated on the success of the race, and so is everyone interested in Californian outdoor sports, outdoor life and athletics. The race advertises the unequaled fitness of California for a contest of this kind, and calls attention to the fact that here, of all places, is that which is most suitable for an International Olympics on a heroic scale."

Q: The modern version of the Los Angeles Marathon started in 1986. What was the original name for this race in 1971: City of Angels Marathon or Griffith Park Marathon?

For more running, visit www.californiasportsastounding.com

A: Griffith Park Marathon.

CALIFORNIA SPORTS BIRTHDAYS

More Fun for September 9

Q: Frank "Peerless Leader" Chance, born in 1877, MLB first baseman, was a player-manager for which team in the Pacific Coast League: the Fresno Raisin Eaters or the Los Angeles Angels?

....

Did You Know?

Pickleball, a paddleball sport that combines elements of badminton, ping pong, and tennis, involves hitting a perforated plastic ball over a net. The sport is played indoors or outdoors on a badminton-sized court and a slightly modified tennis net. Pickleball, which was invented in the mid-1960s, is one of the fastest growing sports in America with over three million participants. It is a fun sport that can be enjoyed by all ages and skills levels.

The Margaritaville USA Pickleball National Championships are held at the Indian Wells Tennis Garden in November. Over 2,000 participants from 46 states and six countries play over 4,000 matches on 45 courts in the week-long event. The venue near Palm Springs boasts the world's largest pickleball championship court. ESPN3 televises the event.

A: The Fresno native was a player-manager for the Los Angeles Angels from 1916 to 1917.

NOTABLE BIRTHDAYS

September 9

1974: Leah O'Brien, born in Garden Grove, softball outfielder, Olympic gold medalist for Team USA in 1996, 2000, and 2004. National Softball Hall of Fame inductee 2009.

1986: Brittney Reese, a native of Inglewood, long jumper, 2012 Olympic gold medalist, 2016 and 2020 Olympic silver medalist, won four outdoor and three indoor World Championships from 2009 to 2017.

Charged Up
September 10, 1960

The Los Angeles team in the American Football League started out with two assistants who would make Super Bowl history. In the meantime, the team needed a nickname. Frank Leahy, former Notre Dame coach and Los Angeles general manager announced that the team's nickname will be the "Chargers." The *San Bernardino Sun* noted that "the nickname was selected in a contest which drew 12,000 nominations. The winning name was submitted by Gerald Courtney of Los Angeles who received an expense paid trip to Mexico City for two. The same name was also submitted by 250 other entrants after Courtney's entry was received." Owner Barron Hilton liked the name "because they were yelling "charge" and sounding the bugle at Dodger Stadium and at USC games."

Their first game was at home in the Los Angeles Memorial Coliseum. Coach Sid Gilman had Jack Kemp as his starting quarterback. Kemp ran for one touchdown and passed for two more, and kicker Ben Agajanian converted on three extra points as the Chargers rallied to beat the Dallas Texans 21-20. Team officials were worried about the small attendance of 17,724. Los Angeles would win the Western Division ahead of the rival Oakland Raiders, but lose to the Houston Oilers in the AFL title game 24-16.

The team lost money and moved to San Diego in 1961. Those Chargers would win the 1963 AFL title with a 51-10 electrocution of the Boston Patriots at Balboa Stadium. The Chargers stayed in San Diego till 2017 when they returned to Los Angeles. The Chargers new home is SoFi Stadium, which opened in 2020 on the former site of the Hollywood Park Racetrack in Inglewood.

Sid Gillman's two assistants would eventually win Super Bowls. Offensive assistant Al Davis eventually coached and owned the Oakland Raiders. He guided them to Super Bowl wins in 1976 and 1980. Defensive line coach Chuck Noll became head coach of the Pittsburgh Steelers and led them to four Super Bowl wins between 1975 and 1980.

Q: What Charger offensive tackle was a Pro Football Hall of Fame inductee in 1979: Ernie Wright or Ron Mix?

For more football, visit www.californiasportsastounding.com

A: Ron "The Intellectual Assassin" Mix. The USC graduate was named to the AFL All-Time Team in 1970.

CALIFORNIA SPORTS BIRTHDAYS
More Fun for September 10

Q: Randy "The Big Unit" Johnson, born in 1963, at 40 years, 256 days old became the oldest Major League pitcher to achieve: the most shutouts, strikeouts, or pitch a perfect game?

. . . .

Did You Know?

Charger quarterback Jack Kemp attended Occidental College in 1953 and played defensive back, placekicker, punter, and quarterback for the football team. He was also an accomplished javelin thrower.

A: Johnson pitched a perfect game on May 18, 2004 as the Arizona Diamondbacks beat the Atlanta Braves 2-0.

NOTABLE BIRTHDAY
September 10, 1943

Hilda Gurney, born in Los Angeles, 1976 Olympic bronze medalist in equestrian dressage, team, open.

Oakland Señores
September 11, 1960

Oakland was awarded the American Football League's eighth franchise on January 30, 1960. The league didn't favor Oakland, but Los Angeles Chargers owner Barron Hilton threatened to forfeit his franchise unless a second team was placed in California. The team didn't have a home field, but used San Francisco's Kezar Stadium and Candlestick Park plus Oakland's Frank Youell Field until establishing a lengthy stay at the Oakland Coliseum in 1966.

This team also needed a nickname. The *Oakland Tribune* held a contest that drew over 10,000 entries, but initially ended in a dull thud. Emerging as the winner on April 4 was a name that "symbolized the history, strength, and solidarity of old-world California." "Senors," which misspelled senores. Fans protested. Even the Oakland City Council passed a resolution lamenting the choice of "Senors." General Manager Chet Soda and a committee changed the name to Raiders ten days later. The Raiders played their first home game on September 11 as they lost 37-22 to the Houston Oilers at Kezar Stadium.

Al Davis became head coach of the team in 1963 and built it into of the most successful NFL franchises. He coached till 1965 then owned the team till his death in 2011. His lengthy career included work as a scout, assistant coach, head coach, general manager, AFL commissioner and owner. Davis was an innovator. He was the first NFL owner to hire an African American head coach, Art Shell, and a female chief executive Amy Trask. Davis also hired Tom Flores, the second Hispanic head coach in the NFL.

The Raiders stayed in Oakland from 1960 to 1981. They won Super Bowl XI played at the Rose Bowl on January 9, 1977 with a 32-14 thrashing of the Minnesota Vikings. Four years later they won Super Bowl XV with a 27-10 rout of the Philadelphia Eagles. A lack of Oakland stadium renovations prompted a move to Los Angeles in 1982. They won another Super Bowl with a 38-9 drubbing of the Washington Redskins on XVIII on January 22, 1984. Davis moved his team back to Oakland in 1995 and the franchise stayed there till 2019. His son Mark Davis is the team's principal owner and managing general partner. Unfortunately, the Raiders were not able to secure a new stadium to replace the deteriorating Oakland Coliseum. Mark relocated the "Senores" to Nevada where they officially changed their name to the Las Vegas Raiders on January 22, 2020.

Q: Who is the first California coach to win a Super Bowl with the same team in two cities: John Madden or Tom Flores?

For more football, visit www.californiasportsastounding.com

A: Tom Flores, a native of Sanger, coached Super Bowl winners with the Oakland Raiders (XV) in 1981 and the Los Angeles Raiders (XVIII) in 1984.

CALIFORNIA SPORTS BIRTHDAYS

More Fun for September 11

Q: Henri LaBorde, born in 1909, won a silver medal at the 1932 Olympics in what field event: the discus throw or shot put?

. . . .

Did You Know?

THE HOLY ROLLER GAME

The Raiders scored with ten seconds left as they beat the San Diego Chargers 21-20 at San Diego Stadium in 1978. Raiders quarterback Kenny Stabler fumbled at the Chargers 24-yard line. As the ball moved forward at the 12-yard line Oakland running back Pete Banaszak batted it with both hands forward to tight end Dave Casper who batted it, kicked it, and recovered it into the end zone for a game tying touchdown. The NFL upheld the touchdown but amended its rules after the season to prevent a recurrence of the play. Raiders announcer Bill King said, "The Raidershave scored on the most zany, unbelievable, absolutely impossible dream of a play!"

A: The San Francisco native won a silver medal in the discus throw at the 1932 Olympics held in Los Angeles.

Agility and Coordination
September 12, 1850

A reference to this sport was published just three days after statehood. The practitioners of this activity need agility and coordination, but also strength, balance, and endurance.

In June of the following year, the *Sacramento Daily Union* announced an exhibition by a gymnast named Mr. Brewer on the horizontal bar performing many hard and difficult feats. Five months later, gymnastics was offered at the new amphitheater owned by Mr. Lewis. In 1852, the *Daily Alta* California reported that a venue offering gymnastics would open in San Francisco on Merchant Street opposite the Union Hotel. Gymnastic associations then grew steadily throughout California in the late 1850s.

Q: Which California men and women gymnasts medaled at the 1984 Olympics in Los Angeles? Hint: there were four total: two men and two women.

For more gymnastics, visit www.californiasportsastounding.com

A: Pete Vidmar of Los Angeles and Van Nuys native Mitch Gaylord won gold in the men's team competition. Long Beach native Michelle Dusserre and Santa Clara's Tracee Talavera earned silver medals for the USA women's team.

CALIFORNIA SPORTS BIRTHDAYS
More Fun for September 12

Q: Albert "Albie" Pearson, born in 1934, MLB outfielder, was a 1963 All-Star with what California team: the Los Angeles Dodgers or the Los Angeles Angels?

Did You Know?

The first California schools to win the NCAA men's and women's gymnastics titles are crosstown rivals. Jack Becker coached the USC men to the 1962 title, while the UCLA women's team coached by Valorie Kondos Field won the 1997 crown.

A: The Alhambra native played for the Los Angeles Angels from 1961 to 1966.

NOTABLE BIRTHDAY
September 12, 1951

Eric Lindroth, born in Huntington Beach, water polo player, 1969, 1971 and 1972 NCAA champion with UCLA, 1972 Olympic bronze medalist, USA Water Polo Hall of Fame inductee 1988.

NOTABLE EVENT
September 12, 2000

Dave Hansen of the Los Angeles Dodgers set a Major League record with his seventh pinch hit home run of the season. The Long Beach native smashed the home run in the Dodgers' 5-4 loss on the road to the Arizona Diamondbacks. Fountain Valley's Craig Wilson, who played for the Pittsburgh Pirates, tied the record in 2001.

Racing in Long Beach
September 13, 1932

Long Beach Motor Speedway opened to motorcycle racing in 1932. American Motorcyclist Association champion Lloyd "Sprouts" Elder raced on opening week and drew a sellout crowd of 6,000 fans. Fresno's famous motorcycle champion was the biggest draw in the 20-event program. The venue was ideal for short track racing. The track was one fifth of a mile in length, 30 feet wide, and had flat turns. Motorcycle races were popular for about 20 years, but faded in the early 1950s.

Cars, not motorcycles, were the next big racing event in town. Drive fast forward more than 40 years and we arrive at the Long Beach Grand Prix in 1975. British expatriate and Long Beach resident Chris Pook had an idea. Why not have a race similar to the Monaco Grand Prix, but through the streets of Long Beach? The City Council didn't believe this doable until American race car driver, constructor, and owner Dan Gurney teamed with Pook to organize the race.

British driver Brian Redman won the first race, a Formula 5000 event, on September 28, 1975. The Grand Prix changed to a Formula One race the next year. What started in 1975 has grown into a three-day event with over 180,000 fans. Long Beach now claims the longest running major street race in North America. A highlight of race week is the induction of new members to the Long Beach Motorsports Walk of Fame in downtown.

Q: Who was the first California born driver to win the Grand Prix of Long Beach: Alexander Rossi or James Vasser?

For more auto racing, visit www.californiasportsastounding.com

A: James Vasser, a native of Canoga Park, won the race on April 14, 1996. He averaged 96.281 mph, the second fastest in race history.

CALIFORNIA SPORTS BIRTHDAYS
More Fun for September 13

Q: Carl Shy, born in 1908, basketball player, won a gold medal in the first ever Olympic basketball tournament held in what country: the USA, Finland, or Germany?

. . . .

Did You Know?

Phil Hill and Dan Gurney were the two charter inductees to the Long Beach Motorsports Walk of Fame. Hill, a resident of Santa Monica, became the first American to win the Formula One World Drivers Championship in 1961. Gurney was the first American to win races in sports cars, Formula One, NASCAR, and Indy cars. He was inducted into several motor sport halls of fame.

A: Shy, a native of Los Angeles, played basketball at the 1936 Summer Olympics held in Berlin. Team USA beat Canada 19-8 in a game played outside in driving rain.

NOTABLE BIRTHDAY
September 13, 1990

Jamie Anderson, born in South Lake Tahoe, snowboarder, won gold medals in the Women's Slopestyle Event at the 2014 and 2018 Winter Olympics. She is the first female snowboarder to win more than one Olympic gold medal.

NOTABLE EVENT
September 13, 2017

The International Olympic Committee awarded Los Angeles the right to host the 2028 Summer Olympics.

Running Away from Tigers
September 14, 1991

San Diego State Aztec running back T.C. Wright was injured with 3:55 to go in the first quarter against the University of the Pacific. The offense needed help. A reserve running back entered the game and the 24,408 fans at Jack Murphy saw one of the amazing performances in college football history. This back rushed for an NCAA record 386 yards, seven touchdowns, a two-point conversion, and 44 points! The Tigers couldn't catch him as he averaged more than a first down per carry, 10.4 yards per try. After the game he told the *San Diego Union*, "Golly, this kind of stuff doesn't happen much to freshman. The offensive line blocked like hell for me." The running back went on to the NFL and the Hall of Fame. His name is Marshall Faulk.

AZTEC GAME OR BUST

Attending the game that day was Aztec superfan Tom Ables. The San Diego State alumnus and proud Navy veteran saw his first Aztec game in 1946 when he was sports editor of the school newspaper. The following year, he was named the school's first sports publicity director. Ables missed only six Aztec road games since his freshman year. Between 1964 and 2015 he attended 600 consecutive Aztec games, home and away. After that first game in September 1946, he never missed a home Aztec football game the rest of his life. His last game was October 14, 2017, two days before he died. Ables attended 788 games! He also found time to attend over 1,000 Aztec basketball games.

Q: Which Aztec head coach was an innovator in football passing offenses and later coached the San Diego Chargers: Sid Gillman or Don Coryell?

For more football, visit www.californiasportsastounding.com

A: Don Coryell coached the Aztecs from 1961 to 1972 and the Chargers from 1978 to 1986. He won over 100 games as both a college and NFL coach. His innovative offense was called, "Air Coryell." John Madden was the defensive coordinator for Coryell and the Aztecs 1964-1966. He coached the Oakland Raiders to the Super Bowl title in 1977.

CALIFORNIA SPORTS BIRTHDAYS
More Fun for September 14

Q: Jerry Coleman, born in 1924, was a radio announcer and manager for which professional baseball team: the California Angels or the San Diego Padres?

....

Did You Know?

San Diego State's new Snapdragon Stadium seats 35,000 fans, but is expandable to a capacity of 55,000 or more to meet a possible return of a National Football League franchise. Snapdragon is the home of the San Diego Wave FC of the National Women's Soccer League and the San Diego Legion of Major League Rugby. The stadium will host the World Lacrosse Championship. Adjacent to the stadium are 80 acres of park, recreation, and open spaces including a 34-acre water park.

A: The San Jose native announced San Diego Padres games from 1972 to 2014, except for a break managing the team in 1980.

NOTABLE EVENT
September 14, 1975

UC San Diego named Judy Sweet as the first female college athletic director in America. The Tritons won 26 of their 30 national championships during her tenure. In 1991 she was elected as the first female president of the NCAA.

NOTABLE BIRTHDAY
September 14, 1986

Courtney Mathewson, born in Orange, water polo attacker, 2012 and 2016 Olympic gold medalist.

A Surf City
September 20, 1959

Huntington Beach lifeguard chief Vince Moorhouse organized the first annual West Coast Surfboard Championships. The event, now known as the U.S. Open of Surfing, was a one-day competition with 75 contestants who competed in 15-minute heats. Seal Beach resident Jack "Mr. Excitement" Haley won the men's division, while San Diego's Linda Benson, all four feet eleven inches of her, navigated her eight-foot-two-inch board to take the women's title. Louie Tarter of Huntington Beach won the boys competition.

Moorhouse was an innovator as chief of the lifeguards. He transformed the lifeguards into an elite crew whose surf rescue techniques have been adopted worldwide. After his death Moorhouse was honored with a memorial monument, the renaming of the lifeguard headquarters in his name, and an Honor Roll plaque.

The U.S. Open is now a week-long event at Huntington Beach Pier, and the largest surfing competition in the world. Over 500,000 fans attend each year. The competition is a qualifying event for the Santa Monica based World Surf League. A memorable highlight during the week is the addition of new inductees to the Surfing Walk of Fame and the Surfers' Hall of Fame across from the pier.

Q: Who won the contest the following year in 1960, Mike Haley or Ron Sizemore?

For more surfing, visit www.californiasportsastounding.com

A: Jack Haley's brother Mike won the men's title, while Linda Benson repeated as women's champion in 1960 and 1961.

CALIFORNIA SPORTS BIRTHDAYS
More Fun for September 20

Q: Eric "E-Rock" Turner, born in 1968, National Football League player, was the highest choice in the NFL draft for what position: receiver, defensive back, or running back?

. . . .

Did You Know?

NASCAR's first stock car race in California was held on April 8, 1951 on a half mile dirt oval. Marshall Teague drove his Hudson Hornet to victory in the 100-mile race at Carrell Speedway in Gardena before over 10,000 fans. Johnny Mantz of Long Beach steered a Nash Ambassador to second place.

Bob "Barky" Barkhimer promoted NASCAR in California. He developed Stockton 99 Speedway as the first track west of the Mississippi River to join NASCAR and tracks in Oakland, Fresno, San Jose, and Hughes Stadium in Sacramento soon followed. The Berkeley native ended his career as senior Vice-President of NASCAR.

A: The Ventura native played defensive back for three NFL teams. He tragically died of stomach cancer at the age of 31.

NOTABLE EVENT

September 20, 1988

El Cajon's Greg Louganis wins the Olympic gold medal in the 3-meter springboard diving event, one day after hitting his head on the diving board in the preliminary round. He won his fourth career gold medal one week later in the 10-meter platform event.

Maroon Racquet
September 23, 1957

This 10-year-old girl loved sports, any kind of sports. She loved basketball, track, and softball. She played shortstop for the softball team that won the all-city public parks championship. Football? She played halfback on her neighborhood team. Those sports faded away, so her father suggested golf, swimming, or tennis. Golf was too slow. She wasn't a water person. Tennis was the choice. Her parents took her to Brown's Sporting Goods on Atlantic Avenue in Long Beach, and she found a super looking racquet with maroon strings and a maroon handle.

Her first lesson was in September of 1954 at Houghton Park in Long Beach. Clyde Walker of the Parks and Recreation Department gave the lesson that started a world class career. Her Mom picked her up in the family's 1947 Chevrolet convertible. Mom asked, "How was it?" The youngster said, "Just great. I want to play tennis forever. I am going to be the number one tennis player in the whole world." Mom said, "That's fine, dear," and drove her home.

Billie Jean King did just that and much, much more. Her first California title was on September 23, 1957, when she won the girls 15-year-old division at the Pacific Southwest Tennis Tournament at the Los Angeles Tennis Club.

King went on to a hall of fame career of 39 Grand Slam titles, including 12 in singles, 16 in women's doubles, and 11 in mixed doubles. She was the #1 ranked player in the world six times from 1966-1975. In 1973, 90 million people worldwide watched her sweep Bobby Riggs in the "Battle of the Sexes," 6-4, 6-3, 6-3. No other sporting event has played a more significant role in developing greater respect and recognition for women athletes. Off the court she campaigned for equal prize money for men's and women's tennis. Thanks to her efforts in 1973, the U.S. Open was the first tournament to offer equal prize money to both sexes.

Her greatest contributions have been as a pioneer for equality and social justice. She won several awards including the Presidential Medal of Freedom in 2009, America's highest civilian honor. She was the first female athlete to be honored. *Life* magazine named her one of the "100 Most Important

Americans of the 20th Century." In 2014, she founded the Billie Jean King Leadership Initiative a non-profit dedicated to addressing the critical issues required to achieve diverse, inclusive leadership in the workforce. Her autobiography, *All In*, published in 2021 was a national bestseller.

Q: What Long Beach sports venue was named after Billie Jean King?

For more tennis, visit www.californiasportsastounding.com

A: The Billie Jean King Tennis Center located at Recreation Park has eight courts and LED lighting for evening play. The center has professional instruction and equipment rental and a pro shop.

CALIFORNIA SPORTS BIRTHDAYS
More Fun for September 23

Q: David "Dave" Turner, rower, 1948 Olympic gold medalist in the coxed eights with his brother Ian. Where did they attend school: Stanford or UC Berkeley?

. . . .

Did You Know?

The National Tennis Center in New York, home of the U.S. Open, was renamed the USTA Billie Jean King National Tennis Center in 2006 in honor of her contributions to tennis, sports, and society both on and off the court. She was the first woman to have a major sports venue named in her honor.

A: The Oakland native and his brother attended UC Berkeley.

NOTABLE BIRTHDAY
September 23, 1930

Don Edmunds, born in Santa Ana, race car driver and car builder, 1957 Indianapolis 500 Rookie of the Year.

Multisport at MB
September 25, 1974

California's first triathlon was held in San Diego. A San Diego Track Club newsletter announced that "The First Annual Mission Bay Triathlon, a race consisting of segments of running, bicycle riding, and swimming, will start at the causeway to Fiesta Island at 5:45 P.M. September 25. The event will consist of 6 miles of running (longest continuous stretch, 2.8 miles), five miles of bicycle riding (all at once), and 500 yards of swimming (longest continuous stretch, 250 yards). Approximately two miles of running will be barefoot on grass and sand. Each participant must bring his own bicycle. Awards will be presented to the first five finishers. For further details contact Don Shanahan or Jack Johnstone."

Forty-six athletes paid the $1 entry fee. The race started with a run, continued with cycling two loops around Fiesta Island, and finished with a swim, plus a crawl up a steep dirt bank to finish. There were no sleek bikes in this race—in fact most entrants used a beach cruiser for their bike! Don and Jack accommodated late finishers by illuminating the course with car headlights. Bill Phillips finished in first place.

Q: What participant would organize the first Ironman Triathlon in Hawaii: John Collins, Tom Warren, or Dave Scott?

For more triathlon, visit www.californiasportsastounding.com

A: John Collins, who finished in 22nd place with a time of 71 minutes.

CALIFORNIA SPORTS BIRTHDAYS
More Fun for September 25

Q: Kim Bokamper, born in 1954, NFL defensive end, played in how many Super Bowls with the Miami Dolphins: two or three?

. . . .

Did You Know?

Susan Williams of Long Beach was the first American triathlete to win an Olympic medal. She won the bronze medal at the 2004 Olympics. Susan finished the .93 mile swim, 25 mile bicycle race, and 6.2 mile run with a time of 2:05:08.92.

Several Californians have won the Ironman World Championship in Hawaii. San Diego's Tom Warren won the 1979 race, the second one ever held. Glendale's Mark Allen won six titles from 1989 to 1995. Scott Molina of Pittsburg took the 1988 crown, Davis native Dave Scott, was a six-time winner from 1980 to 1987, and Scott Tinley of Santa Monica won the February 1982 race.

A: The San Diegan played in Super Bowls XVII and XIX with the Dolphins.

NOTABLE EVENT
September 25, 1979

The California Angels won their first American League Western Division title in Jim Fregosi's first full season as manager. His baseball team gave Kansas City the royal flush 4-1 at Anaheim Stadium. Nearby at Disneyland, the amusement park officials excitedly recognized the Angels' title with a proclamation.

Ramming Around
September 29, 1946

The National Football League's first Los Angeles team was based in Chicago. The Los Angeles Buccaneers were strictly a road team and had players from California colleges. They were named for Los Angeles to showcase football talent from the Golden State. The Buccaneers one and only NFL season was in 1926 when they finished in sixth place. California football fans saw them in person four times, but only in exhibition games held in Los Angeles and San Francisco during January of 1927.

Los Angeles welcomed the next NFL team in 1946. They were the defending NFL champions as the Cleveland Rams. The only team to move after a championship season. Their nickname was chosen because it was "short and would fit easily into a newspaper headline." This team would rent the Los Angeles Memorial Coliseum under the condition that they integrate their roster with African American players.

The team was anchored by three Californians. Bob Waterfield played quarterback, punter, and placekicker. He was the NFL Rookie of the Year the previous season. African American players Kenny Washington and Woody Strode were the first to sign NFL contracts in the modern era. Their signing helped reintegrate the NFL after more than a 10-year gap. Both had played football at UCLA with Jackie Robinson. Kenny was an All-American running back, and Strode an offensive end. Their team was called the Los Angeles Rams. They opened the season on September 29 with a loss at home to the Philadelphia Eagles 25-14.

The first Super Bowl in franchise history was practically a home game as the Rams played at the Rose Bowl in Pasadena, only 14 miles from the Coliseum.

The 1980 Super Bowl between the Rams and the Pittsburgh Steelers was close until the visitors pulled away in the four quarter for a 31-19 win.

They played at the Coliseum till 1979, then moved to Anaheim Stadium from 1980 to 1994. Their hope was to sellout the smaller stadium and avoiding the NFL blackout rule, which prohibited games from being shown on local television 72 hours before kickoff. This move didn't work as fans blamed the owners, and owners blamed the outdated stadium and shrinking fan support. California lost the team as it moved to St. Louis from 1995 to 2015. St. Louis eventually had its own stadium woes and NFL owners voted to approve the Rams relocation back to Los Angeles in 2016. SoFi Stadium opened in 2020 as the new home for the Rams, who share the venue with the NFL's Los Angeles Chargers. The Rams made history soon as they became the first California team to win a Super Bowl playing in its home stadium with their 23-20 victory over the Cincinnati Bengals on February 13, 2022.

Q: What is the name of the Rams' mascot: Rammer the Bammer, Rampage, or Running Rams?

For more football, visit www.californiasportsastounding.com

A: Rampage. He wears the number one (#1). He replaced Ramster, the St. Louis based mascot who lasted a few seasons.

CALIFORNIA SPORTS BIRTHDAYS
More Fun for September 29

Q: Alphonzo Bell Sr., born in 1875, tennis player, won two medals at the 1904 Olympics in what events: singles and doubles, or singles and mixed doubles?

Did You Know?

The Los Angeles Rams became the first NFL team to have all of its games both home and away, televised. KNBH (standing for NBC Hollywood) broadcast the first game on September 17, 1950. The Chicago Bears beat the Los Angeles Rams 24-20 at the Coliseum. Attendance was 18,219 as many fans watched the game at home.

A: Bell, a Los Angeles native, was a silver medalist in the men's doubles and a bronze medalist in the men's singles.

OCTOBER
OH, BOY

Solly is Jolly
October 4, 1897

The rematch fight was big news statewide. The *San Francisco Call* distributed bulletins each round.

Solomon "Solly" Garcia Smith, featherweight boxer and Los Angeles native, had lost to world featherweight champion George Dixon by knockout four years earlier. Dixon was strongly favored again, but the bout in San Francisco at Woodward's Pavilion gave Smith plenty of support from California boxing fans. Solly was also a distance runner and that endurance helped him wear down the champ over 20 rounds.

Bulletins were displayed at "the Call" agencies throughout California such as the Golden Eagle Hotel in Sacramento, Buttleman's cigar store in Marysville, Hotel Julian in Woodland, and J. O. Simm's Saloon in Chico. In Los Angeles it was noted that not since the 1896 presidential election with William McKinley had this much interest been shown in a public event. Over 1,000 fans stood at the Call agency on Spring Street to read the bulletins of each round as they were placed by slide projector upon a large screen, and cheered as the news was pleasing to the fans and friends of either boxer.

Smith won and claimed the World Featherweight title. Solly, the son of a Mexican mother and Irish father, was the first world champion of Hispanic ancestry.

Q: How much prize money did Solly win?

For more boxing, visit www.californiasportsastounding.com

A: He earned a nice payday of $4,000 (approximately $120,000 in today's dollars). Dixon took home $1,000.

CALIFORNIA SPORTS BIRTHDAYS
More Fun for October 4

Q: Jered Weaver, born in 1982, MLB pitcher, three-time All-Star 2010-2012, pitched a no-hitter for which California team?

· ·

Did You Know?

The first California vs. Hawaii outrigger canoe race from Catalina Island to Newport Dunes Aquatic and Recreational Park was held on September 20, 1959.

Several people organized the event. Among them were Ira Dowd, Newport Dunes president, Norm Durkin, special events director, Tommy Zahn, paddleboard champion/surfer/lifeguard. Hawaii's Albert "Toots" Minvielle helped procure the canoes, while Noah Kalama coached the California crew. Hawaiian Olympic swimming champion and surfing legend Duke Kahanamoku was the grand marshal for the 32-mile race.

California's team had only trained for two months. They finished in 5 hours, 32 minutes, only 16 minutes behind the talented Hawaiian crew. The Californians paddled for 2.5 hours when their 30-foot canoe capsized mid channel. They recovered within minutes and finished the race.

A: The Northridge native pitched a no-hitter for the Los Angeles Angels on May 2, 2012 as they beat the Minnesota Twins 9-0 at Angel Stadium of Anaheim.

NOTABLE BIRTHDAYS

October 4

1910: Frank Booth, born in Los Angeles, swimmer, member of the Los Angeles Athletic Club, 1932 Olympic silver medalist in the 4 x 200-meter freestyle relay.

1993: Aubree Munro, a native of Brea, softball catcher, 2016 and 2018 World Champion with Team USA, 2020 Olympic silver medalist.

Coliseum Baseball
October 4, 1959

This baseball game had so many firsts, how do you decide which was first? 92,394 fans at the Los Angeles Memorial Coliseum attended the first World Series game played in California. This was the first and only World Series played at the Coliseum. It was also the first World Series game to exceed 90,000 in attendance. The Los Angeles Dodgers sent them home happy with a 3-1 victory over the Chicago White Sox in game three of the series. Dodger starter Don Drysdale pitched seven innings and reliever Larry Sherry preserved the win. The Dodgers became the first team to go from 7th place in one season to World Champions the next. The World Series win was their first in Los Angeles and marked the first championship for a California team.

Sherry went on to finish all four Dodger victories with two wins and two saves, and earn the World Series MVP Award.

The Dodgers clinched the series by wearing out the Sox 9-3 in Chicago four days later. The winning players share broke the $10,000 barrier and paid a record $11,231.

Q: What is the all-time attendance record for a baseball game at the Coliseum?

For more baseball, visit www.californiasportsastounding.com

A: The Dodgers celebrated their 50th anniversary of their move to Los Angeles by playing the Boston Red Sox in an exhibition game on March 29, 2008. A world record 115,300 fans attended the game.

CALIFORNIA SPORTS BIRTHDAYS
More Fun for October 4

Q: Who was the first American female windsurfer to win the World Championships: Cheryl Tiegs or Cheryl Swatek?

. . . .

Did You Know?

Governor Jerry Brown signed a bill on August 20, 2018 making surfing the official state sport of California. Surfer and state assemblyman Al Muratsuchi coauthored the Assembly Bill (AB) #1782 with legislator Ian Calderon. The Legislature declared: "California is home to a number of world-famous surf breaks like Malibu, Trestles, Mavericks, Rincon, Steamer Lane, and Huntington. The world's first neoprene wetsuit, a modern staple of surfing, was invented in California's San Francisco Bay area. California pioneered the science of surf forecasting at the University of California's Scripps Institution of Oceanography, allowing surfers around the world to predict when and where to go surfing."

A: Los Angeles native Cheryl "Cheri" Swatek, born in 1963, won the 1975 and 1976 International Windsurfer One Design Class World Championships.

NOTABLE BIRTHDAY
October 4, 1956

Doug Padilla, born in Oakland, distance runner, ranked #1 in the world in 1983 for the 3,000-meter run.

The Seven Species of a Mascot
October 5, 1991

The National Hockey League moved into San Jose with the May 9, 1990 founding of a new expansion team. Four months later, they gave it a name. The club received over 5,000 suggestions ranging from California and nearly every other state and Canadian province. There was even one entry from Italy! Proposed names included the Blades, Alcatraz Techs, Condors, Faults, Fog Horns, Golden Skaters, Integrated Circuits, Piranhas, Redwoods, Screaming Squids, and Sea Lions. Team executive Matt Levine described the nickname as "relentless, determined, swift, agile, bright and fearless, and we want to have an organization that has all of those qualities, too." Team officials didn't choose the most popular name, the Blades. They picked the Sharks. Seven species of sharks live in the "Red Triangle" area of the Pacific in the Bay Area. The team's logo includes a triangle.

San Francisco's Cow Palace was the team's home for the first two years. The first home game was October 5, 1991 as they lost to the Vancouver Canucks 5-2. Three days later the Sharks extinguished the Calgary Flames 4-3 for the first their first win. The Sharks moved into their new home, the San Jose Arena in 1993.

The highlight of the 1994 season was the quarterfinal playoff series against the top seeded Detroit Red Wings. The eighth seeded Sharks had the fewest shots on goal out of all 26 teams during the regular season. San Jose shocked the hockey world and knocked out Detroit in seven games. They would go on to face the Toronto Maple Leafs but lost in the conference semi-final.

San Jose skated to the Stanley Cup Final during the 2015-2016 season. The Sharks' home rink had been renamed a few years earlier as the SAP Center at San Jose. Everyone calls it the "Shark Tank." The Sharks chewed through Los Angeles, Nashville and St. Louis, but fell to the Pittsburgh Penguins in the final series 4-2.

Q: What is the name of the San Jose Sharks mascot?

For more hockey, visit www.californiasportsastounding.com

A: S.J. Sharkie was named on April 15, 1992. Sharkie has been selected to represent the team at the NHL All-Star Game over 20 times and assisted in dropping the ceremonial first puck at the 1997 All-Star Game in San Jose.

CALIFORNIA SPORTS BIRTHDAYS
More Fun for October 5

Q: William Corbus, born in 1911, placekicker and offensive lineman, led what college team to the first of three Rose Bowls from 1934 to 1936?

Did You Know?

San Jose Sharks left winger Matt Nieto was born in Long Beach. He was selected by San Jose in the 2011 NHL draft. Nieto was the first California born player selected by the Sharks in franchise history.

A: The San Francisco native played for the Stanford Indians. He was Stanford's first two-time All-American in 1932 and 1933. Corbus was inducted into the College Football Hall of Fame in 1957.

NOTABLE BIRTHDAYS
October 5

1913: Willard "Russ" Letlow, born in Dinuba, NFL guard and tackle, NFL champion with the Green Bay Packers 1936 and 1939. Attended the University of San Francisco.

1960: David "Dave" Wilson, Long Beach native, 1984 Olympic silver medalist in the men's 100-meter backstroke, gold medalist in the 4 x 100-meter medley relay.

A World Series and a Corvette
October 6, 1963

He won the first game of the World Series by striking out 15 New York Yankees and besting their ace Whitey Ford. Their rematch was in game four at Dodger Stadium. Los Angeles led the series 3-0.

Sandy Koufax pitched the Los Angeles Dodgers to a 2-1 win over the New York Yankees and clinched the World Series. The win completed a four game sweep and was the first time the Dodgers won the deciding game of a World Series at home. Dodger pitchers were superb, holding the Yankees to a puny .171 team batting average. The Yankees never had the lead in any game. This showdown was also the first time that Los Angeles and New York teams had met for a major professional sports championship.

Koufax won the World Series MVP for his two complete game victories. He was given the award by *Sport* magazine. Weeks later at a luncheon in New York City, Sandy also received a new Corvette, which was moved onto the sidewalk for photographs. During the luncheon a New York City policeman issued a $15 parking violation ticket and left it on the windshield. Baseball fan revenge?

Q: What was Sandy Koufax's nickname?

For more baseball, visit www.californiasportsastounding.com

A: The Man with the Golden Arm.

CALIFORNIA SPORTS BIRTHDAYS
More Fun for October 6

Q: Helen Wills Moody, born in 1905, tennis player, won how many Grand Slam titles?

....

Did You Know?

The first annual California amateur outdoor speed skating championship races were held February 14, 1930 as part of the winter carnival at Yosemite National Park.

The Yosemite Winter Club, the first outdoor amateur winter organization in California, organized the event. They were assisted by the California Skating Association. The purpose of the association was to develop speed skating and hope that California would have several representatives for the 1932 Olympic Winter Olympics in Lake Placid, New York. Contestants raced on a meager 220-yard track— the smallest speed skating track measurement accepted by the U.S. Amateur Skating Union. A crowd of over 2,000 from all over the state watched as Thomas Meagher of the Oakland Ice Arena won the men's race and Oakland's Gladys Brittain won the women's division.

Derek Parra of San Bernardino is the first Californian to win Olympic medals in speedskating. Parra won two medals at the 2002 Winter Olympics. He skated to a gold medal and world record time of 1:43.95 in the 1,500 meters and added a silver medal in the 5,000 meters.

A: Moody, a native of Centerville, won 31 Grand Slam titles in singles, doubles, and mixed doubles. She was also a 1924 Olympic gold medalist in singles and doubles.

NOTABLE BIRTHDAYS

October 6

1972: J.J. (Jeral Jamal) Stokes, born in San Diego, NFL wide receiver from 1995 to 2003, Super Bowl Champion XXXVIII with the New England Patriots.

1995: Justine Wong-Orantes, born in Torrance, volleyball player, 2020 Olympic gold medalist for the U.S. women's national team.

Pin Fun
October 9, 1847

A newspaper reference to this target sport appeared almost three years before statehood. The San Francisco based *California Star* reported that "Smith's New Bowling Alleys, in Pacific Street, are liberally and deservingly patronized. The good old amusement of bowling will form one of the agreeable and rational pastimes of approaching winter hours."

Another early reference appeared on November 4, 1848 when the *Californian* published the ad, "Shades Tavern and Bowling Alleys, corner of Pacific and Stockton Streets, San Francisco."

THE CALIFORNIA GOAT OF BOWLING

Walter Ray "Deadeye" Williams Jr. of San Jose holds the record for the most all-time standard Professional Bowlers Association records (47) and the most PBA earnings of over $5 million. He was the first player in history to reach over 100 total PBA titles that include PBA tour, PBA Regional Tour, PBA50 and PBA50 Regional. Williams was named PBA Bowler of the Decade 2000-2009 after he won his 7th Player of the Year award at age 50. "Deadeye" won at least one PBA Tour title in 17 consecutive seasons from 1993 to 2009. He has bowled 110 career perfect 300 games in PBA competition. Walter was inducted into the PBA Hall of Fame in 1995 and the United States Bowling Congress Hall of Fame 2005 and is considered America's greatest bowler.

Q: What were the bowling venues sometimes called during the 1850s: bowling saloons or hardball houses?

For more bowling, visit www.californiasportsastounding.com

A: They were sometimes referred to as bowling saloons.

. . . .

Did You Know?

Hall of Fame bowler Walter Ray "Deadeye" Williams Jr. was also a six-time World Horseshoe Pitching champion between 1978 and 1994. Walter had many practice sessions over the years where he would bowl and pitch horse-shoes in the same day. The most notable tournament situation was in June of 1993 when he won the PBA Northwest Classic tournament in Kenne-wick, Washington and that same afternoon drove 33 miles down the road to Hermiston, Oregon and pitched in a horseshoe tournament in which he finished second! He would often miss a bowling tour event to pitch in the world championships.

. . . .

Did You Know?

Judy Seki Sakata of Los Angeles was the first woman west of the Mississippi River to bowl a sanctioned 300 game. She rolled her perfect game at the 1957 Southern California Women's Match Game Championship at the South Bay Bowling Center in Redondo Beach. Sakata, a 177 average bowler, won a new 1957 Ford Thunderbird among other prizes.

NOTABLE BIRTHDAY

October 9, 1950

Brian Downing, born in Los Angeles, MLB catcher, outfielder, and des-ignated hitter, 1979 All-Star with the California Angels.

Row, Row, Row, Your California Boat
October 9, 1850

A sport that raced boats using oars appeared just one month after statehood. The first newspaper reference to rowing was published on the front page of the *Sacramento Transcript*, which reported that "A boat race came off yesterday, around Bird Island, near the mouth of the harbor. We could not learn the particulars, but heard that the whale boat of a Mr. Stanley won the race."

On October 21, the *Daily Alta California* described another boat race "The yacht America, or rather the last news, has set all Whitehall crazy. We recorded, a week or so since, a race that came off between one of oar Yankee boats and an English craft around Bird Island, at the end of which Whitehall threw up its tarpaulin. The Bird Island affair was merely the morning star to the Isle of Wight affair. And now the jolly wights of Long Wharf think they can whip the world. Another race is to come off. But this time Mr. Bull hauls in his horns and keeps in the background, where he was when the America dropped anchor and demanded the silver cup. The race is to be between the Yankee boat Tom K. Battelle, and a Dutch craft. The stake is now being arranged, and will probably be $500. The Yankee boat is to be pulled by two men, with two oars each. oars. The boat is nineteen feet long. The race will be around Groat Island." On October 28 the boats were ready. $100 bets were placed by each side. The Dutch emerged victorious by 50 yards despite the Americans claim that the Dutch cheated since their coxswain had assisted one of their oarsmen. After all this the *Daily Alta California* observed that "Boat races seem to be in fashion now a days."

Q: What Northern California towns with inland ports provided waterman for early competitive rowing? **A:** Vallejo **B:** Stockton **C:** Sacramento **D:** All of these

For more rowing, visit www.californiasportsastounding.com

A: All three towns.

CALIFORNIA SPORTS BIRTHDAYS
More Fun for October 9

Q: Hank Pfister; born 1953, professional tennis player, won Grand Slam doubles titles in 1978 and 1980 at which tournament, Wimbledon, French Open, or Australian Open?

....

Did You Know?

Bob Barde and Pat Cunneen wrote a history of San Francisco's South End Rowing Club, which was established in 1873 as the oldest rowing club west of the Mississippi River. The club promotes rowing, swimming, handball, and running. Their book is titled *Sport and Community at the Dock of the Bay*.

Marine Stadium in Long Beach was the first manmade rowing course in the United States. It was the venue for the 1968 and 1976 United States men's Olympic rowing trials and the 1984 United States women's Olympic rowing trials. The stadium was registered as a California Historical Landmark in 1994.

A: Pfister, a Bakersfield native, won the French Open doubles title in 1978 and 1980.

NOTABLE BIRTHDAY
October 9, 1999

Nicholas Boris "Nick" Itkin; born in Los Angeles, foil fencer, 2020 Olympic bronze medalist in the team competition.

CALIFORNIA SPORTS BIRTHDAYS
More Fun for October 9

Q: Velma Dunn, born in 1918, diver, won a silver medal at the 1936 Olympics in what event?

A: The 17 year old Monrovia native won the silver medal in the women's 10-meter platform.

Saints Slaughtered
October 9, 1920

Nate Schandling was in a heap of trouble. Only five days earlier he had been named head coach by "Brother" Vantasian, St. Mary's moderator of athletics. The team lost the football season opener to Stanford 41-0 and had fired their previous coach the week before. On this day, they traveled to Berkeley to challenge the California Golden Bears. The enrollment of Nate's College was 71 students. Berkeley's enrollment was 2,906 students and they were a national football powerhouse and were the first of California's Wonder Teams that would win national titles from 1920 to 1923.

The game resulted in the biggest margin of defeat in California college football history. Nate and the Saints were slaughtered. Berkeley Golden Bear coach Andy Smith substituted throughout, punted, played conservatively, but the game spiraled out of control. The Berkeley eleven scored 18 touchdowns. Jesse "Duke" Morrison ran for five. The score was 85-0 at halftime. Berkeley's student newspaper *The Daily Californian* loved the shutout. "One hundred and twenty-seven to nothing! Scoreboards aren't built to record such figures, yet they tell the tale of California's touchdown-intoxicated Bruins in the Saturday afternoon 'track meet' with St. Mary's."

Five days after the game, St. Mary's Graduate Manager Le Fevre and Brother Vantasian announced that the remainder of the season was cancelled due to player injuries. The team returned in 1921 and had a 4-3 season under new coach Edward "Slip" Madigan. In 1926 the newly named St. Mary's Galloping Gaels went undefeated at 9-0-1 and claimed the championship of the short-lived Northern California Athletic Conference.

In 1930 Gaels coach Madigan, 33 players, and 150 fans traveled in a special 16 car Santa Fe train dubbed the "World's Longest Bar" to New York. St. Mary's was going to play a regular season game against mighty undefeated Fordham, a team that had outscored opponents 181-9. Stadium officials established a section of stands for St. Mary's graduates, but a newspaper reported that "only six could be found in the city." The Galloping Gaels upset the Fordham University Rams 20-12 on November 15 at the Polo Grounds. Substitute Bill Beasley intercepted a pass and returned it 60 yards for the game winning touchdown with only a few minutes left. Fordham's loss was their first in 16 games dating back to 1928. The Gaels returned to California and wore derbies at parades to Oakland's Athens Athletic Club and San Francisco's City Hall to celebrate the win. St. Mary's dropped their football program in 1950, revived it in 1970, but ended it in 2004 due to budget cuts.

Q: Who gave the St. Mary's football team their nickname?

For more football, visit www.californiasportsastounding.com

A: Pat Frayne, sports editor for the *San Francisco Call-Bulletin*, used "Galloping Gaels" during the 1926 season because many of the players were Irish or Scottish by name.

CALIFORNIA SPORTS BIRTHDAYS
More Fun for October 9

Q: Terry Schroeder, born in 1958, water polo player, won consecutive silver medals at which Olympics?

Did You Know?

Unranked St. Mary's, in their first bowl game, won the 1939 Cotton Bowl Classic over the 11th ranked and undefeated Texas Tech Red Raiders 20-13.

A: The Santa Barbara native won silver medals at the 1984 and 1988 Olympics. Terry was inducted into the U.S. Water Polo Hall of Fame in 1998 and the International Swimming Hall of Fame in 2005.

NOTABLE EVENT
October 9, 1989

Art Shell made history when he took the field as the head coach of the Los Angeles Raiders. Shell, who was promoted mid-season from assistant, became the first African American to coach an NFL team since Fritz Pollard served as a player-coach with the Akron Pros in 1921. The Raiders defeated the New York Jets 14-7 at Giants Stadium.

Kings and Seals
October 14, 1967

California joined the National Hockey League with two expansion franchises in 1967. The Oakland based franchise had four names in 11 years! What started as the California Seals became the Oakland Seals, then Bay Area Seals, and finally the California Golden Seals. They moved to Cleveland in 1976.

A Canadian businessman who liked nicknames brought the NHL franchise to Los Angeles. He instructed the team's announcers to give nicknames for each player. Fans rooted for "Cowboy" Bill Flett, Real "Frenchy" Lemieux, Eddie "The Jet" Joyal, Eddie "The Entertainer" Shack, and Juha "Whitey" Widing. He also chose the team colors of purple and gold that matched the Los Angeles Lakers. His team was going to be associated with royalty. A team naming contest was held and fans submitted 7,649 entries. Newspapers reported that the owner said, "He was 'looking for a name that would be symbolic of leadership in hockey, and that we intended, over the years, to build a hockey dynasty.'" Pasadena's Harry J. Mullen was the "king" of entries and received a color TV and season tickets for the L.A. Kings' first NHL season. Thirty-one other fans submitted the same name, but after Mullen's postmarked entry.

Los Angeles won the first game in franchise history by conquering the Philadelphia Flyers 4-2 at the Long Beach Arena. Their new home at the Forum in Inglewood opened two months later.

THE "MIRACLE ON MANCHESTER"

On April 10, 1982, this was playoff hockey at the Forum located on Manchester Boulevard. The Kings, who had finished in 4th place in their division had barely made the playoffs. They had 24 more losses than Wayne Gretzky and the first place Edmonton Oilers. The Kings completed the largest comeback in NHL playoff history, from losing 5-0 to winning the game 6-5 in overtime. The Kings would go on to win the five-game series, but lose in the next round.

Six years later Gretzky was joined the Kings in a trade that shocked the hockey world. "The Great One" was now a King. He promoted the sport in

California and made the Kings a playoff worthy team.

They didn't win a championship with Gretzky, but won their first Stanley Cup in 2012 by skating past the New Jersey Devils 4-2. They added another title in 2014 with a 4-1 win over the New York Rangers. Kings' announcer Bob Miller loved it all. He announced 3,351 games during his 44-year career.

Q: Who was the first Californian to play for the Los Angeles Kings: Clark Noah or Noah Clarke?

For more hockey, visit www.californiasportsastounding.com

A: Laverne native Noah Clarke. He scored an assist, his first point, in his first National Hockey League game. The Kings crushed the Edmonton Oilers 4-2 at the Staples Center on December 16, 2003.

CALIFORNIA SPORTS BIRTHDAYS
More Fun for October 14

Q: Jared Goff, born in 1994, NFL quarterback, tied what league record?

· ·

Did You Know?

Los Angeles won the 2014 Stanley Cup and became the first team in NHL history to win three game sevens on the road in a single postseason. They beat San Jose 4-3 after losing the first three games, the Anaheim Ducks 4-3 after being behind 3-2, and then Chicago 4-3. The finished with a Stanley Cup win over New York.

A: The Novato native tied the NFL record for most completions in a game with 45. Jared, playing for the Los Angeles Rams, tied Drew Bledsoe's mark in 2019 at the Memorial Coliseum versus the Tampa Bay Bucaneers.

Speed, Strength, and Height
October 15, 1978

San Diego basketball fans had an NBA team before. The San Diego Rockets stayed from 1967 to 1971, but were bought and relocated to Houston. Seven years later, NBA owners voted to let the Buffalo Braves move to San Diego. A new nickname was needed, so a public poll of over 700 entries picked a winner. Local fan Frank Kowalski chose the name. The *Desert Sun* reported his entry as "writing in reference to the fast-moving ships that Clippers means speed, strength and height, all associated with basketball."

The Clippers played their first home game at the San Diego Sports Arena on October 15, 1978 as they lost to the Denver Nuggets 98-94. They finished the season fifth place in their division, but would climb no higher for the next six years. Owner Donald Sterling and the NBA traded lawsuits over his intention to relocate to Los Angeles, but in the end the team moved north in time for the 1984 season.

The newly named Los Angeles Clippers started play at the Los Angeles Memorial Sports Arena from 1984 to 1999, and played occasional games at the Arrowhead Pond of Anaheim 1994 to 1999. Downtown's Staples Center has been the team's home since 1999. In 2024, the Clippers new arena is the 18,000 seat Inglewood Basketball and Entertainment Center. It is located just south of SoFi Stadium, home of the NFL's Los Angeles Chargers and Los Angeles Rams.

An NBA title has eluded the Clippers so far. Forward Blake Griffin and guard Chris Paul anchored the best team in franchise history from 2013 to 2014. They won the Pacific Division, beat Golden State in the first round of the playoffs, but lost to the Oklahoma City Thunder in the semifinals. In 2021, the Clippers made it to the Western conference finals against the Suns and Chris Paul, the former Clipper.

Q: What California born UCLA forward and Basketball Hall of Famer played his final year for the Clippers during the 1985-1986 season?

For more basketball, visit www.californiasportsastounding.com

A: Berkeley native Jamaal Wilkes.

CALIFORNIA SPORTS BIRTHDAYS
More Fun for October 15

Q: Susan DeMattei, born in 1962, was the first American woman to medal in which Olympic biking event?

....

Did You Know?

Natalie Nakase is an assistant coach with the Agua Caliente Clippers of the NBA G League. In 2014, during the NBA Summer League, she made history as the first woman to sit on the bench as an NBA assistant.

A: The San Francisco native won a bronze medal in cross country mountain biking at the 1996 Olympics.

NOTABLE EVENT
October 15, 1988

Los Angeles Dodgers outfielder Kirk Gibson, too weak to take batting practice, stood up on his sprained right knee and strained left hamstring just in time. He entered game one of the World Series against the Oakland A's as a pinch hitter against All-Star reliever Dennis Eckersley. The Dodgers were losing 4-3 in the bottom of the ninth, but had Mike Davis on second base via a walk and a stolen base. Gibson stared down the 3-2 count and on the eighth pitch of the at bat, crushed a low curveball over the right field wall to win the game. Gibson never batted again in the series. The underdog Dodgers won in five games. His fist pump as he circled the bases is an iconic image in sports history.

Wicket Ways
October 16, 1851

A bat and ball game with wickets, bails, and stumps was introduced to Californians just after statehood in 1850. The first newspaper account of cricket appeared in 1851. The *Sacramento Union* announced that "Mr. John S. Lewis who has been engaged capturing grizzlies for the last three months, has just erected a magnificent amphitheater on J street, between 11th and 12th, in which to hold his performances. The dimension of the enclosure are 50 by 75 feet and walls over 12 feet in height. Mr. Lewis intends making his amphitheater a sort of gymnasium, where the citizens may resort and enjoy themselves in the sports of cricket, jumping, and boxing."

By 1852, the Bay Area was an early hub of activity as the San Francisco Cricket Club headed by George Aiken and the Occident Cricket Club promoted the sport.

Southern California's first cricket club was formed in Los Angeles. The *Los Angeles Herald* reported on June 18, 1887 that "Our sport loving friends will be pleased to learn that a cricket club has been organized in this city under the name of the Los Angeles Cricket Club. It numbers already twenty-five members, mostly British and Colonial, but we are informed that American admirers of Old England's national game are cordially invited to cooperate." Ten days later on June 28, the *Herald* added this note "The paraphernalia for the new cricket club arrived from the East recently, and the club had its first practice game at Sixth-street park yesterday afternoon. After the play, there was a meeting of the club in Mr. Gardiner's office in the Stephenson block."

Cricket is still played statewide. The Northern California Cricket Association organizes matches at over 35 grounds ranging from Hayward and Santa Clara to Sacramento. Van Nuys is home to the Southern California Cricket Club, which offers competition at over 10 clubs from San Diego to as far north as Bakersfield.

Q: Where is California's largest cricket venue?

For more cricket, visit www.californiasportsastounding.com

A: The Leo Magnus Cricket Complex is a group of four cricket grounds located inside Woodley Park in Van Nuys.

CALIFORNIA SPORTS BIRTHDAYS
More Fun for October 16

Q: Peter Asch, born in 1948, water polo player, earned what medal at the 1972 Olympics?

. . . .

Did You Know?

USA Cricket, the governing body for the sport in America, is based in Los Altos, CA.

A: The Monterey native won a bronze medal for Team USA. He was an All-American at UC Berkeley from 1967 to 1969. Peter was inducted into the USA Water Polo Hall of Fame in 1984.

NOTABLE BIRTHDAY
October 16, 1953

Susan "Sue" Pedersen, born in Sacramento, swimmer, was 15 years old when she won four medals at the 1968 Olympics. Sue won gold medals in the 4 x 100-meter medley relay and the 4 x 100-meter freestyle relay. Pedersen claimed a silver medal in the 100-meter freestyle as California teammates Jan Henne and Linda Gustavson made it a sweep for Team USA. Her second silver came in the 200-meter individual medley when she finished behind Santa Cruz teammate Claudia Kolb.

Oakland x 3
October 17, 1974

Golden State baseball fans had their first all-California World Series October 12-17, 1974. The National League champion Los Angeles Dodgers had the best record in baseball, winning 12 more games in the regular season than their foe, the Oakland Athletics of the American League. This World Series looked like a mismatch. Oakland was the two-time defending World Series champion, but the underdog. The Dodgers also seemed to have more fans. Their average home attendance led the majors with 32,500 per game, while the Athletics attracted 10,441 fans per game at the Oakland Coliseum, the third lowest in baseball.

Oakland responded with terrific pitching and timely hitting to win the series 4-1. Starting pitchers Catfish Hunter, Ken Holtzman, and Blue Moon Odom had strong outings. Reliever and series MVP Rollie Fingers finished with a win and two saves. The Athletics won game five at home 3-2, in fact four of the five games ended in that score. World Series excitement reached Oakland just in time to host the three home games. Baseball fans converged on the Coliseum to support their team. The Athletics had 49,347 friends for each game.

15 years later the A's added another World Series title with a 4-0 sweep of the San Francisco Giants in the 1989 Earthquake Series. The earthquake forced a 12-day gap between games two and three while San Francisco's Candlestick Park was inspected, but had only minor damage.

Q: What Modesto born left fielder won the Gold Glove award and All-Star honors for the Athletics in 1974?

For more baseball, visit www.californiasportsastounding.com

A: Joe Rudi, who finished second in the American League MVP voting to fellow Californian Jeff Burroughs of the Texas Rangers.

CALIFORNIA SPORTS BIRTHDAYS
More Fun for October 17

Q: Bob Seagren, born in 1946, pole vault gold medalist at the 1968 Olympics, belonged to which track club: Santa Monica Track Club, West Valley Track Club, or the Southern California Striders?

....

Did You Know?

The Oakland Athletics were the first Major League team from California to win three consecutive World Series.

A: Seagren, a native of Pomona, competed for the Southern California Striders track club.

NOTABLE BIRTHDAYS
October 17

1944: Marilyn White, born in Los Angeles, sprinter, 1964 Olympic silver medalist in the 4 x 100-meter relay. Competed for the Los Angeles Mercurettes track club.

1966: Tommy Kendall, race car driver from Santa Monica, Motorsports Hall of Fame inductee 2015.

Warriors in the West
October 23, 1962

The Philadelphia Warriors basketball team relocated to San Francisco in time for the 1962-1963 NBA season. They brought Hall of Famer Wilt Chamberlain and a fast break attack to the West Coast. However, their home games were not always played in Northern California. Warriors basketball debuted at the Cow Palace on October 23 with a 140-113 grinding of the Detroit Pistons. Bob Feerick, who had played and coached at Santa Clara University, was named Warriors head for the inaugural season. The following year Los Angeles native Alex Hannum took over and earned NBA Coach of the Year honors.

The San Francisco Warriors were renamed the Golden State Warriors in 1971. They played six home games at the San Diego Sports Arena, but the rest at the Oakland Arena. None were played in San Francisco.

In 1975 Al Attles coached the Warriors to their first title in California. Rick Barry was voted NBA Finals MVP and Jamaal Wilkes was Rookie of the Year.

The team's 40-year NBA title drought ended with titles in 2015, 2017, and 2018. Coach Steve Kerr had a roster full of All-Stars including "Splash Brothers" Stephen Curry and Klay Thompson, and forwards Kevin Durant and Draymond Green.

San Francisco opened a new home for the Warriors in 2019. The Chase Center seats 18,064 for basketball. The arena is part of Thrive City, the 11-acre mixed-use, privately-financed complex in San Francisco's Mission Bay neighborhood. It is home to retail stores and restaurants in the surrounding district.

Q: Who led the Warriors in scoring during their inaugural season?

For more basketball, visit www.californiasportsastounding.com

A: Wilt Chamberlain averaged 44.8 points a game. The "Big Dipper" was traded to the Philadelphia 76ers in 1965.

CALIFORNIA SPORTS BIRTHDAYS
More Fun for October 23

Q: Gene Brito, born in 1925, NFL defensive end, first team All-Pro from 1955 to 1958 with the Washington Redskins. He finished his career as a second team All-Pro in 1960 for which California team?

....

Did You Know?

On March 29, 2021, Kate Scott became the first woman to announce a regular season game for the Golden State Warriors on radio station KGMZ-FM 95.7 The Game. Scott provided play by play, while Mary Murphy added color commentary. Kerith Burke hosted the pregame and postgame shows for the all-female broadcast team.

A: The Huntington Park native played for the Los Angeles Rams from 1959 to 1960.

NOTABLE BIRTHDAYS
October 23

1922: Ewell "The Whip" Blackwell, Fresno native, MLB pitcher, 1952 World Series champion with the New York Yankees.

1960: Wayne Rainey, born in Downey, motorcycle road racer, 500cc World Champion 1990 to 1992, AMA Motorcycle Hall of Fame Museum inductee 1999.

7th Heaven Baseball
October 27, 2002

The Anaheim Angels baseball team didn't win their own division. They did, however, peak at the right time. There were plenty of contributors. Left fielder Garrett Anderson provided the hitting with 29 home runs and 123 runs batted in. Pitcher Jarrod Washburn registered 18 wins against only six losses on a staff that allowed the fewest runs in the American League. The Angels qualified as a wild card team in the playoffs, and disposed of the New York Yankees and Minnesota Twins, teams they had a losing record against during the regular season. Second baseman Adam Kennedy batted .357 versus the Twins and won the league championship series MVP award. They had earned their first American League pennant.

Yes, the Halos were headed to the World Series. The only remaining hurdle was National League Champion San Francisco Giants. Down five runs in the seventh inning of game six, the Angels rallied for a 6-5 win and forced a game seven at home. They were outhit 6-5, but cobbled together 4 runs and beat the Giants 4-1. Third baseman Troy Glaus finished the series with eight runs batted in and the MVP award. The Angels, who had started their Major League franchise in 1961, celebrated their first World Series Championship! *The Los Angeles Times* captured the euphoria with the headline: "7th Heaven as Angels Win Series."

Q: Angels right fielder Tim "King Fish" Salmon was honored with what baseball award in 2002?

For baseball, visit www.californiasportsastounding.com

A: Salmon won the Hutch Award, given to the player who best exemplifies the fighting spirit and competitive desire of the late baseball manager Fred Hutchinson, by preserving through adversity. Hutchinson died of lung cancer at the age of 45.

CALIFORNIA SPORTS BIRTHDAYS
More Fun for October 27

Q: Leon "Bip" Roberts, born in 1963, MLB second baseman and outfielder, played for which two California teams?

. . . .

Did You Know?

Nolan Ryan, in his first year with the California Angels, struck out the side on nine pitches against the Boston Red Sox at Anaheim Stadium on July 9, 1972.

Garrett Richards, pitching for the Los Angeles Angels, tied that immaculate inning record on June 4, 2014 on the road versus the Houston Astros. Richard struck out three Californians: Jon Singleton, Matthew Dominguez, and Chris Carter.

A: Roberts, a Berkeley native, played seven years with the San Diego Padres between 1986 and 1995 and ended his career with the Oakland Athletics in 1998.

NOTABLE BIRTHDAY
October 27, 1959

Kelly Rickon, born in San Diego, rower, 1984 Olympic silver medalist in the women's coxed quadruple sculls.

Kicking and Punching
October 29, 1978

Taekwondo kicked and punched its way into California in the 1960s. The first major competition was held in 1976 when Cal's men and women swept the inaugural National Collegiate Taekwondo Championships held at UC Berkeley and directed by Ken Min.

In 1978 Howard University won, followed by UC Berkeley and UC Santa Cruz. Cal dominated the tournament, winning 23 titles from 1990-2015.

The inaugural World Games in 1981 showcased taekwondo at Toso Pavilion on the Santa Clara University campus. Taekwondo was one of 15 sports contested during the games.

Riverside's Charlotte Craig and Cerritos native Jimmy Kim are world-class practitioners. Craig won a bronze medal at the 2007 World Championships in the 49 kg division. Heavyweight Kim earned silver in the 83 kg division at the 1987 Worlds, plus a gold at the 1988 Olympic Games demonstration event.

California has several tournaments. Two of the most prominent are the California State Championships held in Fresno and the California Open Taekwondo Tournament in Torrance.

Q: What are the five basic rules of taekwondo?

For more on taekwondo, visit www.californiasportsastounding.com

A: The five basic rules are courtesy, integrity, perseverance, self-control, and indomitable spirit.

CALIFORNIA SPORTS BIRTHDAYS
More Fun for October 29

Q: Austin Hooper, born in 1994, NFL tight end and Pro Bowler, played for what famous high school football program in Concord?

. . . .

Did You Know?

Taekwondo is from the Korean words tae (foot), kwon (hand), and do (path) and dates back to 50 BC when martial arts were developed.

A: The San Ramon native played for the De La Salle High School Spartans.

NOTABLE BIRTHDAY
October 29, 1981

Amanda Beard, born in Newport Beach, won seven Olympic medals from 1996 to 2004. She swam for the Irvine Novaquatics swim team.

NOTABLE EVENT
October 29, 2018

Golden State Warriors guard Klay Thompson shoots down the NBA record previously held by teammate Stephen Curry for most three pointers in a game with 14 as the Warriors crushed the Bulls 149-124 in Chicago. Klay scored 52 points in only 27 minutes.

NOVEMBER
NOT IN MY
HOUSE

Spike Monica
November 2, 1925

Beach volleyball dug, passed, and spiked its way to California in the first quarter of the 20th century. The first mention of beach volleyball appears to be on May 14, 1924 when the Venice based *Evening Vanguard* wrote, "With the advent of summer, beach sports again cast their shadows into the limelight. The sand stretches between Venice and Santa Monica come in for their share of attention from those who enjoy a good game of catch, or volleyball."

Santa Monica outdoor volleyball courts were referenced in November 1925 as the *Los Angeles Times* announced: "groundbreaking ceremonies for the new Breakers Club will take place January 1, 1926. The new clubhouse will be within half a block of the Edgewater Beach Club and the Casa del Mar. It will have the largest private beach, it is stated, of any beach club to date, with 343 feet of sand directly in front of the club building."

VOLLEYBALL CHAMPIONSHIPS EXPLODE

The first Pacific Coast Outdoor Volleyball Championships were held at Santa Monica Canyon State Beach in 1948. Manny Saenz teamed with Al Harris to win the title before 3,500 fans.

Many Southern California cities launched tournaments in the 1960s and the sport became popular statewide. The California Beach Volleyball Association was founded in 1965 and is the governing body for the sport.

California's most prestigious tournament is the Manhattan Beach Open, which started in 1960. Women joined the competition six years later. The tournament started as an amateur event, but is now part of the Association of Volleyball Professionals, the biggest pro beach tour in America. Over 60,000 fans attend the event. Karch Kiraly is the men's record holder with 10 wins, while Kathy Gregory and Kerri Walsh Jennings are tied with seven wins each for the women. Winners receive a volleyball shaped plaque in the Volleyball Walk of Fame spanning the length of the Manhattan Beach Pier.

Q: Who is the first California school to win the NCAA Beach Volleyball Championship?

For more on beach volleyball, visit www. californiasportsastounding.com

A: The USC Trojans coached by Anna Collier swept the Florida State Seminoles 3-0 to win the inaugural tournament in 2016. The Trojans repeated as champions in 2017 by edging Pepperdine 3-2.

CALIFORNIA SPORTS BIRTHDAYS
More Fun for November 2

Q: William "Little Bill" Johnston, born in 1894, is the first Californian to win the men's singles title in which Grand Slam tennis tournament?

. . . .

Did You Know?

The 2016 Olympic women's gold medal match was full of California players. Misty May-Treanor and Kerri Walsh Jennings won their record third consecutive gold medal when they defeated the team of Jennifer Kessy and April Ross 2-0.

A: Johnston, a San Francisco native, won the 1923 Wimbledon singles title. He was the runner-up In the U.S. Open a record six times.

NOTABLE BIRTHDAYS
November 2

1941: Dave Stockton, born in San Bernardino, professional golfer, PGA Championship winner in 1970 and 1976.

1952: Scott Boras, a native of Sacramento, sports agent specializing in baseball. University of the Pacific Athletics Hall of Fame inductee (baseball player) 1995.

LA 33
November 5, 1971

The Los Angeles Lakers named a new team captain before the game as Wilt Chamberlain replaced the retired Elgin Baylor, the only captain since the Lakers moved to California 11 years before. Chamberlain then hauled in 25 rebounds and guard Gail Goodrich poured in 31 points at the Forum as the Lakers topped the Baltimore Bullets 110-106. There were no losses for a while. A long while. The Forum Faithful had seen the start of the longest winning streak in major professional sports history: 33 wins.

Los Angeles racked up 69 wins during the regular season, then on May 7th 1972 they disposed of the New York Knicks for California's first NBA title.

THE NEXT GENERATION—BABY BOOMERS
Laker basketball dominated the NBA in the '80s as they earned titles in 1980, 1982, 1985, 1987, and 1988. The "Showtime" era had Magic Johnson, Kareem Abdul-Jabbar, James Worthy, and several other stars. A title drought lasted for over a decade.

THEN, GENERATION X
Coach Phil Jackson took over and the tandem of center Shaquille O'Neal and guard Kobe Bryant won titles from 2000 to 2002. O'Neal was traded, but Jackson and Bryant still added championships in 2009 and 2010. Kobe finished his 20-year Laker career in 2016 and the Lakers rebuilt their roster.

THE FOURTH GENERATION—MILLENNIALS
Three-time NBA champion forward LeBron James joined the team in 2018 followed by All-Star center Anthony Davis. The elite duo brought the Lakers another title in 2020. Playoff games were played in the NBA bubble in Orlando, an isolation zone to protect players from the COVID-19 pandemic. Lakers president Jeanie Buss made history as the first female controlling owner to guide her team to an NBA title.

Q: What team and future Laker ended the Lakers 33 game-winning streak?

For more basketball, visit www.californiasportsastounding.com

A: The Lakers lost on the road to the Milwaukee Bucks 120-104 on January 9, 1972. Bucks center Kareem Abdul-Jabbar dominated the Lakers with defense and scored 39 points. He would be traded to Los Angeles three years later and go on to win five NBA titles with the Lakers between 1980 and 1988.

CALIFORNIA SPORTS BIRTHDAYS
More Fun for November 5

Q: Bill Walton, born in 1952, two-time NBA champion and basketball hall of famer, and brother Bruce, NFL offensive lineman, are the first brother combination to set what record?

. . . .

Did You Know?

The 1971-1972 Los Angeles Lakers team had five basketball hall of famers: forward Elgin Baylor (1977), center Wilt Chamberlain (1979), and guards Jerry West (1980), Gail Goodrich (1996), and Pat Riley (2008).

A: Bill and Bruce Walton of San Diego are the first brother combination to play in the Super Bowl and win an NBA championship. Bruce played for the Dallas Cowboys in 1976, while Bill won the NBA title with the Portland Blazers the following year.

NOTABLE EVENT
November 5, 2016

Horse racing's Breeders' Cup was held at Santa Anita Park for a record ninth time and set an attendance record of 118,484 for the two-day event. The showcase event was the $6 million Breeder's Cup Classic between three-year-old Arrogate and North America's richest racehorse California Chrome. Arrogate, ridden by Mike Smith, rallied from six lengths behind to win by half a length. Smith recorded his 25th Breeder's Cup win. California Chrome was still voted 2016 Horse of the Year with wins in seven of eight starts and career earnings of over $14 million.

Trojan Tradition
November 14, 1888

USC's football team has played in 22 California cities from San Diego to Berkeley with some surprising results. Their grand tradition of football dates back to a home game in 1888. The Trojan media guide describes the first game played as between the University and the Alliance Athletic Club on a vacant field bordered by Grand, Hope, Eighth, and Ninth Streets, south of Bovard Field. The University, coached by Henry H. Goddard and Frank Suffel, and captained by Will Whitcomb, triumphed 16-0.

Howard Jones delivered the Trojans their first national title 40 years later when his 1928 team recorded a 9-0-1 record. Jones added five more championships between 1929 and 1939.

Twenty years later in 1959, *The Citizen-News* announced that "USC hired a talented but relatively obscure assistant, John McKay." The new hire revitalized the program and achieved national titles in 1962, 1967, 1972, and 1974. His halfback Mike Garrett became the first Trojan to win the Heisman Trophy. McKay often entertained the media with serious, humorous, and sarcastic quotes. When recruiting his son, Johnny "J.K.," he said, "I had a rather distinct advantage. I slept with his mother." In 1972, after his eventual national champions beat Stanford 31-20 on the road, he said, "I'd like to beat Stanford by 2,000 points. They have no class. They're the worst winners we've ever gone up against." Stanford head coach Jack Christiansen retorted with "I don't want to get into a urinating contest with a skunk."

USC has won over 500 games in Los Angeles since 1888 and owns one of the most intimidating home field advantages in college football. The Trojans have a winning record in most California cities, but not quite all. Ontario, Santa Ana, Riverside and Long Beach are on the winning side. The Chaffey College Panthers clawed the Trojans at Ontario 32-6 in 1893. Six years later Santa Ana High School playing at home shutout the University 11-0. USC played the Sherman Institute in Riverside and Long Beach in 1902 and 1904, but fell 28-0 and 17-0. Traveling to Claremont has resulted in a record of 3-3-3, including two ties in 1918, the first with the Whittier State School, and the second with the Pomona College Sagehens.

USC claims 11 national championships (1928, 1931, 1932, 1939, 1962, 1967, 1972, 1974, 1978, 2003, 2004). There were seven other years (1929, 1933, 1976, 1979, 2002, 2005, 2007) in which the Trojans were named a national champion by at least one legitimate poll. The national title list includes teams coached by Howard Jones, John McKay, John Robinson, and Pete Carroll.

Q: Which USC team and coach made history as the first to receive a unanimous first place vote in the polls by the Associated Press and United Press International?

For more football, visit www.californiasportsastounding.com

A: The 1972 team coached by John McKay finished 12-0. USC capped the season with a 42-17 rout of #3 Ohio State. Trojan fullback and game MVP Sam "Bam" Cunningham scored four touchdowns. Coach McKay won his 100th career game.

CALIFORNIA SPORTS BIRTHDAYS
More Fun for November 14

Q: Jim Brewer, born in 1937, won the 1965 World Series with what California team?

. . . .

Did You Know?

USC's last on-campus varsity football game was played on September 29, 1923, when they beat the Cal Tech Engineers 18-7 before about 10,000 fans at Bovard Field. The following week the Trojans played their first game at the Los Angeles Memorial Coliseum. USC squashed the Pomona Sagehens 23-7.

A: The Merced native pitched for the Los Angeles Dodgers.

NOTABLE EVENT
November 14, 1989

Livermore native Mark Davis won the National League Cy Young Award as a relief pitcher for the San Diego Padres.

Long Bridge and Catalina
November 19, 1876

Swimming pools, or tanks as they were called, appeared in California as early as 1861. The first newspaper account of a swimming race was an open water event at San Francisco's Long Bridge on November 19, 1876. The race was between Santa Cruz swimmer William H. Daily and Mexico's Alonzo Marino. *The Daily Alta California* reported of a "swimming race off Long Bridge in the presence of 3,000 spectators on Mission Wharf, and many on boats. The start was postponed until nearly two o'clock, and then made against the tide setting in; distance of 300 yards, from the wharf house, south, around a stake boat, and return." Daily won the race and was given an elegant gold medal by Mr. Munson of the Railroad Saloon.

CATALINA OR BUST

In Southern California, the newsworthy open water event was the first swim across the Catalina Channel on January 15, 1927. The course was from Avalon on Santa Catalina Island to Point Vicente, a distance of 22 miles, one mile further than the English Channel. 102 swimmers, including 15 women entered, but only one swimmer completed the crossing. George Young won the Wrigley Ocean Marathon swim in 15 hours, 44 minutes, and 30 seconds. An estimated crowd of over 15,000 fans watched him finish. Three days later Young was rewarded with a first place check of $25,000. The event was funded by chewing gum magnate William Wrigley Jr. who declared, "it was worth every penny spent to witness the magnificent effort of all the entrants and the remarkable achievement of Young."

Q: Who was the first woman to swim the Catalina Channel?

For more swimming, visit www.californiasportsastounding.com

A: Long Beach's Myrtle Huddleston swam the channel three weeks after Young. Myrtle, who only had a few months training, had a frightening swim. She was bitten four times by a barracuda, lost 17 pounds, drank whiskey during the swim, was lost in the heavy fog, and was carried back several miles due to adverse currents. Myrtle bled profusely and staggered onto the rocks, fell back into the water to be picked up by members of her party and placed in the convoy boat. Her swim was disputed because she drank alcohol. Nevertheless, she finished with a time of 20 hours and 42 minutes. So far, no movie has been made of the treacherous swim.

CALIFORNIA SPORTS BIRTHDAYS
More Fun for November 19

Q: James Lawrence Mora, born in Los Angeles, 1961, football coach, was a defensive coach with what two NFL teams from California?

....

Did You Know?

America's largest swim tank was dedicated on April 23, 1925. The Fleishhacker Pool in San Francisco opened in conjunction with the AAU national championships. The municipal outdoor saltwater pool was 1,000 feet long, 150 feet wide, and contained 6,500,000 gallons of water. Water was pumped, filtered and heated from the Pacific Ocean just 650 feet away. There was room for 10,000 bathers! The pool was so big that lifeguards patrolled the waters with rowboats. Costly repairs caused the pool to close in 1971.

San Diego's Florence Chadwick swam the Catalina Channel in 1952 in a time of 13:45:32, almost two hours faster than the men's record by George Young. Her crossing was televised by KNBH-TV, Channel 4. Chadwick had already made history as the first woman to swim the English Channel in both directions in 1950 and 1951.

A: Mora coached the San Diego Chargers defensive backs from 1985 to 1991. He was a defensive backs coach and coordinator with the San Francisco 49ers from 1997 to 2003.

NOTABLE BIRTHDAY
November 19, 1947

Bob Boone, born in San Diego, MLB catcher and manager, 1980 World Series champion, 4-time All-Star. Played for the California Angels 1982-1988.

Girl Ball-Kickers
November 19, 1892

The *San Francisco Call* provided the first record of a basket ball (originally spelled as two words) game on a college campus. The game they were playing was soccer. The lengthy title shouted "GIRL BALL-KICKERS. Berkeley Beauties Have a Glorious Game. THE SEMINARY MAIDENS WIN. They Defeat the Co-Eds in One of the Liveliest Tussles Girls Ever Engaged In."
The article recounted that:

"Nine of the best-looking "co-eds" are limping about the State University grounds covered all over with bruises, and nine pretty little maids, covered all over with glory are wasting their pin money on arnica and court plaster in Miss Head's fashionable seminary in Berkeley.

Mr. Magee, the instructor in physical culture, is responsible for it all, for it was he who, at an unguarded moment, introduced to his fair lady pupils the latest Eastern fad called "Basket-ball." Instructor Magee Innocently gave the girls a chance when he arranged two clothesbaskets, one on each end of the gymnasium, the other day. He produced a leather ball weighing about six pounds, and divided his fair pupils in physical culture into two teams of nine each. "Now, ladies, this game is called basketball and consists in one trying to put the ball into one of these baskets and the other crew doing everything possible to prevent the accomplishment of the feat. "The side that succeeds in basketing the ball the greatest number of times is the winner."

They were dressed, or costumed, in blue gymnasium costumes with gold ribbons. With various luck the score stood 4 to 4 after the eighth struggle, and my favorites, the little ones from the Head Seminary, who were called the "Kids" by the lofty co-eds, came out winners by landing the ball in a splendid manner. But, oh, how happy were they all, "Now we have a game that beats their old football all to pieces," they said, as they painfully filed out of that gymnasium, wrapped in cloaks to hide their torn costumes and shapely figures from the masculine eyes, for there was a company of students drilling on the campus."

Q: "Basketball" was originally described by California sportswriters as a mixture of what three sports?

For more basketball, visit www.californiasportsastounding.com

A: The *Chico Weekly Enterprise* on November 25, 1892 described "basketball" as a mixture of "polo, handball and football."

CALIFORNIA SPORTS BIRTHDAYS
More Fun for November 19

Q: David "Dave" Dunlap, born in 1910, rower, won an Olympic gold medal in the coxed eights at which Olympics: 1928, 1932, or 1936?

....

Did You Know?

BASKETBALL
Cheryl Miller of Riverside Polytechnic High School scored 105 points as the Bears mauled the Norte Vista High School Braves 179-15 on January 26, 1982. ESPN and NBC televised the game at Riverside's home court.

SNOWBOARDING
The first World Snowboarding Championships were held at Soda Springs in 1983. This is recognized as the first snowboard halfpipe contest. Tom Sims, founder of Sims Snowboards and a world champion skateboarder, organized the event with Mike Chantry, a snowboard instructor at Soda Springs.

San Diego's Shaun White won three gold medals in snowboarding in the halfpipe event at the Winter Olympics from 2006-2018.

A: The Napa native won the medal at the 1932 Olympics held in Los Angeles.

NOTABLE EVENT
November 19, 2019

LeBron James tallied 25 points, 11 rebounds, and 10 assists as the Los Angeles Lakers quieted the Oklahoma City Thunder, 112-107. James became the first player in NBA history to record a triple-double against all 30 franchises.

Indoor Baseball
November 20, 1891

The first reference to indoor baseball, which is now known as fast pitch softball, appeared in the *Los Angeles Herald* which announced, "The public will have a chance to see a game of indoor baseball at Hazard's pavilion next Tuesday night, between the Tufts-Lyons and the Los Angeles club. This will be the first indoor game of baseball ever played in this state."

Q: When was the first NCAA Division I Softball Championship held in California?

For more softball, visit www.californiasportsastounding.com

A: The tournament was held at the Twin Creeks Sports Complex in Sunnyvale on May 29, 1988. UCLA pitcher Lisa Longaker shutout Fresno State 3-0. The tournament returned to Sunnyvale in 1989. UCLA repeated as champions by beating Fresno State 1-0 with strong pitching from Tiffany Boyd. California never hosted the tournament again because the NCAA moved to a permanent site in Oklahoma City.

CALIFORNIA SPORTS BIRTHDAYS
More Fun for November 20

Q: Haley Anderson, born in 1991, open water swimmer, is an Olympic medalist in what event?

. . . .

Did You Know?

Softball coach Jim Liggett guided Carlmont High School in Belmont to a state record 1,009 victories from 1976 to 2016. He finished his career with an 82.3 percent winning percentage.

A: The Santa Clara native won a silver medal in the 10-kilometer event at the 2012 Olympics.

NOTABLE EVENT
THE PLAY
STANFORD VS. CALIFORNIA AT MEMORIAL STADIUM

November 20, 1982

The Stanford football team had just scored and led California 20-19 in the 85th Big Game with four seconds left. Stanford quarterback John Elway's last game was almost over. Just stop the Golden Bears kickoff return and game over, right? What happened next was The Play, the nickname for one of the most memorable plays in college football history. California, short one player on their return team, fielded the kickoff. Kevin Moen started a five lateral play with teammates Richard Rogers, Dwight Garner, and Mariet Ford. Was this play legal? The third lateral from Garner to Rogers was controversial because Stanford players claimed that Garner's knee touched the ground while he was still in possession of the ball. Did he graze the turf? Garner asserted he did not. TV replays were inconclusive. The NCAA did not implement instant replay rules till 2005.

The final lateral was from Ford to Moen who ran the last 25 yards. But by then all 144 Stanford Band members, some cheerleaders, plus at least 11 illegal players were on the field. Moen weaved through the band members, then finished his run by colliding with Stanford trombone player trombone player Gary Tyrrell. California had scored an astounding 25-20 win.

The dispute between the two rivals continues. Winner of the Big Game is awarded a trophy known as the Stanford Axe. Whenever Stanford holds the Stanford Axe, the plaque is altered in protest so that the outcome reads as a 20–19 Stanford victory. When Cal keeps the Axe, the plaque is changed back to the official score of California 25 Stanford 20.

Mission Dolores Wrestling
November 24, 1851

Mission Dolores in San Francisco was the site of the first and very quick wrestling match. The *Daily Alta California* described it as, "The principal attraction was the wrestling match between Ira Cole and Mr. Wilson. The match was for five hundred dollars a side, and to be decided by the two throws out of three. Cole threw Wilson to the mat without any difficulty. The time employed for two rounds was not more than four minutes. Wrestling is a manly art, and if people will desire such amusements on Sunday, it is much better than the brutal bull and bear fights that appear to have become very popular of late. It is a test of skill and strength, and, under proper circumstances, wrestling matches might be made very interesting."

INTERESTING WRESTLING UPDATES

Darrell Vasquez made history in 2002 as the first CIF four-time high school state champion. His Bakersfield High School Drillers set a state record of 226.5 points to win the team title.

Several California wrestlers have earned gold medals at the Olympics. Brothers Dave and Mark Schultz won the 74 kg and 82 kg freestyle gold at the 1984 Olympics in Los Angeles. Henry Cejudo earned a gold medal at the 2008 Olympics in the 55 kg division, while four years later Bakersfield's Jake Varner took the 96 kg freestyle crown.

Q: Who is the first American woman to win an Olympic medal in wrestling: Patricia Miranda or Randi Miller?

For more wrestling, visit www.californiasportsastounding.com

A: Manteca native Patricia Miranda won the bronze medal at the 2004 Olympics in the 48 kg (105.8 lbs.) weight class. Randi Miller of Berkeley won a bronze medal in the 63 kg (138 lbs.) weight class at the 2008 Olympics.

CALIFORNIA SPORTS BIRTHDAYS
More Fun for November 24

Q: David Hansen, born in 1968, MLB infielder and pinch hitter, set what Major League record in 2000?

....

Did You Know?

Stephen Abas of Logan High School in Union City set a state record with 406 takedowns during the 1995 season. He went on to become a three-time NCAA Division I wrestling champion in the 125 pound weight division at Fresno State. Stephen won a silver medal wrestling in the 121 pound weight division at the 2004 Olympic Games.

A: The Long Beach native hit seven pinch hit home runs for the Los Angeles Dodgers. His record was tied a year later by fellow Californian Craig Wilson who played for the Pittsburgh Pirates.

NOTABLE EVENT
November 24, 1970

Stanford quarterback Jim Plunkett was named the winner of the Heisman Trophy as the most outstanding player in college football.

NOTABLE BIRTHDAY
November 24, 1979

Carmelita Jeter, born in Los Angeles, sprinter, won three gold medals in the 4 x 100-meter relay and 100-meters at the World Championships 2007-2011. She also won Olympic gold, silver, and bronze at the 2012 Olympics competing in the 100 and 200 meters, plus the 4 x 100-meter relay.

Spartans Supremacy
November 26, 1962

The San Jose State Spartans coached by Dean Miller became the first integrated team to win the NCAA Division I Cross Country Title. These Spartans were ready for the challenge. Coach Miller had prepped the team with training sessions running up 4,265-foot Mount Hamilton, a mountain in the nearby Diablo Range. They were also the first California team to win the crown.

Danny Murphy was the top Spartan finisher in third place, followed by Ron Davis, Jeff Fishback, Ben Tucker, and Horace Whitehead. The Black runners Davis, Tucker, and Whitehead overcame frequent racial slurs, tossed beer cans on road runs, and housing discrimination just to make it to the starting line. They ignored the racism and had supportive teammates. The result? An 11-point victory over the runner-up Villanova Wildcats.

Spartan runners repeated as champs in 1963 with a 15-point victory over the Oregon Ducks. Fishback, Murphy, and Tucker dominated by finishing third, fifth, and eighth. Coach Miller had rejected prejudiced comments about his team all season long. He said "I don't care if they're black, white, striped, or polka dot. All I'm interested in is how fast they can run, how far they can run, and whether they're willing to commit physically and mentally to being a champion. We run seven days a week, 365 days a year. I think we set a precedent."

Q: Where did Dean Miller coach before arriving at San Jose State?

For more cross country, visit www.californiasportsastounding.com

A: Mira Costa High School in Manhattan Beach. He recruited Danny Murphy from that team to join him at San Jose State.

CALIFORNIA SPORTS BIRTHDAYS
More Fun for November 26

Q: Lynne Jewell, born in 1959, sailor, won a gold medal in what two person sailing event at the 1988 Olympics: catamaran, laser, or dinghy?

. . . .

Did You Know?

California's first yacht club was founded in San Diego on March 6, 1852.

Major J. McKinstry, United States Army, Judson Ames, Esq., and John C. Cremony, Esq., were the organizers of the Pacific Pioneer Yacht Club. The news traveled statewide, with the *Daily Alta* and the *Sacramento Union* reporting that "The first Yacht Club on the Pacific coast has been established at San Diego." It is unclear when the club ceased.

The San Francisco Yacht Club, founded in 1869, is the oldest operating yacht club west of the Mississippi River. Based in tranquil Belvedere Cove, the SFYC is one of the most elegant and exclusive yacht clubs in America. The club has hosted local, national, and international regattas.

A: The native of Burbank won a gold medal in the women's two-person dinghy with teammate Allison Jolly. The duo sailed past competition from 21 countries.

NOTABLE BIRTHDAYS
November 26

1908: Lefty Gomez, born in Rodeo, MLB pitcher, 5-time World Series champion and 7-time All-Star for the New York Yankees from 1930-1942. National Baseball Hall of Fame inductee 1972.

1956: Marty Smith, born in San Diego, professional motocross racer, American Motorcyclist Association 125cc champion 1974 and 1975, 500 cc in 1977, inducted into the AMA Motorcycle Hall of Fame in 2000.

Ancient Sport
November 28, 1895

The first newspaper reference after statehood to this ancient sport appeared in the *Sacramento Transcript*. On September 12, 1850, the paper reported on horse racing and the $1,000 purse at the Union Race Course. "A match of much interest comes off to-day between Warner's famed mare and a horse owned by Mr. Vischer. The mare's exploits have rendered her the favorite, but the "sporting gents" have been so bit of late that we have no faith in their judgment."

1890S MODERN RACETRACK OPENS

California's first modern racetrack opened on Thanksgiving Day 1895. The Ingleside Racetrack impressed sportswriters. The *San Francisco Call* proclaimed, "California is to be congratulated on having a racecourse fit for the "sport of kings" and one that compares favorably with any in the country."

Fans reached the new venue mostly by steam cars and the electric trolley line. Both hauled their cars over new roadbeds for the first time. The steam cars from Third and Townsend streets carried 1,200 people each trip and reached the track in twenty-four minutes. The electric cars carried 140 people at one load and took fifty minutes from Third and Mission streets. The more adventurous fans used the wagon road and tied up their carriages, buggies, and coaches to trees and posts.

An estimated 12,000 fans enjoyed the inaugural festivities. First winner on the new track was Semper Lex, in the Palace Hotel Stakes. The Pacific Coast Jockey Club managed the racetrack. The track hosted races till December 30 of 1905, four months before the Great Earthquake.

Q: What other major racetrack opened in the Bay Area before 1900?

For more horse racing, visit www.californiasportsastounding.com

A: San Bruno's Tanforan Racetrack opened on September 4, 1899. Racing lasted till 1964, when a fire destroyed the facility.

CALIFORNIA SPORTS BIRTHDAYS
More Fun for November 28

Q: Whitney Engen, born in 1987, is a World Cup champion in what sport: softball, volleyball, or soccer?

. . . .

Did You Know?

San Mateo's Bay Meadows Racetrack and Santa Anita Park in Arcadia opened up less than two months apart. Bay Meadows opened on November 13, 1934 and Santa Anita followed on Christmas Day of that year.

"Swaps," was the first California thoroughbred elected to the National Museum of Racing and Hall of Fame in 1966. The earliest horse from California in the Hall is the "Emperor of Norfolk." The "California Wonder" raced from 1887 to 1888, but was not inducted until 100 years later in 1988.

A: Soccer. Whitney, a native of Torrance, played defender and helped the U.S. win the FIFA Women's World Cup in 2015.

NOTABLE BIRTHDAY
November 28, 1969

Robb Nen, born in San Pedro, MLB pitcher, 1997 World Series champion with the Florida Marlins, three-time All-Star with the San Francisco Giants 1998, 1999, and 2002. San Francisco Giants Wall of Fame inductee 2008.

Sharp-Pointed Missiles
November 29, 1896

This sport requires that players bare-handedly throw small sharp-pointed missiles at a round target. Originating in Europe, it took almost 40 years to reach California's shores.

The *Los Angeles Times* published the first reference with the article, "The Game of Darts." Subtitled "An Amusing and Inexpensive Pastime for Half-Holidays," the article described it as, "There are very few practical games that a boy of small means can get up for the entertainment of his friends without any expense, or which do not require a roomy playground. Here is an instructive game that will afford many hours of amusement, will cost nothing to make up, can be played as well in a small yard as on an extensive lawn, and is easily prepared by any boy."

TOSSING TOURNAMENTS CAME LATER

California's first major tournament lasted from 1970 to 1999. The North American Open Dart Tournament was hosted by the Southern California Darts Association and held at the Veteran's Auditorium in Culver City. 250 players vied for $2,000 in prize money. John Lowe and Stacy Bromberg dominated the tournament for several years, winning 12 and 14 titles in the men's and women's divisions. The final tournament attracted over 2,000 players from 48 states and a purse of $45,000.

Sacramento's Camellia Classic is one of the leading tournaments statewide. The tournament started in 1977 and is organized by the Sacramento Valley Darting Association.

Q: Who is the first California woman to win the singles title at the World Cup of Darts?

For more darts, visit www.californiasportsastounding.com

A: Torrance native Sandy Reitan won the 1983 World Cup held in Scotland.

CALIFORNIA SPORTS BIRTHDAYS
More Fun for November 29

Q: Jim Derrington, born in 1939, MLB pitcher, set what major league record on September 30, 1956 playing for the Chicago White Sox?

....

Did You Know?

Tom Fleetwood of Bellflower helped cofound the American Dart Organization in 1976 which started with 30 clubs and 7,500 players. The Southern California Darts Association which had started in 1963, was a charter member. ADO has grown to over 250 clubs and over 50,000 members.

The standard distance in darts is 7 feet 9.25 inches from the throwing line to the front face of the dart board. Dartboards are hung on the wall with the center of the bullseye at five foot eight inches from the floor, a height established based on the eye level of a six-foot man.

A: The native of Compton was the youngest starting pitcher at 16 years and 306 days. He lost the game 7-6 to the Kansas City Athletics.

NOTABLE EVENT
November 29, 1966

The San Francisco Warriors outlasted the Chicago Bulls 108-101 in the first NBA game played at the new Oakland-Alameda County Coliseum Arena.

NOTABLE BIRTHDAY
November 29, 1974

Michael Penberthy, born in Los Gatos, NBA guard, won NBA titles with the Los Angeles Lakers in 2001 as a player and 2020 as an assistant coach.

DECEMBER
DYNAMIC

PacWest in CA
December 1, 1992

When the PacWest conference lost two members in 2005, it ceased to be a NCAA recognized conference. The Pacific West Conference was originally formed in 1992 when the Great Northwest Conference, a men's conference, merged with the Continental Divide Conference, a women's conference containing some of the same members.

In 2006, Notre Dame de Namur University became the first California school to join the new PacWest conference and it was reinstated by the NCAA as a Division II conference.

Conference expansion and contraction have resulted in 11 members, with eight in California. These are the Academy of Art University Urban Knights, Azusa Pacific University Cougars, Biola University Eagles, Concordia University Irvine Eagles, Dominican University of California Penguins, Fresno Pacific University Sunbirds, Holy Names University Hawks, and Point Loma Nazarene University Sea Lions. The remaining three members are in Hawaii. All PacWest schools have full NCAA Division II status.

Azusa Pacific is the most successful California member with over 30 conference titles since joining in 2012. Cougar teams have dominated women's cross country, men's indoor and outdoor track and field, women's outdoor track and field, and men's tennis. The Cougars ended their football program in 2020 due to fiscal constraints. Azusa Pacific was the only NCAA Division II school in California with a football program.

Q: The PacWest Conference is based in what city: San Francisco, Irvine, or Los Angeles?

For more PacWest and other college conferences, visit www. californiasportsastounding.com

A: Irvine

CALIFORNIA SPORTS BIRTHDAYS
More Fun for December 1

Q: Jennifer Fetter Isler, born in 1963, yachtswoman, two-time Olympic medalist, world champion, is the first woman inductee of which hall of fame?

. . . .

Did You Know?

The PacWest's largest basketball arena is the Kezar Pavilion, home court of the Academy of Art Urban Knights. The indoor arena in Golden Gate Park has a seating capacity of 4,000 and was built in 1924.

A: The La Jolla native joined the Sailing World Hall of Fame in 2005. She was also inducted into the National Sailing Hall of Fame in 2015.

NOTABLE BIRTHDAYS
December 1

1912: Harry "Cookie" Lavagetto, Oakland native, MLB infielder, All-Star with the Brooklyn Dodgers 1938 to 1941, nicknamed "Cookie" by Oakland Oaks president Victor "Cookie" Devincenzi when he played for the Pacific Coast League baseball team in 1933.

1979: Stephanie Trafton, San Luis Obispo native, first California-born Olympic gold medalist in the discus at the 2008 Olympics.

NOTABLE EVENT
December 1, 1974

Jacqueline Hansen of the San Fernando Valley Track Club set a women's world best time of 2:43:54.6 in the Western Hemisphere Marathon in Culver City.

PCC to Conference of Champions
December 2, 1915

The path from Pacific Coast Conference to Pac-12 went through four names and several members. The PCC was founded at a meeting at the Imperial Hotel in Portland. Four schools, the University of California at Berkeley, the University of Oregon, the University of Washington, and Oregon Agricultural College (now Oregon State University) joined as charter members. The *Los Angeles Herald* reported that Cal graduate manager "Johnny Stroud of the Bears is looking after the interests of the University of California."

Pacific Coast Conference play began in 1916 and, one year later, Washington State College (now Washington State University) was accepted into the league, with Stanford University following in 1918. The PCC expanded to eight teams in 1922 with the admission of the University of Southern California and the University of Idaho. In 1924, the University of Montana joined the league roster and in 1928, the PCC grew to 10 members with the addition of UCLA.

The PCC disbanded in 1959 and was replaced by the Athletic Association of Western Universities from 1959 to 1968, the Pacific-8 from 1968 to 1978, the Pac-10 from 1978 to 2011 to reflect the addition of Arizona and Arizona State, and finally the Pac-12 after Utah and Colorado joined on July 1, 2011.

OVER 500 NCAA CHAMPIONSHIPS

California's four members remain the California Golden Bears, Stanford Cardinal, UCLA Bruins, and USC Trojans. The Pac-12's nickname is "Conference of Champions" since it has won more NCAA national team titles than any other conference. Stanford, UCLA, and USC have the most NCAA team titles in history. The trio have over 100 NCAA Division I championships each, more than twice the amount of the fourth highest university. Stanford University has dominated the Directors' Cup, given annually by the National Association of Collegiate Directors of Athletics to the most successful school in collegiate athletics. The Cardinal won over 25 consecutive Cups starting in 1994. The Pac-12 sponsors 24 sports, 11 for men, and 13 for women.

Q: Which Pac-12 school won the 500th NCAA title in conference history?

For more Pac-12 and other college conferences, visit www. californiasportsastounding.com

A: The University of Washington Huskies won the NCAA Division I Women's Rowing Championships on May 31, 2017. Defending champion California finished second.

CALIFORNIA SPORTS BIRTHDAYS
More Fun for December 2

Q: John "Sevo" Severson Jr., born in 1933, surfer, editor, author, artist, photographer, filmmaker, founded which monthly magazine?

....

Did You Know?

UCLA became the first school to win 100 NCAA Division I titles as the women's water polo team beat Stanford 5-4 at the Joint Forces Training Base - Los Alamitos on May 13, 2007. Bruins coach Adam Krikorian was in the middle of a five-year reign as NCAA champions from 2005-2009.

A: *Surfer* magazine. Severson, a Los Angeles native, was a Surfing Hall of Fame inductee in 1991. He received the Surfer Poll Lifetime Achievement Award in 2011. The magazine ended publication in 2020.

NOTABLE BIRTHDAY
December 2, 1968

Darryl Kile, born in Garden Grove, MLB pitcher, pitched the final no-hitter at the Houston Astrodome with a 7-1 win for the Astros over the New York Mets on September 8, 1993. Plate umpire Edward Montague, a San Francisco native, officiated the game.

Anita Place to Race Horses
December 7, 1907

California's largest horse racing venue opened in 1907. The *Los Angeles Herald* predicted that when the racetrack opens the "Sport of Kings" will be placed on a higher plane in California than ever before." An advertisement before opening day by the Los Angeles Racing Association touted the "Most beautiful racing park in America and the best class of horses ever brought to the Pacific Coast."

Fans traveled from Los Angeles through miles of lemon and orange groves, with a view of mountains in the background. The track was located in Arcadia at a ranch owned by Elias "Lucky" Baldwin. Admission was $1. The featured race of the day was the Pomona Handicap. Marc Anthony, ridden by G. Burns, won $2,050 for first place.

Horse racing at Santa Anita Park lasted till 1909 when the California Legislature outlawed the sport. The venue's grandstand burned to the ground in 1912. Voters approved legalizing pari-mutuel wagering on horse racing on June 27, 1933 and two months later the first bets were placed on races at the San Joaquin County Fair in Stockton. Santa Anita reopened on Christmas Day 1934. The first Santa Anita Handicap was held two months later in February and offered $100,000 making it the richest horse race in American history at the time. Seabiscuit raced to victory in the 1940 race after two failed attempts. 1940 also included the introduction of the starting gate.

World War II interrupted racing in 1942. Racing resumed in 1945 and the venue established itself as one of America's greatest racetracks. Among the elite horses that raced there were 1978 Triple Crown winner Affirmed, John Henry who won two Santa Anita Handicaps, and Spectacular Bid, who went undefeated in 1980.

Santa Anita was the preferred track for several great jockeys, including Hall of Famers such as Laffit Pincay Jr. and Bill Shoemaker. The equestrian events of the 1984 Olympics were held at Santa Anita. Two years later, the track hosted the first of several Breeders Cup World Championships. In 2016, the event drew a record two-day attendance figure of 118,484.

Q: What Los Angeles horse racing venue opened four years before Santa Anita Park?

For more horse racing, visit www.californiasportsastounding.com

A: Ascot Park opened on Slauson Avenue in Los Angeles on Christmas Eve 1903 as the "Finest Race Course West of New York." The venue lasted until March 30, 1907. Los Angeles incorporated some land into its city limits that included the racetrack, but city law prohibited gambling so Ascot Park closed.

CALIFORNIA SPORTS BIRTHDAYS
More Fun for December 7

Q: Bennie Edens, born in 1925, coached football for 48 years at which Southern California high school: Long Beach Poly, Mater Dei, or Point Loma?

. . . .

Did You Know?

The first California-born jockey to win the Santa Anita Handicap was Corey Nakatani of Covina in 2000. Corey won aboard General Challenge, owned by John Mabee of Golden Eagle Farm in Ramona. Nakatani also raced at Del Mar and compiled over 100 stakes victories there from 1991-2017. He ranks among the top 15 jockeys of all time with earnings of over $234 million.

Santa Anita Park with a capacity of 85,000 and the Del Mar Thoroughbred Club at 44,000 are the two largest horse racing venues in the Western United States.

A: Edens, a San Diego native, coached the Point Loma High School Pointers from 1950 to 1998. He was named the 1981 California Athletic Director of the Year, 1992 California High School Coach of the Year, and 2002 NFL High School Coach of the Year. Edens coached several future NFL stars such as cornerback Eric Allen, defensive tackle La'Roi Glover, and receiver J.J. Stokes.

DLS 151
December 7, 1991

Bob Ladacouer's Spartan football team had just lost to the Pittsburg High School Pirates 35-27 at the Oakland Coliseum. The loss in the North Coast Section class 3A championship game broke a 34-game winning streak for his team. The Spartan's were attempting a comeback as the Pirates held a precarious 28-27 lead. That's when their running back/defensive back Percy McGee intercepted a Spartan pass and returned it 77 yards with 2:09 remaining and sealed the win. Bob's team had lost only five times in the previous seven years by a combined total of just 12 points.

It was time to start a new winning streak. He had nine long months until the 1992 season started. That next game started an unprecedented football winning streak in American high school history.

Previously, Michigan's Hudson High School Tigers owned the national record of 72 consecutive wins. Bob Ladouceur and the De La Salle Spartans more than doubled that achievement. They kept winning all through the end of the 2003 season. The 2004 season opener was on the road against the Bellevue High School Wolverines before 24,987 fans at Seattle's Qwest Field. Finally, after 151 games, the Spartans lost. The 39-20 defeat ended an era. His teams were voted 11-time national champions between 1994 and 2012 by various media, but more wins were on the horizon.

Bob coached California state football champions in 2007, 2009, 2010, 2011, and 2012. He retired in 2013 with a record of 399-25-3 as California's all-time winningest high school football coach.

Q: When was the first winning football season in De La Salle history?

For more football, visit www.californiasportsastounding.com

A: 1979 when 25-year-old Bob Ladouceur coached the team to a record of 6-3.

CALIFORNIA SPORTS BIRTHDAYS
More Fun for December 7

Q: Kyle Hendricks, born in 1989, MLB pitcher, 2016 World Series champion with the Chicago Cubs. What is his nickname?

. . . .

Did You Know? Part 1

The De La Salle Spartans won over 310 consecutive football games against Northern California teams beginning in 1991. The Spartans are a member of the East Bay Athletic League, but do not compete for the league title in football.

A: The Newport Beach native is nicknamed "The Professor."

. . . .

Did You Know? Part 2

The *San Francisco Examiner* announced their 1993 San Francisco-Prep Metro All-Star Football Team. Jayce of Goree of Oakland High School was named Player of the Year.

Goree led his team to the Oakland Section Silver Bowl Championship with a 11-1 record. Also named first team quarterback was Cy Simonton of Pittsburg High School. Honorable mention went to quarterback Tom Brady and wide receiver Chris McLaughlin of Serra High School. Brady went on to play at the University of Michigan and the NFL. His astounding career includes winning a record seven Super Bowls between 2002-2021.

NOTABLE BIRTHDAY
December 7, 1963

Shane Mack, born in Los Angeles, MLB outfielder, competed in the 1984 Olympic demonstration baseball tournament at Dodger Stadium, 1991 World Series champion with the Minnesota Twins.

Marvelous Miners
December 9, 1949

San Francisco's team in the All-American Football Conference moved to the National Football League in 1949 when the leagues merged on December 9, 1949. Their first NFL game was on September 17, 1950 when they lost to the New York Yanks 21-17 at Kezar Stadium.

Tony Morabito owned the team along with partners in the Lumber Terminals of San Francisco Allen E. Sorrell, E.J. Turre and brother Victor. Morabito, a San Francisco native, had played football at St. Ignatius High School and the University of Santa Clara before injuries ended his athletic career. His partner Sorrell named the team "49ers" after the voyagers who had rushed to the West for gold. Morabito is credited with bringing San Francisco its first major league professional sports franchise, several years ahead of pro baseball, basketball, and hockey.

The 49ers were the NFL's team of the '80s, winning Super Bowls XVI (1981), XIX (1984), XXIII (1988), and XXIV (1989). Head coaches Bill Walsh engineered the famed "West Coast Offense," that was ahead of its time. Quarterback Joe Montana ran the offense. All-Pro cornerback/safety Ronnie Lott provided the backbone of their tenacious defense. San Francisco added Super Bowl XXIX (1994) to their trophy case as quarterback Steve Young directed a 49-26 pounding of the San Diego Chargers and set a Super Bowl single game record of six touchdown passes.

Many stadiums have housed the team over the years. Kezar Stadium was home for the 49ers from 1946 to 1970, then Candlestick Park 1971 to 2013. The Loma Prieta earthquake forced a one game move to Stanford Stadium in 1989. The 49ers moved to Santa Clara and settled into the new Levi's Stadium in September of 2014.

Q: What was the name of the San Francisco 49ers cheerleading team when they played at Kezar Stadium?

For more football, visit www.californiasportsastounding.com

A: The Niner Nuggets, which were known as the only singing cheerleader squad in the NFL. They are now called the Gold Rush Cheerleaders.

CALIFORNIA SPORTS BIRTHDAYS
More Fun for December 9

Q: Sheryl Johnson, born in 1957, field hockey player, won an Olympic bronze medal in what year?

· ·

Did You Know?

The San Francisco 49ers, Los Angeles Dons—an All-America Football Conference team that folded in 1949—and the NFL's Los Angeles Rams were the first California teams to play a "big four" (MLB, NBA, NFL, NHL) sport.

A: The Palo Alto native won a bronze medal at the 1984 Olympics held in Los Angeles. Johnson was inducted into the USA Field Hockey Hall of Fame in 1994.

NOTABLE EVENT
December 9, 1985

San Francisco 49er wide receiver Jerry Rice began a National Football League streak of 274 consecutive games with a reception in a 27-20 loss to the Los Angeles Rams at Candlestick Park. Rice finished the game with 10 receptions for 241 yards and a 66-yard touchdown pass from Joe Montana. His streak ended almost 19 years later in September of 2004.

NOTABLE BIRTHDAY
December 9, 1995

McKayla Maroney, born in Aliso Viejo, gymnast, 2012 Olympic gold medalist in team competition and silver medalist in vault.

Indoors and Out
December 10, 1881

The *Los Angeles Times*, which initially published under the name of the *Los Angeles Daily Times*, printed its first sports column just six days after the paper's debut on December 4, 1881. The first column was spelled as "Indoor and Out," which was changed to "Indoors and Out" the following week. Readers were entertained with a "Review of the Past Week's Sporting Happenings." This is evidently the first regularly published sports column in Southern California, though several newspapers had limited sports coverage from statehood till 1881. Among the Southern California newspapers were the *Los Angeles Star* in 1851, *San Diego Union* (1868), *Los Angeles Express* (1871) and the *Los Angeles Herald* (1873). Northern California newspapers included the *Sacramento Union* from 1851, San Francisco's *Evening Bulletin* in 1855, and the *Morning Call* the following year.

Q: Which Northern California newspaper published a weekly sports column as early as 1884: *Daily Alta California* or the *Daily Examiner*?

For more sports, visit californiasportsastounding.com

A: The *Daily Alta California* published the column Sports and Sporting on July 20, 1884.

CALIFORNIA SPORTS BIRTHDAYS
More Fun for December 10

Q: Rachel Fattal, born in 1993, water polo player, won gold medals at which two Olympics?

Did You Know?

The *Los Angeles Times* published their first distinct Sunday sports section on August 30, 1903. The actual name was the "Sporting Section" and was four pages long. Editors declared that "events of local and general interest in the broad fields of sport, amusement and recreation will be placed before readers in compact form. Los Angeles is becoming more and more a sporting center. Readers will find pleasure in the Sporting Section, and the part, complete in itself, can be detached for individual use."

Plenty of sports were covered including baseball, boxing, fishing, golf, horse racing, hunting and tennis. Bowling was also popular. The paper reported that "Interest in bowling is increasing. Cool weather has brought men to their best. Mrs. F.N. Porter of Los Angeles made a score of 220 on the Coronado alleys of that city. It is the highest score at ten pins ever made on this coast by a lady."

A: The native of Seal Beach won gold at the 2016 and 2020 Olympics for Team USA.

NOTABLE EVENT
December 10, 2019

Garden Grove native Troy Polamalu was inducted into the College Football Hall of Fame. USC strong safety and All-American in 2002. Named to the NFL Pro Bowl eight times from 2004-2013. Super Bowl champion XL and XLIII with the Pittsburgh Steelers.

Round Ball
December 15, 1900

This team sport played with a round ball between two teams of 11 players became popular in California as early as 1900. The first newspaper article about soccer appeared in the *San Francisco Call* with a headline in all caps: "WANDERERS AND VAMPIRES PLAY A "SOCCER" GAME. The Vampires of San Francisco will play a match of association football, or "soccer" as enthusiasts term it, this afternoon on the Presidio athletic grounds against the Oakland Wanderers, captained by Douglas Erskine."

Soccer became popular quickly, and by 1902 there were several clubs in Los Angeles, Sacramento, and San Francisco. That same year the growth led to the formation of the California State Football Association. The San Francisco Soccer League was founded in 1902 and remains the oldest American soccer league in continuous existence. Notable teams still in existence include the Olympic Club formed in 1916, the San Francisco Italian Athletic Club founded a year later, and the San Francisco Vikings Soccer Club formed in 1922.

One of America's oldest state tournaments started in 1904. Originally called the California State Senior Challenge Cup, it is now known as the State Cup. This tournament was instrumental in growing the sport statewide.

Q: Who was the first California school to win the NCAA Division I Men's Soccer Championship?

For more soccer, visit www.californiasportsastounding.com

A: The University of San Francisco Dons beat the Long Island University Blackbirds 5-2 at California's Memorial Stadium on December 3, 1966. The Dons finished their season 11-0-1, their tie with the California Golden Bears in a game played at San Francisco's Balboa Stadium.

CALIFORNIA SPORTS BIRTHDAYS
More Fun for December 15

Q: Jason Brown, born in 1994, figure skater, won an Olympic bronze medal in what event?

. . . .

Did You Know?

John Velho of Richmond High School set a boys national soccer record with 158 assists during his career from 1984 to 1987.

Kelly Berkemeier, goalkeeper for St. Mary's High School in Stockton, set a girls national soccer record with 32 shutouts during the 1999 season.

A: The Los Angeles native won bronze in the team event at the 2014 Winter Olympics.

NOTABLE EVENT
December 15, 2019

The Jacksonville Jaguars rallied to beat the Oakland Raiders 20-16 in the final scheduled game at the Oakland Coliseum. A little over a month later, on January 22, 2020, Oakland was officially renamed the Las Vegas Raiders and moved to Nevada.

NOTABLE BIRTHDAY
December 15, 1987

Mikey Garcia, born in Oxnard, professional boxer, trained at La Colina Youth Boxing Club, held world championships in four different weight classes 2010-2018.

Pinch, Punch, Kick, Choke, and Jab
December 26, 1909

A Japanese martial art involving takedowns, pins, and chokeholds arrived in California just before 1910.

The earliest reference to judo in California was in the *Los Angeles Times*, which wrote about a match between Eddie Robinson and an unnamed Japanese opponent. Judo was described as "rough stuff pure and simple and a combination of brutal football playing, rough house wrestling, and prize fighting combined, added to all the possessed by a quick, alert man who knows the weak points of the muscles and the location of the nerve centers. In judo one can pinch, punch, kick, choke, jab the eyes with the fingers, trip up and make helpless in any way, shape, or form."

Jigoro Kano of Japan, the founder of judo, exhibited the sport during his visit to San Francisco in 1912. Judo then spread to Bakersfield, Fresno, and Sacramento in the 1930s.

YOSHI UCHIDA BUILDS A POWERHOUSE

San Jose became California's judo hub behind the work of Yoshi Uchida. He started the judo program at San Jose State University in 1946 and coached into a national powerhouse. The Spartans dominated the first National Collegiate Judo Association national championship in 1962 and now have over 50 titles. Uchida coached the Spartans for over 70 years and was the USA head coach at the first Olympic Judo Tournament in 1964. That team included San Jose State judoka Ben Nighthorse Campbell, the first Native American on the judo team, and Paul Maruyama, who coached the USA judo team at the 1984 Olympics in Los Angeles.

Q: Who is the only other California school to win the NCJA national title?

For more judo, visit www.californiasportsastounding.com

A: The Fresno State Bulldogs won championships in 1985 and 1988.

CALIFORNIA SPORTS BIRTHDAYS
More Fun for December 26

Q: Glenn "Mr. Outside" Davis, born in 1924, Army football halfback, 1946 Heisman Trophy winner. What high school stadium was dedicated in his name?

. . . .

Did You Know?

Dr. Henry Stone, Chairman of the Physical Education Department and wrestling coach at UC Berkeley, teamed with Yoshi Uchida to improve the sport of judo. He introduced weight classes at senior level contests and convinced International Olympic Committee President Avery Brundage to approve the entry of judo at the 1964 Olympics. Stone was the first Chairman of the AAU National Judo Committee. Dr. Stone organized and was the first president of the Amateur Judo Association.

San Jose State University is one of six USA Judo National Training Sites. The building on the San Jose State campus that houses the judo dojo was renamed Yoshihiro Uchida Hall in 1997.

A: Davis was born in Claremont and attended Bonita High School in La Verne. In 1989 Bonita's football venue was dedicated as Glenn Davis Stadium.

NOTABLE BIRTHDAY
December 26, 1905

Donald "Don" Blessing, born in Hollister, rower, 1928 Olympic gold medalist in the coxed eights. He was the coxswain of the undefeated UC Berkeley team that won the 1928 season, Olympic Trials, and Olympics.

. . . .

Before This Book Ends

NAIA HEADS WEST
The National Association of Intercollegiate Athletics (NAIA) moved west when it launched the Golden State Athletic Conference in 1986, followed by the California Pacific Conference in 1995. The Azusa-based GSAC has 10

members, including eight in California. Life Pacific College, Westmont College and William Jessup University are all Warriors. Other members include the Hope International University Royals, Menlo College Oaks, San Diego Christian College Hawks, Vanguard University Lions, and The Master's University Mustangs. Conference members have won over 45 national titles in over 10 men's and women's sports.

Cal Pac, or the California Pacific Conference is based in Oakland. Members compete in 15 men's and women's sports. The largest conference in the West includes 11 schools from the Golden State. Biggest of all is the University of California, Merced Golden Bobcats with over 7,000 students. Southern California members include the University of Antelope Valley Pioneers, La Sierra University Golden Eagles, Marymount California University Mariners, Providence Christian College Sea Beggars, University of Saint Katherine Firebirds, Soka University of America Lions, and the Westcliff University Warriors. Northern California is represented by the California State University Maritime Academy Keelhaulers, Pacific Union College Pioneers, and the Simpson University Red Hawks.

Last, But Certainly Not Least!

THIS MASCOT IS B.S.

UC Santa Cruz athletic teams have the best mascot and nickname ever. The Banana Slugs. Yes, that bright yellow, slimy, shell-less mollusk commonly found on the redwood forest floor. *Sports Illustrated* and ESPN have named it the best!

In 1980, Santa Cruz joined the NCAA Division III in five sports and were known as the Sea Lions. However, a great number of students favored the Banana Slugs as the nickname. After five years of protests and a two mascot identity, UC Santa Cruz officially changed the name to the Banana Slugs in 1986. The Slugs compete in 15 men's and women's sports as members of the Virginia based Coast to Coast Athletic Conference.

CLOSING STATEMENT

Sports Fans,

You are now one of the experts who can wow their friends, impress on social media, and score many points on the California sports TV quiz show that is sure to be created by someone.

If you have any California sports history facts, please send them to me and we'll add them to my website.

Good luck with all this powerful knowledge, and make sure to use it for good!

Dan Cisco

a.k.a. the California Sports Guy

www.californiasportsastounding.com

ACKNOWLEDGMENTS

This book represents the creativity of many people. Their contributions, suggestions, and ideas made this book far better than just my own effort. It is never about just the author, and I am glad for that!

To Julie Broad and her staff at Book Launchers, thanks for collaborating with me and providing extensive support for each step in the process. Thanks for your help with the early drafts, title, story creation, editing, layout, design, proofreading, and beyond. Thanks to Tim Tester, accomplished writer, sports expert, and story master, who helped immensely with content and presentation. His sense of humor made this project fun. I have a new persona thanks to him. Thanks to Jaqueline Kyle, book production manager, for her meticulous, organized, and detailed input. A sincere thanks to art goddess Cassandra Voors who designed the cover. Thank you to Brian Baker for his copyediting and improvements on my initial submission. Rachel Robertson did a fine job of proofreading and eliminated more than one pesky error. Roy Rocha was a big help in keeping me organized and ahead of deadlines.

Many thanks go to Bob Barde, author of *South End: Sport and Community at the Dock of the Bay*, which contains history of rowing and handball.

Thank you to Olympic Trials marathon qualifier Gary Close for use of his amazing scrapbook on distance running covering Grossmont College and the Jamul Toads Running Club. A great teammate who inspired me to improve each and every day.

Thanks to Rob Russell of Quincy, CA who shared his extensive research on California's ski history.

Thank you to the California Historical Society, and all of the California academic and public libraries that contributed books and other sources.

A sincere thanks to sports fans who gave their time, shared their knowledge, and helped me along the way!

THANK YOU LETTER

Sports Fans,

Thank you for reading. I hope you enjoyed this book and learned a lot of fun facts. This author loves feedback. Please tell me what you loved or didn't like about the book. All this feedback will make the next edition bigger and better.

Here is my humble request. Please post an online review wherever you buy books. Reviews are essential to the success of books and this author is grateful for your input.

Thank You!

Dan Cisco
a.k.a. the California Sports Guy
www.californiasportsastounding.com

REFERENCES

Ables, Tom. *Go Aztecs! A Fan Looks Back at the First 783 Games He Saw, Including the Championship 2016 Season*. San Bernardino: CreateSpace Independent Publishing Platform, 2018.

Anderson, Don. "The Third Carriage Age: June 9, 1860: The First Automobile in San Francisco." June 7, 2020. www.thirdcarriageage.com.

Anguiano, Dani. "Lake Tahoe ski resort changes name to remove racist and misogynistic slur." *The Guardian*. September 13, 2021. https://www.theguardian.com

Ardell, Jean Hastings, and Andy McCue. *The National Pastime, Endless Seasons, 2011: Baseball in Southern California*. Phoenix: Society for American Baseball Research, 2011.

Ardley, Neil. Dictionary of Science: 2,000 Key Words Arranged Thematically. London; Dorling Kindersley. 1995.

Barde, Robert Eric, with Patrick F. Cunneen. *South End: Sport and Community at the Dock of the Bay*. Alameda: Gibbons Press, 2019.

Baxter, Kevin. "Galaxy and LAFC Fans Are Taking New Rivalry Very Seriously." *Los Angeles Times*. March 28, 2018. https://www.latimes.com/sports/soccer/la-sp-galaxy-lafc-20180328-story.html.

Benyo, Richard. *Running Encyclopedia*. Champaign: Human Kinetics, 2001.

Berliner, Don. "The Big Race of 1910." January 2010. https://www.airspacemag.com/history-of-flight/the-big-race-of-1910-9075126/.

Berry, William B. and Chapman Wentworth. *Lost Sierra: Gold, Ghosts, and Skis*. Soda Springs: Western America SkiSport Museum, 1991.

Bishop, Ken. "De La Salle Loses NCS 3A Title and 34-game Win Streak" *San Francisco Examiner*. December 8, 1991. https://www.newspapers.com/clip/73964904/football-last-loss-before-start-of/page 31.

Bohannan, Larry. "From the Vault: That Time When Steph Curry and

Other NBA Stars Played Outdoors in Indian Wells." *Desert Sun.* October 19, 2019. http://www.desertsun.com.

Book Club of California. *Sports in California.* San Francisco: Book Club of California, 1986.

Brand, Steve. "Longtime Track Coach Reflects on Athletes' Lost Year." *San Diego Union-Tribune.* June 17, 2020. https://www.sandiegouniontribune.com/sports/high-school-preps/story/2020-06-17/bob-larsen.

Brandt, Stephen. "History of Soccer in Los Angeles: Ethnic Origins Get Sport Off the Ground." March 20, 2015.
https://www.angelsonparade.com/2015/3/20/8266137/history-of-soccer-in-los-angeles-ethnic-origins-get-sport-off-ground.

Brown, Gary. "San Jose's Historic Feet." October 29, 2012. https://www.ncaa.org/about/resources/media-center/news/san-joses-historic-feet

Bruun, Anders. "The First Aviation Meeting in the USA." The First Air Races. http://www.thefirstairraces.net/meetings/la1001/events.php

Burns, Bob. *The Track in the Forest: The Creation of a Legendary 1968 US Olympic Team.* Chicago: Chicago Review Press, 2018.

Cantwell, Robert. "Run, Rabbit, Run." *Sports Illustrated.* August 27, 1973. https://vault.si.com/vault/1973/08/27/run-rabbit-run.

Chapin, Dwight. "75th Anniversary: St. Mary's Pulled a Stunner in '30." *San Francisco Chronicle.* November 13, 2005. https://www.sfgate.com/sports/article/75TH-ANNIVERSARY-St-Mary-s-pulled-a-stunner-in-2595377.php.

Cherwa, John. "Polishing off the Chrome." *Los Angeles Times.* November 6, 2016. https://www.newspapers.com/image/278014448/?terms=Chrome%20Cherwa%20polishing&match=Page D1

City Slickers Can't Stay with Me: The Coach Bob Larsen Story. DVD. Directed by Robert Lusitana. Encino: Extant Media, 2015.

Clark, Dr. Kristine Setting.. *Undefeated, Untied, and Uninvited: a Documentary of the 1951 University of San Francisco Dons Football Team.* CreateSpace Independent Publishing Platform, 2014.

Crane, Lee. "A Complete History of the Snowboard Halfpipe." *Transworld Snowboarding,* December 1, 1996. https://www.snowboarder.com/

transworld-snowboarding-archive/snowboarding-photos/a-complete-history-of-the-snowboard-halfpipe/.

Crowe, Jerry. "This Right-Hand Man Could Use a Pat on Back." *Los Angeles Times*. March 19, 2007. https://www.latimes.com/archives/la-xpm-2007-mar-19-sp-crowe19-story.html.

Davis, Pepper Paire. *Dirt in the Skirt*. Bloomington: Author House, 2009.

Dean, Penny Lee Dr. "A History of the Catalina Channel Swims Since 1927." 2012. https://swimcatalina.org/wp-content/uploads/2017/02/catalinachannelhistory_wrigley_marathon_swim-1.pdf

Dickey, Glenn. *Just Win, Baby: Al Davis and His Raiders*. New York: Harcourt, 1991.

Dunn, Geoffrey. "Riders Like the Sea Spray." *Santa Cruz Magazine* 4 (Spring 2009): 44-47.

Durham, David L. *California's Geographic Names: A Gazetteer of Historic and Modern Names of the State*. Clovis: Word Dancer Press, 1998.

Erskine, Chris. "Prestige and Wackiness at Catalina Water Ski Race." *Los Angeles Times*. July 16, 2011. https://www.latimes.com/sports/la-xpm-2011-jul-16-la-sp-0717-erskine-catalina-ski-20110717-story.html.

Fimrite, Ron. *Way to Go! A Chronicle of Heroes and Legends of Bay Area Sports*. Mill Valley. Tarquin Books, 1978.

_____. "The Amazing Madigan" *Sports Illustrated*. October 27, 1992. https://vault.si.com/vault/1992/10/27/the-amazing-madigan-he-was-part-coach-part-impresario-part-entrepreneur-part-raconteur-and-slip-madigan-used-all-his-varied-talents-to-turn-the-team-from-tiny-st-marys-college-into-the-fanciest-football-show-in-the-land.

Foster, Chris. "Kings Have Interesting, Some Might Say Colorful History." *Los Angeles Times*. May 27, 2012. https://www.latimes.com/sports/la-xpm-2012-may-27-la-sp-kings-history-20120527-story.html.

Franks, Dr. Joel S. *Whose Baseball? The National Pastime and Cultural Diversity in California, 1859-1941*. Lanham: Scarecrow Press, 2001.

Futterman, Matthew. *Running to the Edge: A Band of Misfits and the Guru Who Unlocked the Secrets of Speed*. New York: Doubleday, 2019.

Garcia, Ken. "Soccer Fever in S.F. Is Not New Outbreak." June 7, 2002.

https://www.sfgate.com/bayarea/article/Soccer-fever-in-S-F-is-not-new-out-break-2830188.php://www.sfgate.com.

Gisclair, S. Derby. "DiMaggio's Other Streak." *Society for American Baseball Research*. 2004. https://www.sabrneworleans.com/publications/derbygisclair/generaladmission/DiMaggiosOtherStreak(09-22-2004).pdf.

Glasgow, Lindsey. "Butcher Boy and the Start of Yacht Racing in San Diego." January 15, 2021. https://www.thelog.com/local/fast-facts-butcher-boy-and-the-start-of-yacht-racing-in-san-diego/

Gnerre, Sam. "Carrell Speedway in Gardena." *The Daily Breeze*. April 26, 2013. http://blogs.dailybreeze.com/history/2013/04/.

Gray, Mike. "What Are We Calling the LA Galaxy LAFC Rivalry?" LAG Confidential. March 26, 2018. https://www.lagconfidential.com/2018/3/26/17164424/what-are-we-calling-the-la-galaxy-lafc-rivalry.

Gustkey, Earl. *Great Moments in Southern California Sports*. New York: Harry N. Abrams, 1990.

Hales, Diane Moore. *A History of Badminton in the United States*. Papillion: United States Badminton Association, 1988.

Hart, Eddie. *Disqualified: Eddie Hart, Munich 1972, and the Voices of the Most Tragic Olympics*. Kent, OH: Kent State University Press, 2017.

Harvey, Randy. "All's Well: Words to Live By for Track Promoter Al Franken—as Long as He Makes the Newspapers." *Los Angeles Times*. January 20, 1989. https://www.latimes.com/archives/la-xpm-1989-01-20-sp-1167-story.html.

Hatfield, David D. *Dominguez Air Meet*. Inglewood: Northrop University Press, 1976.

Hotelling, Neal. *Pebble Beach: The Official Golf History*. Chicago: Triumph Books, 2009.

Jacobs, Michael (Jake). "History of the Catalina Channel Crossing." Accessed August 20, 2021. https://www.scora.org/about-us/catalina-crossing/.

James, Jack. "Bears Swamp St. Mary's Under Record Score of 127-0." *San Francisco Examiner*. October 10, 1920.

Janssen, Frederick William. *A History of American Amateur Athletics and Aquatics with the Records*. New York: Outing Company, 1887.

Jardin, Xeni. "Owen Morse Sets Hang Gliding World Record for Pi-

loting 222.22 miles Over California's Owens Valley." July 3, 2020. https://
boingboing.net/2020/07/03/owen-morse-sets-hang-gliding-w.html.

Jenkins, Bruce. *A Good Man: The Pete Newell Story.* Berkeley: Frog: Distributed by North Atlantic Books, 1999.

Jenkins, Chris. Boys of Summer '61 Celebrate Storied Championship."
San Diego Union. August 27, 2011. https://www.sandiegouniontribune.
com/sports/mlb/sdut-boys-of-summer-61-celebrate-storied-championship-
2011aug27-story.html.

Jurjevics, Rosa. "Their Own Little World: Mission Beach."
San Diego Reader. July 12, 2007. https://www.sandiegoreader.com/
news/2007/jul/12/their-own-little-world-mission-beach/.

Keeley, Steve Bo. *Charlie Brumfield: King of Racquetball.* Free Man Publishing, 2013.

Kiefer, David. "World All-Stars Prove U.S. is Vulnerable." *Santa Cruz
Sentinel.* February 15, 1999. https://cdnc.ucr.edu

Kramer, Anne. *The Ultimate Book of Darts: A Complete Guide to Games,
Gear, Terms, and Rules.* New York: Skyhorse, 2013.

King, Billie Jean, with Kim Chapin. *Billie Jean.* New York: Harper &
Row, 1974.

_____, with Johnette Howard and Maryanne Vollers. *All In: An Autobiography.* New York: Knopf, 2021.

Krikorian, Doug. *Los Angeles Sports Memories.* Charleston: History
Press, 2005.

Lang, Arne K. *The Nelson-Wolgast Fight and the San Francisco Boxing
Scene*, 1900-1914. Jefferson: McFarland & Co., 2012.

Lasseter, Evan. "For Yosh Uchida, Judo is a Way of Life." United States
Olympic and Paralympic Museum. Accessed August 20, 2021. https://
usopm.org/for-yosh-uchida-judo-is-a-way-of-life/.

Lawson, Scott J. and Rob Russell. 2009. "The History of Longboard
Skiing and Revival Races in Plumas County." Presented to the National Ski
Congress and International Ski History Association at Mammoth Lakes.

Liberti, Rita, and Maureen Smith. *San Francisco Bay Area Sports: Golden Gate Athletics, Recreation, and Community.* Fayetteville: University of Arkansas Press, 2017.

Ligon, Phil, Ron Pietila, and John Raue. *OTL: The Sport & the Spectacle*. San Diego: LPR Productions, 1978.

"Los Angeles 1932: California Welcomes the World." September 12, 2017. https://olympics.com/en/news/los-angeles-1932-california-welcomes-the-world.

MacCambridge, Michael. *America's Game*. New York: Random House, 2004.

Martin, Hugo. "Retiring its racist name, historic Squaw Valley resort will become Palisades Tahoe." September 13, 2021. www.latimes.com

McCoy-Murray, Linda. *Quotable Jim Murray: The Literary Wit, Wisdom, and Wonder of a Distinguished American Sports Columnist*. Nashville: Towle-House Publishing, 2003.

McIntosh, Bruce, Rick Obrand, and Bill Peck. *A History of Football in Los Angeles City High Schools*. Los Angeles: Amateur Athletic Foundation of Los Angeles, 1990.

McLaughlin, Mark. "Bold Sierra Nevada Miners Struck 'Gold' in Ski Racing." Accessed August, 20, 2021. https://www.historynet.com/bold-sierra-nevada-miners-struck-gold-ski-racing.htm.

Medrano, Kastalia. "There Is Only One Open-Ocean Waterskiing Race in the World and You Must Watch It." May 31, 2019. https://www.thrillist.com/travel/nation/the-worlds-greatest-ski-race-water-skiing.

Miller, Scott. "After Two Years of Organizing, It's Time to Let the Games Begin." *Los Angeles Times*. July 14, 1988.

Montell, Doug. "University of California Defeats St. Mary's Eleven 127-0." *Oakland Tribune*. October 10, 1920.

Mussato, Joe. "OTL Founders Revel in Tourney's Growth" *San Diego Union*. July 11, 2015. https://www.sandiegouniontribune.com/sdut-otl-tournament-founders-fiestaisland-2015jul11-story.html. "Nearly $160 Million Wagered On 2016 Breeders' Cup; Record Attendance Reported." November 6, 2016. https://www.paulickreport.com/news/the-biz/nearly-160-million-wagered-2016-breeders-cup-record-attendance-reported/.

Newland, James D. "La Mesa's Boys of Summer Were Baseball Heroes." Patch. July 10, 2011. https://patch.com/california/lamesa/la-mesas-boys-of-summer-were-baseball-heroes.

Nusbaum, Eric. *Stealing Home: Los Angeles, the Dodgers, and the Lives Caught in Between.* New York: PublicAffairs, 2020.

Odin. Layla. "Looking Back: This Week in Sports History October 8-14." October 9, 2017. https://sportsretriever.com/stories/looking-back-week-sports-history-october-8-14/.

Olalde, Mark. "'Larger than life': Richard Heckmann, Rancho Mirage Businessman, Philanthropist, Dies at 76." *Desert Sun.* November 1, 2020. https://www.desertsun.com/story/news/2020/11/01/richard-heckmann-rancho-mirage-businessman-and-philanthropist-has-died-76/6114976002/.

Oliver, Myrna. "A. Melin, 77: Introduced Frisbee and Hula Hoop." *Los Angeles Times.* June 30, 2002. https://www.latimes.com/archives/la-xpm-2002-jun-30-me-melin30-story.html.

Ostler, Scott. "A Lap Around the Track." *San Francisco Chronicle.* August 28, 2000.

https://www.sfgate.com/sports/ostler/article/A-Lap-Around-an-Old-Track-3326459.php

Outlaw, Adrianna. "Hawkeye Flock for All Indian Wells' Courts." *Tennis Now.* November 3, 2010. http://www.tennisnow.com/News/Hawkeye-Flock-For-All-Indian-Wells--Courts.aspx.

Park, Roberta. "From Football to Rugby—and Back, 1906-1919: The University of California-Stanford University Response to the 'Football Crisis of 1905.'" *Journal of Sport History.* 11 (Winter 1984): 5-40. https://www.jstor.org/stable/43609112

Payne, Melanie. *Champions, Cheaters, and Childhood Dreams: Memories of the All-American Soap Box Derby.* Akron: University of Akron Press, 2003.

Perelman Richard B., and Mark Meyers. *Unforgettable! The 100 Greatest Moments in Los Angeles Sports History.* Memphis: Towery Publishing, 1995.

Plaschke, Bill. "Hot Soccer in the City? From Now on Banc on It." *Los Angeles Times.* April 30, 2018. https://enewspaper.latimes.com/infinity/article_share.aspx?guid=d3b1c9cf-a15f-4bee-908c-67109bdbf2cd.

———. "Kobe Bryant's Spirit is Present in Lakers' NBA Championship Triumph." *Los Angeles Times.* October 11, 2020. https://www.latimes.com/sports/lakers/story/2020-10-11/lakers-heat-game-6-plaschke.

"Professional Football Teams in Los Angeles." Los Angeles Almanac. Accessed August 20, 2021. http://www.laalmanac.com/sports/sp02.php

Rhoden, William C. "For 66 Years, a Force for Judo in the United States." *New York Times*. April 1, 2012. https://www.nytimes.com/2012/04/02/sports/san-jose-coach-yoshihiro-uchida-a-force-for-judo.html.

Ring, Frances Kroll and the California Historical Society. *Champions in the Sun: A Special Issue of California History, the Magazine of the California Historical Society*. San Francisco: California Historical Society, 1984.

Rodriguez, Alicia. "What Are We Calling the LA Galaxy LAFC rivalry?" March 26, 2018. https://www.angelsonparade.com/2018/3/26/17165594/poll-what-should-we-call-the-lafc-la-galaxy-rivalry-battle-of-los-angeles-el-trafico-hollywood-derby

Ryczek, William J. *Baseball's First Inning: A History of the National Pastime Through the Civil War*. Jefferson: McFarland & Company, 2009.

Sacramento Republic Football Club. "Celebrating 100+ Years of Indomitable Soccer History." July 7, 2016. https://www.sacrepublicfc.com/news_article/show/720609-celebrating-100-years-of-indomitable-soccer-history.

Sakamoto, Kinya, and Michael Flachmann. "The History of Judo in Bakersfield." Accessed August 20, 2021. http://www.csub.edu/judo/history.html.

Seymour, Joey. *San Diego's Finest Athletes: Five Exceptional Lives*. El Cajon: Sunbelt Publications, 2009.

Smith, Chris. "Major League Soccer's Most Valuable Teams 2019: Atlanta Stays on Top as Expansion Fees, Sale Prices Surge." *Forbes*. November 4, 2019. https://www.forbes.com/sites/chrissmith/2019/11/04/major-league-soccers-most-valuable-teams-2019-atlanta-stays-on-top-as-expansion-fees-sale-prices-surge/?sh=35dba3c151b5.

Smith, Michelle. "Clash Now Quaking in their boots." *San Francisco Examiner*. October 28, 1999. https://www.sfgate.com/sports/article/Clash-now-Quaking-in-their-boots-3060953.php

Somrack, F. Daniel. *Boxing in San Francisco*. Charleston: Arcadia Press, 2005.

Springer, Steve. "Those Gaels, What Tales: For St. Mary's, Football Glory Is Just a Memory." *Los Angeles Times*. October 12, 1985. https://www.

latimes.com/archives/la-xpm-1985-10-12-sp-14572-story.html.

Stacey, Olivia. "Joey Chestnut's Net Worth: 5 Fast Facts You Need to Know." Heavy. July 4, 2016. https://heavy.com/sports/2016/07/joey-chest-nut-net-worth-prize-money-salary-record-hot-dog-eating-contest/

Tennis, Mark. *High School Football in California: Amazing Stories on the Gridiron from San Diego to the Golden Gate and Everywhere In Between.* New York: Sports Publishing, 2018.

Thorn, John. "The Knickerbockers: San Francisco's First Base Ball Team?" Our Game (blog). May 14, 2013. https://ourgame.mlblogs.com/the-knickerbockers-san-franciscos-first-base-ball-team-864ab16fc3f8

Van Dyke, Jonathan. "Long Beach Celebrates 30 Races of Being the People's Marathon." *Grunion Gazette.* October 8, 2014.

"Various Makes of Aeroplanes" *Los Angeles Times.* December 12, 1909. (accessed March 14, 2021). https://www.newspapers.com

Wallace, Glenn. "San Diego Was to Racquetball What Hawaii Was to Surfing." *San Diego Reader.* July 25, 1985. https://www.sandiegoreader.com/news/1985/jul/25/rise-and-fall-racquetball/.

West, Phil. "How DC United and the San Jose Clash Got Their Names and Original Look." April 5, 2020. https://www.mlssoccer.com/news/how-dc-united-and-san-jose-clash-got-their-names-and-original-look.

———. "How the San Jose Earthquakes Got Their Name." June 25, 2016. https://www.mlssoccer.com/news/how-san-jose-earthquakes-got-their-name.

Wharton, David. "7th Heaven as Angels Win Series." *Los Angeles Times.* October 28, 2002. https://www.latimes.com/archives/la-xpm-2002-oct-28-me-series28-story.html.

Wilhelm, Chase. "The 17 Tracks NASCAR Has Visited in Califor-nia Through the Years." March 23, 2017 https://www.foxsports.com/nascar/gallery/the-17-tracks-nascar-has-visited-in-california-through-the-years-032317.

Wilson, Wayne, and David K. Wiggins. *LA Sports: Play, Games, and Community in the City of Angels.* Fayetteville: University of Arkansas Press, 2018.

Wolf, Bob. "A Dream Team: El Cajon-La Mesa Stood Tall in '61 Little

League World Series." *Los Angeles Times*. July 5, 1989. https://www.latimes. com/archives/la-xpm-1989-07-05-sp-3072-story.html.

Wright, George, and Bill Peck. *Los Angeles Jefferson High School, 1950: The Greatest Track and Field Team Ever!* San Francisco: Pacifica Sports Research Institute, 2006.

Yakowicz, Will. "It Took Tony Hawk 10 Years (Several Teeth, Some Broken Ribs and Multiple Concussions) to Accomplish His Dream." *Inc*. April 28, 2017. https://www.inc.com/will-yakowicz/tony-hawk-10-year-quest-to-land-900-skateboard.html.

Ziajka, Alan. *Legacy & Promise: 150 Years of Jesuit Education at the University of San Francisco*. San Francisco: University of San Francisco, 2005.

1910 Los Angeles International Aviation Meet at Dominguez Flying Field Committee. 1909-1999. *1910 Los Angeles International Aviation Meet Research Collection*. California State University Dominguez Hills, Gerth Archives and Special Collections SPC-1996-001.

NEWSPAPERS

Amador Ledger
Beach and Bay Press
Californian
California Star
California Spirit of the Times and Fireman's Journal
Chico Enterprise-Record
Chico Weekly Enterprise
Coronado Citizen
Coronado Mercury
Daily Alta California
Daily Blade-Tribune
Daily Breeze
Daily Californian
Daily Evening Herald
Daily Evening Sentinel
Daily Independent Journal
Daily National Democrat
Daily News

Daily Record

Daily Surf

Desert Sun

Eagle Rock Sentinel

Evening Mail

Evening News

Evening Transcript

Evening Vanguard

Fresno Bee

Grunion Gazette

Hanford Journal

Hanford Sentinel

Healdsburg Tribune

Hollywood Reporter

Humboldt Times

Independent

Inyo Independent

La Habra Star

Long Beach Sun

Los Angeles Evening Citizen News

Los Angeles Evening Express

Los Angeles Herald

Los Angeles Times

Lompoc Record

Madera Tribune

Marin County Tocsin

Marin Journal

Marysville Daily Appeal

Mercury News

Mirror News

Modesto Bee

Monrovia Daily News-Post

Morning Press
Morning Union
Mountain Messenger
Napa Daily Journal
Napa Valley Register
Newcastle News
New York Times
Nichi Bei Times
North County Times
Oakland Daily Transcript
Oakland Tribune
Oceanside Daily Blade-Tribune
Orange County Register
Oxnard Press-Courier
Pacific Bee
Pasadena Independent
Placer Argus
Placer County Republican
Placer Herald
Placer Times
Press Democrat
Press-Telegram
Redlands Daily Facts
Redondo Reflex
Riverside Daily Press
Sacramento Bee
Sacramento Daily Record
Sacramento Record-Union
Sacramento Transcript
Sacramento Union
Sacramento Weekly Bee
San Bernardino Sun
San Diego Journal
San Diego Union

San Diego Union and Daily Bee
San Diego Union-Tribune
San Francisco Call
San Francisco Call and Post
San Francisco Chronicle
San Francisco Examiner
San Joaquin Republican
San Jose Mercury News
San Luis Obispo Daily Telegram
San Mateo Times
San Pedro News-Pilot
Santa Ana Register
Santa Barbara Weekly Press
Santa Cruz Evening News
Santa Cruz Sentinel
Sausalito News
Selma Enterprise
Shin Nichibei
Sonoma Democrat
Star-News
Stockton Independent
Times-Advocate
Van Nuys News
Visalia-Times-Delta
Weekly Butte Record
Whittier News
Wilmington Press-Journal

WEBSITES

adamsmotorsportspark.com

adodarts.com

angelsonparade.com

apnews.com

arcadiahistoricalsociety.org

archeryhalloffame.com

arrs.run

baseball-almanac.com

baseball-reference.com

basketball-reference.com

bayareacurling.com

bia.gov

bigwest.org

bleacherreport.com

breederscup.com

breederscupexperiences.com

calbears.com

calbearshistory.com

calhisports.com

calie.org

californiahistoricalsociety.org

calindianhistory.org

calisphere.org

calpacathletics.com

calstategames.org

carodeo.com

catalinaskirace.net

cbva.com

cccaasports.org

cdnc.ucr.edu

chargers.com

cifstate.org

citymb.info

cityofsantacruz.com

clerk.assembly.ca.gov

clippers.com

colinsghost.org

collegerodeo.com

croquetamerica.com

csub.edu

csudharchives.libraryhost.com/repositories/6/resources/234

curling.la

cuyamacacoyotes.com

digitalcollections.archives.csudh.edu

dlshs.org

encyclopedia.densho.org

equibase.com

espn.com

fbref.com

flyingdiscmuseum.com

forbes.com

49ers.com

foundsf.org

foxsports.com

frankenenterprises.com

goaztecs.com

gobulldogs.com

goccaa.org

gostanford.com

gplb.com

greatestphysiques.com

greyhound-racing.info

gsacsports.org

guinnessworldrecords.com

hickoksports.com

historynet.com

hockey-reference.com

horseshoepitching.com

huntingtonbeachsurfingmuseum.org

inc.com

infoplease.com

its.caltech.edu

jimmurrayfoundation.org

juniorworldgolf.com

kcet.org

kpbs.org

la28.org

laac.com

laalmanac.com

lafc.com

lagalaxy.com

lagconfidential.com

lahistoryarchive.org

leginfo.legislature.ca.gov

littleleague.org

majorleagueeating.com

martialartsmuseum.com

missionhillscroquet.com

mlb.com

mlssoccer.com

mopacca.org

motorcyclemuseum.org

nascarhall.com

nba.com

nbcsports.com

ncaa.com

ncaa.org

nchpa.com

ncwsa.com

newspapers.com

nfhs.org

nfl.com

nhl.com

norcalhandball.org

norcalsquash.org

npr.org

oac.cdlib.org

olyclub.com

olympedia.org

olympic.org

ombac.org

outsidelands.org

pac-12.com

paramounticeland.net

patch.com

paulickreport.com

philmickelson.com

polomuseum.com

pro-football-reference.com

profootballhof.com

racingmuseum.org

raiders.com

recsports.berkeley.edu

redbluffroundup.com

runlongbeach.com

sabr.org

santaanita.com

sbnation.com

scdaleague.com

sealslax.com

seecalifornia.com

sfmuseum.org

sfyc.org

shacc.org

sjearthquakes.com

ska.org

skirace.net

slacusbc.com

smcgaels.com

snowboarder.com

soapboxderby.org

socalhorseshoes.weebly.com

socalshowdown.org

socal.ussquash.com

sportsencyclopedia.com

sportsillustrated.com

sports-reference.com

sportsretriever.com

sportingnews.com

statscrew.com

stmarys-ca.edu

stockton99speedway

surfer.com

surfertoday.com

surfmuseum.org

svda.org

swimcatalina.org

teamusa.org

thearmwrestlingarchives.com

thefirstairraces.net

themw.com

thepacwest.com

therams.com

thesciac.org

trackandfieldnews.com

ucirvinesports.com

uclabruins.com

ucsc.edu

ultimatehistory.com

usapickleball.org

usawaterpolo.org

usawaterski.org

usa-wwf.org

ushandball.org

usctrojans.com

useventing.com

usjf.com

usjudo.org

uspa.org

uspolo.org

ussquash.org

vansusopenofsurfing.com

visitlongbeach.com

webarchive.org

wccsports.com

wikipedia.org

wildlife.ca.gov

wnba.com

worldgolfhalloffame.org

worldsurfleague.com

yardbarker.com

LET'S KEEP THE
CONVERSATION
GOING! ——

 Order discounted bulk purchases of the book for your sports teams, sports camps, association or company.

 Book Dan Cisco for interviews or speaking at californiasportsguy@gmail.com

 Join the e-mail list and receive our free newsletter at www.californiasportsastounding.com

GET MORE NEWS AND UPDATES

- 🖑 **WEBSITE** californiasportsastounding.com/
- 🐦 **TWITTER:** @akatheCaliforn1
- 📷 **INSTAGRAM:** @danciscosportsguy
- 💼 **LINKEDIN:** linkedin.com/in/dan-cisco-818214220/

THANK YOU
FOR READING!

Thank you for reading! If you enjoyed CALIFORNIA SPORTS ASTOUNDING! Please leave an online review where you purchased this book. Reviews will help the author make the next edition bigger and better.

Your comments and suggestions are welcome. Together, let's keep CALIFORNIA SPORTS ASTOUNDING! Thank You!